We Don't Quit!

Stories of UAW Global Solidarity

© 2015 by Don Stillman

By Don Stillman

Design by Katerina Barry: www.katerinabarry.com
Copy Editing by Susan Burke
Cover Illustration by Kim Fujiwara

Printed in the United States of America

First printing, April 2015

Library of Congress Cataloging-in-Publication Data

Stillman, Donald Dennis, 1945-
We don't quit: stories of UAW global solidarity / by Don Stillman.
     pages cm
Includes bibliographical references and index.
ISBN 978-1-60358-582-8 (pbk. : alk. paper)
1. International Union,United Automobile Workers of America (CIO)
2. Automobile industry workers—Labor unions—United States.
3. International labor activities—United States. I. Title.

HD6515.A82I5777 2014
331.88'1292220973—dc23

2014015319

Distributed by
Chelsea Green Publishing
85 North Main Street, Suite 120
White River Junction, VT 05001
(802) 295 6300
www.chelseagreen.com

UAW International Affairs Dept.
1757 N Street, NW
Washington, D.C. 20036
(202) 828 8500
www.uaw.org

We Don't Quit!

Stories of UAW Global Solidarity

By Don Stillman

Design by Katerina Barry
Copy Editing by Susan Burke

Distributed by Chelsea Green Publishing, White River Junction, Vermont

Table of Contents

Foreword

On October 14, 2013, in the early morning hours at the gates of the Nissan plant in Canton, Mississippi, shop stewards from Nissan's South African factory and leaders of the powerful National Union of Metalworkers of South Africa (NUMSA) leafleted workers changing shifts. They also danced and sang in the South African union tradition of struggle.

The South Africans' message was simple: Nissan workers everywhere must be treated equally and fairly, whether in Japan, Mexico, South Africa, or the United States. Those workers have the right to organize.

NUMSA's support for the UAW should not be surprising. It is a strong and militant union with a record of solidarity on behalf of workers throughout the world.

More than three decades earlier, the UAW launched its own global campaign against the racist apartheid system. UAW members boycotted Shell, pressured their employers regarding operations in South Africa, and came to the defense of imprisoned union leaders. The stalwart support of the UAW helped the metalworkers of South Africa coalesce into a single union, NUMSA.

You can read about the UAW's fight against apartheid and for South Africa's black trade unions in the first two chapters of Don Stillman's excellent book, *We Don't Quit! Stories of UAW Global Solidarity*. This book gives a behind-the-scenes account of how workers courageously took on apartheid with strong support from the UAW and global allies.

As UAW leaders, we are proud to urge every member and retiree and their families and friends to read this book.

It contains stories of UAW global solidarity that now have been preserved for history. But these stories also provide inspiration for our union's future struggles.

The book comes at a time when we live in a global economy in which so many decisions that impact workers' lives are made by companies and governments beyond our borders. Only the power of workers standing together across those borders can preserve and strengthen the gains we have won over the years at the bargaining table and through the ballot box.

Our leadership and membership have always possessed a strong vision of global economic justice and a deep concern for the human rights of working people everywhere.

In Brazil, for example, our union fought on behalf of autoworkers and other unionists and stood up for Luiz Inacio Lula da Silva, who faced trial and a prison sentence during military rule there. Each day, the UAW attended Lula's 1981 trial to show that the whole world was watching.

Years later, in a democratic Brazil, the people elected Lula as president of their country. In 2013 Lula attended the UAW Community Action Program (CAP) conference and pledged his support for the workers at Nissan in Mississippi who are seeking to join the UAW. Today, Brazilian unions are bringing global attention to rights violations at Nissan USA and have helped win reinstatement for workers who were targeted for firing because of their outspoken support for the union.

The support for the UAW of Lula and the Brazilian unions, like that of the South African unions, serves as a powerful example that global solidarity is a two-way street—one that shows that those we support regularly use their power on behalf of the UAW when we need their help.

As you will read in Chapter 7, at the height of repression in Poland against the freedom movement led by the Solidarność union and Lech Wałęsa, the UAW helped smuggle printing presses into Poland so the workers there could continue to speak truth to power and mobilize the populace. This support, and that of others, helped Solidarność win and hastened the end of the Cold War.

After World War II, the UAW lobbied for the Marshall Plan to rebuild Europe and worked with German industrial unions to build an independent labor movement and ensure that a system of co-determination functioned to further the interests of workers.

In the early 1990s, the UAW worked closely with the German metalworkers' union, IG Metall, and the works councils there. Their solidarity assistance was critical to our organizing Freightliner in Mount Holly, North Carolina, and helped workers there win a good first contract. That success led to more workers at Freightliner and related companies joining the UAW.

Our partnership with our German colleagues is stronger than ever. Today we are working with IG Metall and the German works councils to ensure that American workers have union representation at Volkswagen and Mercedes-Benz, ultimately carving out a new path for unionization in the United States.

The Volkswagen struggle shows how important global solidarity is today. We face a harsh climate in which workers too often are denied the right to join a union. Vicious anti-labor groups spend huge sums to unfairly influence outcomes and their GOP allies use taxpayer funds as anti-union leverage.

Last year, a significant portion of VW's Chattanooga, Tennessee, employees joined UAW Local 42, which is run entirely by workers there. International allies signed a letter of intent with the UAW indicating their support for employee representation by Local 42 that would make the Chattanooga plant a "UAW-represented facility."

That would allow an effective co-determination structure to be established between management and workers and open the way for participation in the Volkswagen Global Group Works Council, which has formally stated that the UAW is its preferred partner in Chattanooga.

In December 2014, the UAW was certified officially as the representative of more than 45 percent of VW's workers there after an independent audit of the workers. We continue to gain additional support and since early 2015 have had the right to meet regularly with management on workplace issues. Our expectation is that VW will recognize the UAW as the sole bargaining representative in Chattanooga.

Progress at VW, and ultimately success there, could not occur without the global solidarity for the UAW from our allies at the German metalworkers' union and the German works councils.

As you read this book, you will see that workers here and abroad faced many dark moments in the past, but fought on and ultimately won the victories they sought.

We don't have time to be passive or feel hopeless. We need optimism and boldness and energy. We need to be smart, and efficient, and focused. And we need to fight for economic, political, and social justice both at home and abroad.

The UAW has a great history of global solidarity, as the following pages describe. We didn't back down then. And we won't back down now.

We don't quit!

Dennis Williams
UAW President

Gary Casteel
UAW Secretary-Treasurer

Introduction

I flew to Sweden for meetings with the Swedish metalworkers' union, known as Svenska Metall, in mid-September 1982. I'd timed the trip to witness the Swedish national elections, hoping to see how unions there did political work.

Walter Reuther, president of the UAW from 1946 to 1970, traveled frequently to Sweden and found inspiration from the Social Democratic economic and social policies that made that country a haven of prosperity and equality.

On the evening of September 19, 1982, my Svenska Metall counterparts invited me to the union headquarters in Stockholm to watch the election returns come in. It was a happy night, with the Social Democratic Party jumping to a big lead after six years of being out of power.

With the victory in hand, Olof Palme, who had led Sweden as prime minister from 1969 to 1976, entered the union headquarters.

I was surprised. Looking back, it would be like Bill Clinton spending election night at Solidarity House in 1992 or Barack Obama coming to UAW headquarters after the networks called the 2008 election.

After half an hour or so, I was introduced to Palme as the new international affairs director from the UAW. I expected merely a quick handshake from the most important man in Sweden that election night.

Instead, Palme asked me to sit down and talk with him.

"There is no union that has a better tradition of global solidarity with workers all over the world than the United Auto Workers," Palme told me. "The UAW steps up on the global stage when it counts.

"You put the power of your members at the service of workers everywhere, particularly those who are oppressed."

I came away not only in awe of Palme, but also very proud of the union I had the privilege to represent. I knew that all of us doing global work at the UAW stood on the shoulders of those who had preceded us and who had fought and won so many battles at home and abroad.

Walter Reuther in his years as UAW president had worked with his brother, Victor, to establish the union as a global player respected throughout the world. Leonard Woodcock, Doug Fraser, Owen Bieber, Steve Yokich, Ron Gettelfinger, Bob King, and Dennis Williams continued to devote UAW resources and clout to advance international labor solidarity.

This book focuses on the post-Reuther era and details stories of UAW global solidarity during the last three decades. There are many excellent books and articles on Reuther's time, but few that describe and analyze global labor events in the 1980s, 1990s, and 2000s.

The UAW leadership recognized this in 2012 and urged me to write about some of the major battles the union took on in support of workers in other countries in those years.

I was honored to have the opportunity to complete this effort with the support of UAW President Dennis Williams and Secretary-Treasurer Gary Casteel, and this book is the result.

In it, readers will find the stories of UAW members and leaders who:

- joined the struggle against apartheid in South Africa and supported the independent black unions there to confront the forces of racism;

- stood up in behalf of unionists in Central America, who faced the horrors inflicted by U.S.-funded death squads and paramilitary forces in the 1980s;
- worked to win freedom for women organizers in Indonesia, oil and gas union leaders in Nigeria, and worker activists in China;
- provided covert shipments of equipment and money to the underground Solidarity movement in Poland under communist-imposed martial law in the 1980s;
- fought for immigration reform after the early years in which immigrants built and strengthened the UAW;
- supported a Brazilian autoworker on trial for strike actions who went on to become president of his country and to support the UAW's Nissan organizing campaign;
- participated in the fight to liberate Kuwait from Saddam Hussein and then demanded that the emirs halt their repression of workers and of labor rights; and
- built close ties to the German metalworkers' union and works councils, which helped Freightliner workers organize into the UAW and win good contracts.

These are just a few of the stories of UAW global solidarity. There are many more that remain to be told, perhaps in a revised and expanded electronic version of this book in the months ahead.

There are some heroes in these pages, but above all it is the members of the UAW who deserve credit for their consistent support of the union's global activism.

Those UAW members showed up at protests against apartheid, at demonstrations urging the release of labor activists in China, at actions along the border with Mexico in support of maquiladora workers, at rallies backing Polish workers striking under martial law, and so on.

Time and time again, UAW local activists and leaders devoted their time and money to fight for workers abroad who faced hostile governments and greedy corporations.

UAW members know that repression abroad hurts both workers there and their counterparts here at home. The UAW has helped foreign workers time and again because it is the right thing to do. And on many occasions, it has been unions from other countries that have supported the UAW in our own organizing and bargaining struggles.

The German metalworkers have backed our ongoing effort in support of workers at Volkswagen in Tennessee and Mercedes-Benz in Alabama. Brazilian, Japanese, South African, and European unions have supported Nissan workers in Canton, Mississippi, who want to join the UAW. Their help has been crucial.

Solidarity truly is a two-way street.

I've tried to tell the stories of UAW members and leaders and the workers and unions that we supported around the world as best as I could reconstruct them decades later.

UAW Solidarity, the union magazine, proved to be an invaluable resource. In my early years at the union, I edited *Solidarity*. Then, in perhaps the best decision I made during my tenure, I hired Dave Elsila to become editor. He did a brilliant job, as I was reminded when I reread 30 years worth of the magazine during my research for this book.

During nearly three decades at the union in Detroit and Washington, D.C., I served six different UAW presidents. Throughout that time, I tried always to maintain a low profile and keep the focus on the issues prioritized by our members and elected leaders. As I wrote drafts of this book, I realized my actions and role on occasion were a part of some events that occurred. I could not ignore that and still convey major elements of certain stories.

The chapters that follow are not in any particular order or chronology. They cover UAW global solidarity in most regions of the world: Africa, Central and South America, Asia, the

Middle East, Europe, and, of course, the help we have received here in the United States.

Much of the union's international affairs work has been conducted in cooperation with global union federations, particularly the International Metalworkers' Federation, which, after a reorganization in 2012, is now known as IndustriALL. I cannot emphasize enough the important role IndustriALL plays as a labor organization that brings together metalworkers and other unionists from across the globe.

The UAW also has had an excellent relationship with the AFL-CIO on most international issues since 1995, when our union joined with others to elect John Sweeney and Richard Trumka to the top posts there. In earlier days, the UAW had some differences on global affairs with the federation that are touched on in this book, but that is seldom the case today.

I should also point out that this book is not an academic study. There remains a need for historians to write definitive accounts of the UAW's history, including its work on global solidarity. Their independent judgments and analysis are required to round out the full story.

Many of the solidarity campaigns described here sound antiquated today. Decades ago we used telexes to communicate with unions around the world and we launched postcard campaigns seeking freedom for jailed worker activists. Today, in the age of the Internet, social media, and viral videos, there are so many more tools through which solidarity campaigns can be waged. Given the velocity of change, the mechanics of solidarity will always be evolving, but the philosophy underpinning the UAW's global efforts remains the same. Workers are stronger together than apart.

There are many more examples of UAW global solidarity that need to be detailed. Every region and local union has been a part of the international struggle. Hopefully, their rich histories can be preserved.

It's important for our members, local union leadership, and staff to know about the UAW's global achievements—not just so we can feel proud, but because awareness of our past international efforts can help shape the union's agenda for the future.

If we know where we've been yesterday, we're better equipped to know where we want to go tomorrow.

Most UAW employers today operate globally, often with little regard for national borders. They salute no flag, but do worship the dollar, the yen, and the euro. Decisions made in Tokyo, Beijing, and Stuttgart now may affect UAW members as much as those made in Detroit, Washington, or on Wall Street.

Knowing how the UAW has fought throughout the world to seek worker gains that someday can lead to a global middle class can inform our union's strategic decisions.

This book on UAW global solidarity also may be helpful to our many allies in the progressive community, who often know little of this history. With time passing and new generations of leadership emerging, it's useful for our friends in the civil rights community to know what a crucial role the UAW played in defeating apartheid and fighting for social justice around the world.

It's also good for religious activists to be aware of how the union joined with people of faith to protest the killing of workers in El Salvador and the repression of Polish workers in Solidarność. It's good for our environmental friends to know how the UAW joined with Friends of the Earth and others to fight the Three Gorges Dam in China.

The book also hopefully will be useful in the broader American labor movement, which at times has been too inward looking on global matters.

A word about the title. At the end of 1981, I sat around the table in UAW President Doug Fraser's office with a number of others who were discussing the imposition of martial law by the communist regime in Poland.

Our own members had suffered from many months of a severe economic downturn during that time.

One of those at the table argued that the UAW should pull back from our aid to the Solidarity union in Poland to conserve resources for the difficult days ahead.

Fraser, who nearly always evidenced optimism, showed a flash of anger as he responded: "This is not the time to cut back our support for the Polish struggle—that's not who we are. The UAW doesn't back away from a fight. And we don't quit."

In the more than 30 years that followed, I frequently remembered Fraser's admonition, particularly when things got tough.

In the aftermath of the NLRB election that was part of our ongoing effort to organize Volkswagen in Tennessee, in early 2014, I listened as Dennis Williams pledged the union would fight on, as it always has.

"We don't quit," he said.

That same fighting spirit propelled the UAW's global solidarity efforts described in this book.

Few people predicted the racist apartheid government of South Africa would be destroyed by a democratic movement led by independent black unions there, with the support of the UAW and its allies. In the darkest of days, we didn't quit.

When Freightliner fought the union's organizing effort in North Carolina and then refused to bargain in the early 1990s, the UAW didn't quit. With crucial help from the German metalworkers, we won that important struggle.

In the 1980s when U.S.-funded death squads killed thousands of trade unionists in El Salvador, the UAW didn't turn away. We fought on every front to support workers there. Today the country is governed by pro-labor allies of the UAW from that time.

Looking forward, the UAW will face many new challenges on the global front.

Despite inevitable ups and downs, our union won't back away from the struggle for economic, political, and social justice.

We don't quit!

Don Stillman
Washington, D.C., November 12, 2014

Acknowledgments

Many people helped make this book possible. I want to thank all of them, even those not named here.

I want to thank UAW President Dennis Williams and Secretary-Treasurer Gary Casteel for their strong support for me and for this project, and also for the skill and tenacity with which they lead the union. Their commitment to global solidarity will strengthen UAW ties with our sisters and brothers throughout the world. I am proud to be a member of the UAW led by Dennis and Gary as they build support for UAW bargaining and organizing from our allies abroad.

I appreciate the help of retired UAW President Bob King, who urged me in 2012 to write this book to document the union's role in global solidarity down through the years.

I also want to thank the UAW officers and regional directors, without whose support this book would not have been possible. They include Cindy Estrada, Norwood H. Jewell, James Settles Jr., Chuck Hall, Rory Gamble, Gerald Kariem, Ken Lortz, Ron McInroy, Gary Jones, Ray Curry, Terry Dittes, and Julie Kushner. My thanks also to Chuck Browning for his help.

For years I have worked closely with Kristyne Peter, who provided invaluable help and advice during this project.

I have done many projects with Katerina Barry, the designer of this book, who is an amazing creative force.

Susan Burke, a superb editor who greatly improved this book, also has my deep gratitude. Thanks also go to Dan Giosta, another great editor, and to Scott Shrake as well.

Steve Beckman read the draft manuscript and offered great ideas, edits, and corrections. He was involved in many of the events described in this book in his role as a member and later director of the International Affairs Department.

John Christensen played an important role in the struggles detailed here. He died in 2003, but his contribution to the UAW lives on. I also want to thank Beverly Jones, who worked with me for more than 20 years.

Dave Elsila, who read the manuscript and offered excellent suggestions, has my sincere thanks. His years as editor of *UAW Solidarity* also provided much of the raw material for this book. I also appreciate the work of other *Solidarity* writers and editors whose work helped record the union's history. Among them: Jeff Stansbury, Michael Funke, Nancy Brigham, Sam Kirkland, Sam Stark, and Andy Neather.

Thanks to Doug Taylor, Vince Piscopo, and Joan Silvi. Also to Leo Baunach, who did a great job providing editorial assistance. Brad Markell and Oscar Paskal read the manuscript and offered excellent suggestions.

Also, thanks to Stanley Gacek, who read the Brazil chapter, and Glenn Adler, who read all of the Africa chapters. Both had great suggestions. Thanks also to Phil Robertson and Earl Brown for their help over the years on labor rights issues in Asia. Tom Lewandowski provided assistance on the Burma chapter.

Janet Shenk and Dave Dyson read the Central America chapters and had many good ideas. Thanks, too, to Cindy Buhl. Susan Meiselas also has my thanks for the use of her Central American photographs. Charles Kernaghan and Barbara Briggs helped shape much of our work on Central America and I thank them.

I'm grateful to all the photographers whose work appears in *We Don't Quit!* Thanks in particular to Earl Dotter, with whom I have worked closely for more than 40 years. His body of work is unsurpassed. Also to Rick Reinhard, who has documented the fight for social justice so well for many years. David Bacon is another superb photographer who has brilliantly recorded workers' struggles in Mexico, Central America, and here at home. Russ Marshall also photographed many stories for *UAW Solidarity.* Thanks also to David Sachs.

The UAW's historical archives are at the Walter P. Reuther Library of Labor and Urban Affairs at Wayne State University. My thanks to Mike Smith, the archivist who provided me with a variety of historical records, publications, and other papers. Also to Elizabeth Clemens for her help.

Thanks also to Susan Klebick, Cheryl Alston, Shalaundia Thomas, Susan Galvan, and Then Tran.

This book is distributed by Chelsea Green Publishing based in White River Junction, Vermont. I am deeply grateful to Margo Baldwin, the publisher, and to Michael Weaver, Sandi Eaton, and Bill Bokermann at Chelsea Green.

Denis MacShane, who worked for years at the International Metalworkers' Federation, read much of the manuscript. He is my friend and I thank him. I also acknowledge and appreciate the great work of Dan La Botz, Lawrence Weschler, Lesley Gill, Bill Quigley, John McClintock, Robert E. Scott, Melvin Kahn, and Philip P. Pan.

Barbara Shailor handled international affairs for the Machinists' union for years and then for the AFL-CIO. I appreciate her help on many of the struggles described herein. I also am grateful for the assistance that many NGOs and human rights groups provided the UAW through the years.

Three others no longer with us shaped my time at the UAW. Steve Schlossberg recruited me and helped me immeasurably in my early years at the union. UAW President Doug Fraser was my boss, my mentor, and my friend. I will always be grateful to him for the trust he placed in me. I also benefited from a close relationship with UAW Vice President Pat Greathouse, whose knowledge of global union issues was exceeded only by his superb skills at the bargaining table.

Important chapters in this book describe UAW President Owen Bieber's strong commitment to international solidarity. I greatly enjoyed working for him. Dick Shoemaker, the union vice president who bargained with General Motors after serving as Bieber's top administrative assistant, also was an ally whose advice I valued highly. I also want to thank Dave Curson, executive assistant to several UAW presidents and a former member of the U.S. Congress.

I have done my best to see this book is accurate and fair throughout. But inevitably with a project of this size and scope, errors may have crept in. Any and all mistakes are my responsibility alone and not that of the UAW, its leadership and staff, or any of those who provided me with help on this book. Every effort will be made to correct any errors in future printings of *We Don't Quit!*, as well as in the electronic version of the book that hopefully will provide expanded and updated materials on global solidarity. If you find an inaccuracy or other editorial problems, please e-mail: uaw.book@gmail.com.

Finally, thanks to my family, to whom I owe so much: my wife, Judy Scott, and my children, Scott Stillman and Sarah Stillman (a UAW member), and to my daughter-in-law, Kara Bischoff, and my granddaughter, Sydney Bischoff Stillman.

CHAPTER ONE

UAW's Crucial Role In The Struggle Against Apartheid
Support Provided To South Africa's Black Unions, Mandela

The Detroit Athletic Club, established in 1887, is a private social club where prominent automotive and industrial leaders have mingled with American presidents, war heroes, and royalty.

On March 3, 1978, UAW President Doug Fraser strode through the six-story clubhouse designed by the famed architect Albert Kahn, past paintings of George Washington and Abraham Lincoln, and up a marble staircase to the ballroom where he would deliver a major address.

The bankers, Big 3 auto executives, stockbrokers, Michigan politicians, and other power brokers respected Fraser. He was a well-known figure in Detroit not only for his strong leadership of the UAW, but also for his many civic achievements, such as helping to reform the Detroit police department.

But on this day, Fraser had a message many in the audience did not particularly like: the UAW would be pulling out all of its funds from banks that did business with South Africa, where the racist apartheid system oppressed millions of people of color.

And the UAW president warned that corporations doing business in South Africa would face a UAW campaign to hold them accountable.

"The government of South Africa continues to brutally suppress blacks and other nonwhites who make up 80 percent of the population," Fraser said. "It is a racist society that refuses to allow black workers even the most basic human rights."[1]

"We in the UAW don't believe that the hard-earned dues money of our 1.5 million members should wind up being used directly or indirectly to aid a country that practices such racist, repressive, and undemocratic policies."

The apartheid system in South Africa had been in place for 30 years when Fraser made his speech. It kicked off a very strong and multiyear commitment by the UAW to oppose apartheid and to support the hope of black workers there for a multiracial democracy. The union joined this struggle when it was unpopular and carried it through to see apartheid dismantled. The victory belonged to the South African workers and others there whose courage won the fight. We were proud to support them.

The word "apartheid" means "the state of being apart." After World War II, the Afrikaner-run National Party segregated the country into four racial groups: "white," "black," "coloured," and "Indian."

Segregation occurred in every area of life. Millions of black South Africans were forcibly relocated into segregated residential areas. They were denied the right to vote. Separate systems were established for education, medical care, and governmental services. Those for blacks were far inferior to those enjoyed by whites.

"I hope that the U.S. corporations with investments in South Africa and the U.S. banks which have loaned $2.2 billion to that country will pursue a course of enlightened self-interest," Fraser told the Detroit Athletic Club audience. "They must recognize that the present policies of the [Prime Minister B.J.] Vorster government can only lead eventually to broadscale economic boycotts, more repression, and finally massive violent destruction."[2] The UAW leader said the union would cooperate with churches, civil rights organizations, human rights groups, and other unions "to wage and lead a campaign to win public and congressional support for concrete actions against apartheid."

The union set aside March 13–21, 1978, for a period of intensified campaigning against apartheid as a commemoration of the Sharpeville massacre that had occurred in 1960. Black South Africans suffered from laws that required them to carry passbooks restricting their free movement about the country. Thousands protested by not carrying their passbooks and turning up for arrest at the Sharpeville Township police station. Police opened fire on the crowd, killing 69 people, including 10 children and 8 women. The massacre set off years of protests against South Africa in many countries.

Fraser also called upon U.S. President Jimmy Carter to do more to fight apartheid in South Africa. He expected to be heard in part because the UAW had played a crucial role in helping Carter win the Democratic nomination and, ultimately, the White House in 1976.

Among the steps the UAW urged President Carter to take were to:

- end all Export-Import Bank insurance, loan guarantees, and discount loans in support of exports to South Africa;
- withdraw all U.S. government services that provided information, encouragement, and assistance to U.S. businesses trading with or investing in South Africa;
- end all DISC benefits, an export tax-saving program, for corporations dealing with South Africa;
- end all forms of nuclear collaboration with South Africa;
- study and present to Congress concrete proposals, as promised in the Democratic Party platform, for tax disincentives to discourage investment and loans to South Africa;
- use the European Economic Community's Code of Conduct as a point of departure to draw up official

guidelines on investments and fair employment practices for the approximately 300 U.S. companies that had invested more than $1.6 billion in South Africa during the preceding two decades; and

- instruct the U.S. directors of such international financial institutions as the World Bank and International Monetary Fund to strongly urge that human rights conditions be imposed in their loans to South Africa.[3]

Fraser pledged the UAW would expand assistance to the union's counterparts in South Africa in the form of trade union education and organizing support. He also said the UAW would use its influence on multinational parent companies to help black workers there get full union recognition in those firms' South African subsidiaries.

Fraser noted that unions around the world "are beginning an intensive effort to lift the banning orders imposed on African trade unionists and those helping African unions."

"We are assisting in the establishment of trade union and human rights for the African majority," he said.[4]

The UAW strategy in the late 1970s correctly foresaw that leverage for change in South Africa could come from pressure on financial institutions loaning money to the apartheid government and on corporations doing business there. The union worked closely with the American Committee on Africa and the Africa Fund to hone this approach.

The apartheid government needed capital and technology from other countries to build its own economic and military power during this period. The initiatives of the UAW and its allies in the anti-apartheid struggle sought to limit or halt those capital/technology flows to South Africa.

Fraser, an immigrant from Scotland, dropped out of high school when he was 18 and eventually became a metal finisher at a Chrysler factory producing cars under the DeSoto nameplate. He won election as president of UAW Local 227, then became a top assistant to UAW President Walter Reuther, and later the union's top negotiator with Chrysler.

He became UAW president in 1977, and it was at Chrysler that the union in 1979 first bargained an innovative breakthrough that allowed the union effectively to block the investment of pension funds in certain companies doing business in South Africa.

Black South Africans frequently suffered violence at the hands of the apartheid government's security forces. This protester had been part of a demonstration against the jailing of union members in the 1980s. Photo by Guy Adams.

Marc Stepp, who had followed Fraser as the union's lead negotiator at Chrysler, was an African American union leader who had devoted much of his life to labor and civil rights struggles. He became one of the UAW's most vocal critics of apartheid.

At a United Nations symposium on transnational corporations held in Detroit in June 1981, Stepp announced that the UAW had named five companies it wanted Chrysler pension fund trustees to cut off from further fund investments: Allegheny Ludlum, Dresser Industries, Eaton Corporation, Newmont Mining, and U.S. Steel.

The 1979–1982 master contract negotiated by Fraser and Stepp contained the provision on investments in companies doing business in South Africa that refused to honor the so-called "Sullivan Principles"—a corporate code of conduct developed by the Rev. Leon Sullivan, an African American minister who served on the board of General Motors Corporation.

Those principles included:

1. Nonsegregation of the races in all eating, comfort, and work facilities.
2. Equal and fair employment practices for all employees.
3. Equal pay for all employees doing equal or comparable work for the same period of time.
4. Initiation of and development of training programs that would prepare, in substantial numbers, blacks and other nonwhites for supervisory, administrative, clerical, and technical jobs.
5. Increasing the number of blacks and other nonwhites in management and supervisory positions.
6. Improving the quality of life for blacks and other nonwhites outside the work environment in such areas as housing, transportation, school, recreation, and health facilities.
7. Working to eliminate laws and customs that impeded social, economic, and political justice *(added in 1984)*.

At the UN symposium, Stepp blasted the South African government for herding blacks into "homelands" where there was little or no infrastructure to provide electricity, water, or other necessary services.

During the mid-1980s, the 4.7 million whites in South Africa had access to about 87 percent of the country's land, while the 20 million blacks lived on only 13 percent of the land. Half of the children born in the designated black areas died before reaching the age of five, according to the American Committee on Africa.[5] South Africa exported more than $2 billion worth of food each year at a time when malnutrition was widespread among people of color there. The white minority took home 64 percent of the country's total income, while the average black manufacturing worker earned only $304 per month, or less than a quarter of what comparable white workers received. Black farm workers earned only $268 per month in this era.

The UAW vice president noted that people of color could not vote in elections there, while whites who made up just 16 percent of the population could.

"The racist government spends $1,650 per student to educate whites," Stepp said, "and only $67 per student to educate blacks."

He also blasted Chrysler itself, because it owned 25 percent of South Africa's largest auto manufacturer at that time, Sigma.

"Recently, black workers at Sigma struck for recognition," the UAW leader said. "They were earning the entry wage of barely more than $1 an hour, which some labor sources estimated to be about one-third the amount needed for subsistence." He also noted that apartheid had created a pool of low-wage labor that U.S. corporations were eager to exploit.[6]

Fraser also addressed the United Nations symposium. He said the UAW believed the Sullivan Principles were inadequate.

"We must toughen our stand by going beyond the Sullivan Principles and widening our ability to disinvest pension and

UAW Vice President Marc Stepp (right) played a crucial role in the union's fight against apartheid. He joined Harry Belafonte, the singer and social activist, in a protest at the embassy of South Africa in Washington, D.C., in 1984. Photo by Rick Reinhard.

other funds that ultimately enable South Africa to maintain the economic and military strength to continue apartheid," the UAW president said.

"Apartheid will fall," Fraser predicted, "but not without a push."

The UAW over the years supported the independent black trade union movement in South Africa and fought apartheid in a wide variety of ways. The union worked very hard to shape its policies based on extensive discussions with our counterparts in South Africa.

Our South African union allies got up every day in the midst of the apartheid system, and they were the ones who had to live with the consequences of the various campaign tactics of the UAW, other unions, civil rights activists, church and human rights groups, and other anti-apartheid campaigners.

The pressure brought by the UAW on banks and companies had real-world consequences on the ground in South Africa. Divestment meant the loss of some jobs, for example. So the UAW engaged in frequent consultations on both its strategy and tactics and accepted guidance from its union counterparts in South Africa.

The resistance that was reignited in the 1970s in South Africa reached a new level in the decade that followed. External solidarity with the anti-apartheid struggle moved in rhythm with internal resistance

On one of my early trips to South Africa in the mid-1980s, the metalworkers' unions arranged for me to meet Cyril Ramaphosa, the president of the National Union of Mineworkers (NUM), then South Africa's largest union. He was a strong figure who later went on to lead the negotiations with the government over the end of apartheid and helped to write South Africa's post-apartheid constitution.

Before coming to the UAW, I had worked at the United Mine Workers after helping to topple the union's corrupt leadership under Tony Boyle, its president. Boyle ended up in prison for murdering his election opponent, for whom I had worked.

Ramaphosa and I hit it off. The NUM staff included a number of extremely competent activists, including Marcel Golding. I recall watching Golding and other researchers at the union producing educational materials for members on new Apple computers (at a time when I was still doing similar work on an old Remington manual typewriter).

A few months after that visit, I got a call from Golding asking for UAW support on a dispute that had developed between the mineworkers' union and Shell Oil.

A black mineworker had been killed in an accident in a mine in Rietspruit that was 50 percent owned by Shell's South African subsidiary. Ramaphosa's union organized a memorial that lasted two hours during a work shift. Shell's mine management responded by suspending four NUM shop stewards.

The conflict quickly escalated. About 800 miners went on strike to get the shop stewards reinstated, and Shell called in security forces who attacked the strikers with rubber bullets and tear gas.

In the aftermath, 129 workers were fired and also evicted from company-owned housing. The strikers were forced back to work at gunpoint.

Shell then issued orders forbidding union meetings and denying shop stewards access to the workers.

I told NUM's Golding that I would inform UAW President Owen Bieber about the union's struggle at Rietspruit and get back to him. Before calling Bieber, I spoke with Ken Zinn, who worked at the United Mine Workers headquarters in Washington, D.C. Zinn confirmed the UMWA knew of the dispute and would be supporting their South African counterpart.

Bieber agreed that the UAW would back the National Union of Mineworkers' call for international action against Shell.

From that decision, the UAW and the UMWA joined with anti-apartheid groups such as TransAfrica and the Free South Africa Movement to launch a boycott of Shell in the United States. Bieber chaired the boycott along with Richard L. Trumka, president of the UMWA (who years later became president of the AFL-CIO).

While the impetus for the action came from Shell's brutal treatment of miners in South Africa, the nationwide boycott of Shell here soon addressed broader issues of the parent company's role in supporting the apartheid government.

Royal Dutch/Shell basically provided South Africa with a vital natural resource the country did not possess: oil.

By refining that oil and selling it to the South African

government for its military and police, we argued that Shell directly fueled apartheid.

Significantly, South African law defined oil as a "munition of war." By investing large amounts of capital in South Africa, Shell played a crucial role in propping up its crisis-ridden economy.

Our case against Shell was strengthened by the fact that both the United Nations and the Organization of the Petroleum Exporting Countries (OPEC) had in place oil embargoes that barred shipments of crude oil to South Africa. Shell clearly had violated those embargoes through purposely convoluted arrangements with oil traders and various middlemen, including those in Oman, Brunei, and elsewhere.

Bieber and Trumka launched the Shell boycott in January 1986 along with Randall Robinson of the Free South Africa Movement. The boycott soon had more than 70 endorsers, including the NAACP, the National Organization for Women, the AFL-CIO, the National Council of Churches, SEIU, and the U.S. Student Association.

"The UAW supports the Shell boycott for two central reasons: first, because of Royal Dutch/Shell's mistreatment of black workers at its Rietspruit mine in South Africa; and second, because Shell provides fuel for South Africa's apartheid economy and security forces repressing blacks there," Bieber later wrote.[7] In a story on the growing pressure the UAW campaign had created, *The Washington Post* wrote: "The Shell boycott is one of the more dramatic examples of the escalating pressures that have faced most multinational corporations operating in South Africa."[8] The article quoted Tony Cimino, a Shell Oil official, stating that "the boycott is a concern to Shell."

"This could adversely affect the business of our dealers and jobbers. They're the ones who see the picketers and have the customers turned away," he said.

A *Business International* report on South Africa also found the boycott had begun to hurt Royal Dutch/Shell:

"A global campaign to force the Royal Dutch/Shell Group to withdraw from South Africa is beginning to draw blood. . . . The growing pressure on the company opens an ominous new chapter in the disinvestment debate, with European activists introducing the same tactics against Shell that have proved so successful in the U.S."[9]

Shell Oil had more than 11,000 gas stations in the United States during this period. It also had a range of other products we urged consumers to avoid, such as tires, batteries, furniture polish, flea collars, and air fresheners.

UAW President Bieber asked members to avoid patronizing Shell gas stations and called upon consumers to cut their Shell credit cards in half and mail them to the AFL-CIO.

The boycott began by targeting 11 cities, including Detroit. UAW members and anti-apartheid activists passed out leaflets at Shell stations that described the company's role in South Africa. Within several months, it was clear the boycott had an impact.

Quickly we had produced "Stop Apartheid, Boycott Shell" bumper stickers, buttons, a wallet-size "Discredit Card" that was "a reminder of your commitment to boycott Shell products," a 16-page guide to why Shell was our boycott target, a 9-minute slide show that featured Bieber and Trumka, posters for stores that read "No Shell Products Sold Here," and a range of leaflets targeted at different audiences.

To combat the boycott, Shell arranged for many of its stations to drop gas prices below their competitors'. The company also tried unsuccessfully to claim it was unrelated to the operations in South Africa.

"Certainly, we are concerned" about the boycott, said Shell's chief spokesperson, Richard Hansen, in 1986, as the campaign grew. "The boycott isn't doing us any good."[10] Shell also sought to counter the negative publicity by arranging news conferences and interviews featuring independent gas station owners operating Shell stations.

In response, we shifted the boycott's focus to stations that were company-owned. The Detroit campaign, for example, spared individual owners and focused picketing at the two stations in the city that were owned directly by Shell.

Much of the energy for the boycott came from the UMWA.

Shell had a 50 percent interest in A. T. Massey Company, where about 1,000 coal miners in West Virginia and Kentucky had been involved in a bitter 15-month strike in 1984–85. When it ended one month before the Shell boycott launched, UMWA President Trumka said the company had conducted "the most vicious reign of terror against working people seen in this country since the 1930s."[11] In addition, the Rietspruit mine in South Africa produced more than 6 million tons of coal annually, and most of it was exported. Because of the low labor costs under the apartheid system, South Africa's coal exports undercut U.S. competitiveness in the international coal market.

UMWA organizer Sidney Hill, who worked full-time on the Shell boycott, told reporters that 1,500 union coal miners had been laid off in the Birmingham, Alabama, area in early 1986.

"Coal miners are responding real well to the call [for a boycott]," Hill said. "We are having no trouble making the link-up with the South African coal industry."

Ken Zinn of the UMWA helped develop a strategy that centered on getting shareholders of Royal Dutch Petroleum Company to demand a special shareholders' meeting to discuss withdrawal from South Africa. Dutch law and the corporation's own bylaws required that an extraordinary shareholders' meeting be conducted if investors holding 10 percent of Royal Dutch Petroleum shares requested the special session.

Working with church groups, other unions, and pension fund administrators, we won commitments of owners of nearly 12 million shares of Royal Dutch Petroleum stock for a special

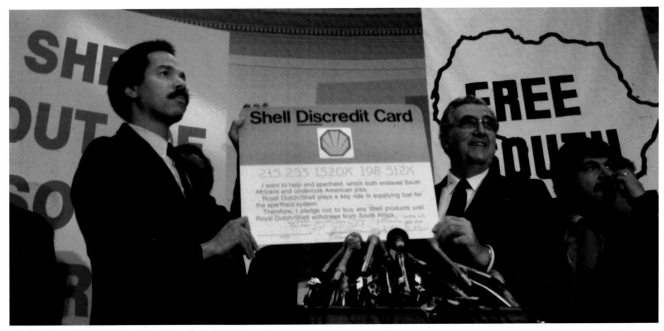

Randall Robinson of the Free South Africa Movement joined UAW President Owen Bieber and United Mine Workers President Richard Trumka to launch the Shell Boycott in January 1986. The boycott had more than 70 endorsers, including the NAACP and the National Organization for Women. Photo by Earl Dotter.

Photo by Earl Dotter.

shareholders meeting. These represented large public employee pension funds, religious institutions, insurance companies, and even some banks.

We would have had even more shares committed to the strategy, but many of the most activist shareholders had chosen to divest themselves of Royal Dutch/Shell stock entirely—actions we also supported.

John R. Wilson, the chair of Shell South Africa, told his senior executives the company "is involved in a struggle for survival" and could be forced to pull out of South Africa. He called the boycott effort led by Bieber and Trumka "an onslaught" and said "we would have difficulty pretending" the Shell boycott was not a major factor in company discussions on its future.

"If the bottom line of Royal Dutch/Shell is adversely affected internationally, the shareholders will have to reconsider their position," Wilson ventured.

The Johannesburg *Sunday Times* carried a headline of "SHELL SHOCK!" and a story that stated: "Any move by Shell to run down its operations would be a heavy psychological blow to South Africa."

We opened another front in the Shell boycott campaign working with the National Council of Black Mayors, whose members included the leaders of Los Angeles, Atlanta, Chicago, and Birmingham. The group resolved that its members would work to divest all city funds from Shell companies, withdraw Shell credit cards issued to city employees, and ban purchases of Shell products by city agencies.

After winning the black mayors' support, we went to the National Black Caucus of State Legislators, and it approved a similar resolution.

In the aftermath, the Los Angeles County Board investors dumped $15 million of Royal Dutch/Shell stock. The City of Detroit sold shares worth $3 million. And Harvard University

got rid of $32 million of stock. Other unions and religious organizations sold more than $12.5 million worth of shares in Shell.

New York City Comptroller Harrison Goldin sent an official demand that Shell stop fueling the South African military and police.

"The provision of goods or services to the (South African) government, its agencies, and enterprises constitutes support for apartheid—a morally reprehensible policy," Goldin said at a press conference with Ken Zinn. "At the same time, we believe that the reckless, public-be-damned attitude evidenced by companies (such as Shell) that continue to make these sales to the Republic of South Africa make them a poor investment."

We also conducted regular informational picketing in front of Shell's legislative offices on Connecticut Avenue NW in Washington, D.C. There was always a small core of UAW staffers from the union's D.C. office, joined by a wide range of other unions as well. Whenever we needed more marchers, Zinn or I would call the Seafarers union, and it would bus recruits from the union's training school in Piney Point, Maryland.

One sign of the effectiveness of our boycott came in 1987, when we got our hands on a secret report called the "Neptune Strategy" through our friend Tim Smith, who ran the Interfaith Center on Corporate Responsibility (ICCR), a group with close ties to church organizations that worked to promote corporate social responsibility.

The "Neptune" report was a 254-page strategy document prepared by Pagan International, a corporate public relations firm that had a long history of fighting boycott campaigns, such as the one conducted against Nestlé. That company sold powdered milk that had resulted in many mothers in developing nations giving up breast-feeding of their infants—some of whom died because Nestlé's powdered formula had to be mixed with water that often was tainted.

Shell had commissioned Pagan to develop a strategy to

counter the Shell boycott by dividing the coalition the UAW had helped create. The "Neptune Strategy" sought to use a former National Council of Churches leader, James Armstrong, to pressure religious leaders to weaken or end support for the boycott. It also detailed the hiring of consultants with close ties to organized labor to water down union support.

I was stunned to find that one such consultant, who had been the labor liaison for the 1984 presidential campaign of Democratic Party nominee Walter Mondale, quietly used his influence against us.

Through Pagan, Shell secretly orchestrated the creation of the Coalition on Southern Africa. It was led by several prominent black clergymen who ostensibly sought to help prepare for a post-apartheid society. In fact, the Coalition was a front group set up by Shell to undermine church support for the boycott and to oppose religious organizations calling for disinvestment.

Shell and Pagan denied any connection with the Coalition, but we quickly learned that Pagan had provided the front group with free office space, had paid for travel by the group's leaders, and covered the cost of telephones for the Coalition.[12] The disclosure of Pagan International's secret plan to divide and conquer the Shell boycott coalition created an uproar. Shell sought to distance itself from Pagan and canceled its $800,000 contract with the company, which was run by Rafael D. Pagan Jr., a former high-level military intelligence operative. Soon, other corporate clients dumped Pagan in the aftermath of widespread negative publicity we helped to generate.[13] Several years later, Pagan International shut its doors for good and filed for bankruptcy.

While Shell continued to resist calls to disinvest from South Africa, the boycott "had a sustained impact on public opinion and imposed significant economic costs on Shell," according to William Minter and Sylvia Hill, who analyzed anti-apartheid solidarity some years later.[14] "More broadly, the wider campaign for divestment and economic disengagement intensified business demands for change in the apartheid system," they found.

Chase Manhattan Bank decided not to roll over a $500 million loan to South Africa, and soon a number of other banks and financial institutions had cut their lending to the apartheid nation.

General Motors then announced it planned to pull out of South Africa. IBM said it would withdraw as well, and so did Citibank.

Between January 1, 1986, the same month the UAW helped launch the Shell boycott, and April 30, 1988, 114 U.S. companies said they would withdraw from South Africa.[15]

The impact was dramatic, Minter and Hill said. "It reflected a fundamental shift in perspective from the assumption that the apartheid regime might continue and successfully reform itself to the view that only a democratic transition could ensure stability in South Africa," they wrote.

At the same time the UAW and its allies put pressure on banks and corporations doing business with the apartheid regime, the union also provided practical assistance to the independent black unions in South Africa.

The UAW sent Dr. Frank Mirer, who directed the union's Occupational Safety and Health Department, to South Africa in 1986 to teach classes organized by the auto and metal unions there. Because most workers spoke English, UAW health and safety materials that detailed various workplace hazards helped South African workers demand safer working conditions.[16] Some of the health and safety seminars were run by the International Metalworkers' Federation (IMF), a global union federation with which the UAW was affiliated. The IMF also worked closely with unions in South Africa.

The UAW had aligned itself strongly with the emerging independent black unions there and had concerns about some

South African IMF affiliates run by whites that continued in the early 1980s to discriminate against black workers. The union sent Vice President Marc Stepp and James Wright, the Region 4 director, to South Africa as part of a fact-finding mission.

After the trip, Stepp and Wright recommended that the IMF expel the racist white unions. Subsequently, in June 1982, those unions were thrown out.

That same year, the AFL-CIO unfortunately gave its George Meany Human Rights Award to Gatsha Buthelezi, the Zulu leader of Inkatha. Buthelezi went on to form a phony labor federation that appeared to be a front for the apartheid government. His Inkatha forces later waged a literal war on the unions in South Africa that included the murders of a number of metalworkers who were allies of the UAW there.

In this period, the AFL-CIO, led by Lane Kirkland, frequently faced criticism from the UAW and other progressive unions for the federation's prioritizing of anti-communism abroad. By honoring Buthelezi, the AFL-CIO marginalized its ability to work with many of South Africa's independent black unions until after Kirkland was forced out and new leadership

UAW local unions carried out much of the union's campaign against apartheid. Sam Meyers, then president of Local 259, rallied support for the Shell boycott in 1987. Photo by Linda Eber.

took over the federation in 1995.

The UAW intervened in the mid-1980s to help our counterpart unions in South Africa and often played a role in their ongoing contract disputes with General Motors and Ford subsidiaries operating there. We helped the National Union of Motor Assembly and Rubber Workers win significant contract gains after intervention by the UAW General Motors Department and UAW Ford Department.

When the National Automobile and Allied Workers Union (NAAWU) sought our help in getting fired members back to work at a subsidiary of Borg-Warner, I arranged a meeting between UAW Vice President Odessa Komer and executives of the parent company in the United States. The intervention succeeded in getting the workers rehired in South Africa.

UAW President Owen Bieber made two trips to South Africa at the invitation of the black unions there to see firsthand the conditions they faced and to show the UAW's solidarity with them.

The first trip occurred in 1986 about nine weeks after the apartheid government had imposed a "state of emergency" that gave it extraordinary powers to repress blacks and other people of color following the success of a May Day strike and continued widespread unrest in the black townships. Estimates of the number of people jailed ranged from 12,000 to 15,000.

"I spoke with numerous union members who had been detained for varying periods of time—from 14 up to 62 days," Bieber reported after the trip. "Some had been tortured by electric shock. Others told me they were beaten with fists, whips, and other devices. Some were being held in solitary confinement with lights on 24 hours a day and TV cameras monitoring them."

Nearly all of them said their interrogations focused almost entirely on their trade union activities. I had organized the trip for Bieber and accompanied him, so I heard firsthand the accounts of these union prisoners.

One said his captors blamed the black unions for "wrecking the economy" of South Africa through their "high" wage demands and militancy.

"I heard four reports of children being held in detention," Bieber said. "The youngest was 8 years old. Others were 9, and groups age 11 and up. The children reported some were taken back to their townships with blankets placed over them with eyeholes cut out so they could see.

"Then they were asked to point out to authorities individuals who allegedly had asked township residents to support community-based rent boycotts and other protest activities. Those who refused to name others were taken back to detention and were said to have been subjected to electric shock."

The UAW president met with two cabinet ministers of the South African government during the trip. He blasted the repression of the black majority by the apartheid regime and raised the issue of the thousands of detainees very strongly.

Bieber found the unions, such as the National Union of Metalworkers of South Africa (NUMSA), to be a crucial force for black empowerment.

"They make up one of the only sectors in which black leadership development has been allowed and in which blacks negotiate across the table from whites," the UAW president said after he returned. "I was impressed with the strong democratic roots in these unions.

"Many concentrated in the early period after legalization on shop floor actions and collective bargaining," he noted. "They built a grassroots base by delivering on economics and improving working conditions. Yet they also recognized over time the need to mobilize against the rigid and racist apartheid political system as unionists and broaden their own political activities beyond the workplace."

During the visit, many of the union leaders and workers we met said they favored disinvestment and the strongest pos-

sible sanctions against the apartheid government. They saw the withdrawal of foreign companies from South Africa as a necessary last resort, given the conditions that existed under the state of emergency and the inadequacies of so-called "reforms"

offered by the government.

The black workers and unionists Bieber and I spoke with emphasized the necessity of corporations bargaining with the unions over the terms of their withdrawal from South Africa and urged that the "wealth" (in terms of plants, equipment, etc.) be kept within the country when disinvestment occurred.

We met with workers at the General Motors plant in Port Elizabeth and at a factory near Pretoria in which Ford had a substantial ownership stake. Later, Bieber and union leaders met with company management to press a number of economic and workplace issues of concern to its black workers.

"One of the unions' key demands was that the companies pay full wages to workers who had been jailed by the government under the state of emergency," Bieber said. "Upon my return to America, I entered into discussions with GM. Subsequently, the firm's South African subsidiary agreed to pay detainees 100 percent of their wages."

This success grew out of some discussions we had as Bieber's trip was being planned. Some of our South Africa allies told me that General Motors and other firms paid white workers their full wages during periods when they were called up to serve in the military or security forces. They went into townships and factories to suppress protests. But the companies refused to treat their workers who were arrested and detained in the same way.

Bieber really homed in on this unequal treatment and raised it forcefully with GM's CEO, Roger Smith. Already sensitive to the negative image its very presence in South Africa presented and wanting to keep peace with the UAW, Smith finally agreed to Bieber's demand to pay the detainees their wages.

But months later, NUMSA leaders contacted me to say that, in fact, local managers for GM still had not honored the deal. Bieber demanded to speak to Smith immediately, and soon he was patched through to the CEO, who was in the air on one of the company's private jets. After some angry conversation, Smith pledged to get involved directly. Soon, the GM detainees' families were getting paid, and other money was set aside to be paid after release.

After Bieber's visit, both GM and Ford sold off direct ownership of their South African operations, although each maintained ties there through licensing and other arrangements.

GM's pullback, however, provoked a bitter strike. It refused to reach agreement with the union on severance and other issues. The apartheid regime sent in police to break the strike, and many of the union activists were fired.

During Bieber's visit in 1986, he demanded to visit Moses Mayekiso, an autoworker who led one of the unions that eventually merged to form NUMSA. He had been jailed for using trade union organizing tactics in his township of Alexandra, near Johannesburg, seeking to improve the horrible living conditions there.

He and four others were charged with treason and sedition and faced death by hanging if convicted. The UAW fought

hard on Mayekiso's behalf, as the following chapter in this book details.

The UAW campaigned as well for others who rotted away in apartheid jails without charge or trial. Many had been tortured and denied access to family members and lawyers.

In 1989, Bieber sent a telex message to Adriaan Vlok, South Africa's minister of law and order, urging him to end the detentions of those held without charge.

"No civilized nation in the world locks people up without charge or trial and just throws away the prison keys," Bieber's telex stated. "That is what the apartheid government has done, and it is reprehensible."

The UAW president had been moved in part by a message he received from the Southern African Catholic Bishops' Conference, which passed on information from Diepkloof Prison in Johannesburg where some prisoners had been held for nearly three years without any charges or trial.

"We now have embarked on a hunger strike in an attempt to highlight our detention and the restrictions on our organizations and bodies," the detainees' communication said. "We call on you as Christians and concerned individuals to bring our plight to all and to pressure the government to release us."

I had been in South Africa the week before Bieber sent his telex to Vlok. NUMSA leaders had told me their union had at least eight members imprisoned in brutal conditions. I

passed that news on to the UAW president and told him at least two members of NUMSA were on the hunger strike: Andrew Mzobe, who was held in Modderbee Prison in Springs, South Africa, and Amos Mathonsi, whose location I could not verify.

In a press statement that followed, Bieber reported:

"While in South Africa, Stillman met with lawyers who represent a number of the detainees still incarcerated who were participating in the hunger strikes. They told him of the severe human anguish and detrimental psychological and physical condition of many of their detained clients. Many of them are youths who are likely to suffer lasting effects from being held in prison with so little hope for so long."

The UAW president decided to dramatize the union's concern for the detainees' plight. On February 17, 1989, he announced that he and other UAW leaders would join the hunger fasts in support of the black South African prisoners being held without charge.

He said the UAW joined with its allies in South Africa to urge the detainees to suspend their own hunger strikes because many were in extreme physical danger after not eating for 24 days or more.

"I began this fast at 6 a.m. today to make a moral statement about the outrageous injustice being inflicted by the apartheid government, which has kept more than 1,000 blacks locked up for as long as two-and-one-half years without charge or trial," Bieber said.[17] He said that at the end of his fast 48 hours later, another UAW leader would begin fasting for 48 hours, followed by a third and so on.

"This will be a 'rolling fast' with someone from the UAW fasting at all times until the detainees are released or at least through to our convention in mid-June," he said.

"The South African detainees have done their part through the hunger strikes to pressure the government. Now's the time for us to pick up their struggle and shine the spotlight of international scrutiny on apartheid's jails."

The pressure had an impact. We heard from church leaders, including Anglican Archbishop Desmond Tutu, that the government would free some detainees. And within a few weeks, hundreds of them were released, including many trade unionists.

It was a victory of sorts, but Bieber said he could not and would not forget the other detainees who remained locked in apartheid jails.

The UAW also played a crucial role in the fight against apartheid by pushing the United States to adopt tough sanctions on South Africa.

When President Ronald Reagan took office in 1981, he soon gave a speech expressing his support for South Africa's apartheid government, largely due to its backing of America in the Cold War.

P. W. Botha, the South African president, shrewdly manipulated both Reagan and British Prime Minister Margaret Thatcher by playing to their fears of the Soviet Union's developing influence in Africa. Botha warned of a revolution in South Africa that would result in a Marxist takeover and a black-run government aligned with the Soviet Union.

Reagan worried about Angola, where the government had welcomed Cuban military forces and allied itself with the Soviets. Namibia, which was on the path to independence, also posed dangers of aligning with the left, Reagan believed. The apartheid government played on the conservatives' fear that all of Africa would go Marxist if apartheid opponents took power in South Africa.

Soon, the Reagan administration was giving economic and military aid to the apartheid government. He called his policy "constructive engagement" and said the United States would provide positive incentives for South Africa to slowly move away from the apartheid system. The conservative Republican strongly rejected sanctions and disinvestment, the policies advocated by the UAW as part of a broad international consensus that included the United Nations and most other countries.

Opposition to Reagan's constructive engagement policy mounted shortly after he was reelected to a second term in 1984. A sit-in occurred at the South African embassy in Washington, D.C., the day before Thanksgiving, led by Randall Robinson of TransAfrica; Mary Francis Berry, who had chaired the U.S. Civil Rights Commission; Walter Fauntroy, D.C.'s at-large member of Congress; and Eleanor Holmes Norton, who had chaired the Equal Employment Opportunity Commission.

All were close allies of the UAW, and they formed the core of the Free South Africa Movement.

On November 28, 1984, UAW Vice President Marc Stepp went to the embassy to deliver a letter from Bieber to the South African ambassador demanding the release of jailed unionists.

Stepp was arrested along with U.S. Representative Ron Dellums, a leader of the Congressional Black Caucus.

"I went to jail proudly to express my outrage over the arrest without charges of 13 black South African union leaders and to protest the racist policies of the white-minority government there," Stepp said.

The embassy officials had refused to accept the UAW letter. When the UAW leader refused to leave, he was handcuffed behind his back and forced to spend the night in jail.[18] "Americans cannot afford to sit idly by and see their U.S. tax dollars supporting . . . near-slavery conditions that exist in the rich country of South Africa," Stepp said after his arrest. "President Reagan cannot continue calling for free trade unions in Poland yet not do the same in South Africa."

Danny Glover, the award-winning film actor and activist,

UAW President Owen Bieber and Vice President Ernie Lofton were arrested at the embassy of South Africa in April 1985 during an anti-apartheid protest. Photo by Rick Reinhard.

joined other UAW leaders at new protests at the embassy, as did Harry Belafonte, the famous singer and ally of progressive causes.

After the series of arrests including Stepp, and later Bieber and another UAW vice president, Ernie Lofton, the South African ambassador complained to the White House that the protests were the equivalent of the seizure of the United States embassy in Iran that led to the 1980 hostage crisis.

The UAW had pushed Congress to enact economic and political sanctions against South Africa since the early 1970s when Dellums had introduced such legislation. The Democrats in the Senate tried to pass a sanctions bill in 1985, but could

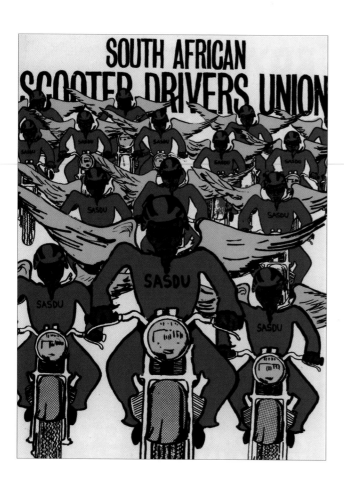

not overcome a Republican filibuster.

The next year, following the continued protests, a weakened bill did pass, but Reagan vetoed it. The Republican president called the bill "economic warfare" and called in Pik Botha, the apartheid government's foreign minister, to help rally GOP support for his veto.

Both the Senate (78–21) and the House (313–83) voted to override the Reagan veto of the Comprehensive Anti-Apartheid Act. It was the first time in the 20th century that a president had a foreign policy veto overridden.[19] Reagan had suffered a huge rebuff of his support for the apartheid regime. He lost many Republicans on the override vote. In 1989 after Reagan left office, the nonpartisan General Accounting Office studied the impact of the Anti-Apartheid Act and found the Reagan administration failed to enforce basic elements of the law.

UAW President Bieber played a major role in the sanctions debate. Reagan had directed Secretary of State George Shultz to establish an Advisory Committee on South Africa. Shultz, who had earlier served as secretary of labor, respected Bieber's achievements at the bargaining table and his leadership on global issues. He named Bieber to the committee, whose other members included CEOs of IBM and General Motors, former attorney general Griffin Bell, and the leader of the Christian College Coalition.

Bieber pressed the committee to recommend tough sanctions against South Africa. The group's 72-page report in 1987 stunned the Reagan administration because it had handpicked the members.

It criticized the Reagan policy on South Africa and said the United States should join with other nations to expand international sanctions on the apartheid government. Those included a ban on new investments in South Africa, a halt to loans to the apartheid government, curbs on South African exports and imports, termination of landing rights for South African Airways, and others.

The UAW sent observers to the 1994 election in South Africa. Nelson Mandela's last big campaign rally occurred in Durban. Photo by Don Stillman.

The committee said Reagan's policy of constructive engagement with the apartheid government had "failed to achieve its objectives."

Bieber shared that view, but filed a dissenting opinion included in the report. The UAW president called for even more potent sanctions. He also foresaw Reagan's failure to enforce South Africa sanctions, stating: "There is no room for a difference between the laws of the United States and the policy of this administration."[20]

All of the pressure on the apartheid government from outside South Africa, including that of the UAW and its allies, helped, but it was the courage and perseverance of workers and others inside that country that ultimately toppled that ugly, racist system.

Hundreds of thousands of workers in unions affiliated with the Congress of South African Trade Unions (COSATU) kept the heat on the government every day. Church leaders, such as Archbishop Desmond Tutu and the Rev. Beyers Naude, and their followers campaigned relentlessly against apartheid. Town-

ship activists fought back through street and yard committees.

South Africa, in 1990 led by F. W. de Klerk, faced popular uprisings and internal resistance at home and sanctions and embargoes on the global front. De Klerk and other apartheid leaders concluded the system no longer could be sustained and that a path toward multiracial democratic elections was preferable to the possibility of escalating internal resistance that could end in a violent overthrow of the white minority government.

They began repealing apartheid laws and engaging in private discussions with the African National Congress. De Klerk, who had replaced P. W. Botha after he suffered a stroke, lifted the ban on the ANC and ordered the release of Nelson Mandela from Victor Verster Prison after 27 years of confinement.

On February 11, 1990, Mandela left prison finally free at last. He gave a speech in Cape Town that was televised worldwide. In it, he reaffirmed his commitment to peace and reconciliation with the white minority, called for the apartheid regime to negotiate "so there may no longer be the need for armed struggle," and urged that black South Africans have the right to vote in elections at all levels.

UAW President Bieber immediately sent Mandela a letter inviting him to visit the union in Detroit. It was an invitation Mandela accepted as part of a U.S. tour in June 1990. By then, Mandela and the ANC had begun "talks about talks" over the terms of a negotiated settlement with de Klerk and other government officials.

On his tour of the U.S., Mandela arrived at Detroit Metro Airport on June 28, 1990, where he was met by a group led by Bieber, who took him to Ford's Dearborn Assembly Plant.

"Hundreds of autoworkers waited in the steamy plant for hours, and sent up a tremendous cheer when Mandela appeared," the *Detroit Free Press* reported.

UAW President Bieber and Vice President Ernie Lofton presented Mandela with a jacket with his name and the union logo on it and with an honorary lifetime UAW membership card.

Mandela beamed his approval, held up the card for all to see, and told the crowd: "The man who is speaking is not a stranger here. The man who is speaking is a member of the UAW. I am your flesh and blood. I am your comrade."[21] The then 71-year-old leader of the African National Congress told UAW workers that he felt joy and strength from his visit to Local 600.

"You are not only workers at this plant . . . you are the men and women who are responsible for the health of the economy of this country," he said.

Mandela praised the UAW for its "unswerving" record of support for the struggle of black South African workers and the union's many years of work against apartheid.[22] Bieber told Mandela the union was honored that he chose a UAW plant

as the only factory he visited on his tour of the United States.

"The UAW is proud of the fact that we have long supported the proposition that the apartheid government system in South Africa has to go, and we pledge to you today our support here in this country," the UAW president said.

Those traveling in the Mandela delegation, including CO-SATU Vice President Chris Dlamini, said black unionists and anti-apartheid activists in South Africa credited the UAW for leading the U.S. labor movement's drive for sanctions and for providing substantial support for black unions in South Africa.[23] Mandela, who stayed at the Westin Hotel in Detroit, invited Bieber to go walking with him near the Detroit River. They talked about revenge and why Mandela rejected it.

"He said there's nothing to be gained by retribution," Bieber said, recalling Mandela's words to him that "I'm just interested in building a better country for all of [our] citizens."[24]

UAW President Owen Bieber and Vice President Ernie Lofton (left) presented Nelson Mandela with a UAW jacket and honorary membership card. Mandela told the crowd: "The man who is speaking is a member of the UAW. I am your flesh and blood. I am your comrade." Photo by Daymon Hartley.

Over the next few years, Mandela and the ANC reached agreement with de Klerk and the government on an interim constitution, creation of a constitutional court, a "bill of rights," and a range of transitional measures.

But the most important achievement was the agreement to hold the multiracial election that occurred on April 27, 1994. It established a government of national unity led by Mandela.

The UAW sent a delegation to help monitor that historic election, which included M. L. Douglas of Local 22; Gordon Fleming of Local 600; Harold Sheldon of Local 668; Eula Booker Tate of Local 372; Eddie Thomas Sr. of Local 961; and Dan Wainaina of Local 600. John Christensen of the International Affairs Department and I also went to South Africa to be part of the monitoring effort.

While there, I saw firsthand the huge turnout by millions of black South Africans who had never before cast ballots for those who governed them.

John Gomomo, an autoworker who then led COSATU, took me with him as he voted for the first time near his home in Uitenhage. It was a moment of great pride for him, and incredibly moving for me as well.

Several days before in Johannesburg, I had been reminded that the struggle was not over. Christensen and I stayed at a small hotel downtown. I had sought press accreditation from the ANC in order to be able to move freely around the polling places where voting occurred.

When I called the ANC press operation at the Carlton Hotel nearby, I was told the photographer who would take the photo for my press card was out and I should come an hour later than planned.

During that hour, right-wing white extremists set off a bomb that created a huge crater on Bree Street, the route I would have taken to the Carlton Hotel. The blast killed 7 people and injured at least 13 others. It destroyed most of the block.

The author at the site of a bombing by far right political forces opposed to South Africa's 1994 election of Nelson Mandela as president. Photo by John Christensen.

After observing the election, Christensen and I flew back from Port Elizabeth to Johannesburg. As our plane neared Jan Smuts Airport, the pilot announced we would be circling for at least an hour because there had been an explosion at the airport.

It turned out the bombing had been committed by members of the AWB, a far-right Boer-Afrikaner extremist group.

The area of the explosion was closed off, but when I went to the airport two days later to fly back to the United States, I found the bomb had exploded just a few feet away from a rental car counter where I had stood for 45 minutes a few days before while waiting for a friend, Frank Greer, who was a media adviser to Mandela.

Neither bombing dampened the high spirits that millions of previously disenfranchised black South Africans felt. Not only had they been able to vote for the first time, but they had also elected an ANC government led by Nelson Mandela to replace the hated apartheid regime.

December in South Africa is a summer month. The earth in Mandela's childhood village of Qunu was warm as workers in 2013 dug the grave near a tent in which tribal leaders wearing animal skins later joined with international digni-

South African children gathered on election day, 1994. Photo by Don Stillman.

taries. They all watched the final steps of Mandela's long walk to freedom.

Mandela's casket was draped in the South African flag in the tent, and a crescent of 95 candles burned nearby—one for each year of his life.

Mourners listened as the sounds of the national anthem, "Nkosi Sikelel iAfrika"—"God Bless Africa"—drifted over the village.

South Africa's current president, Jacob Zuma, told the crowd: "We shall not say good-bye, for you are not gone. You'll live forever in our hearts and minds."[25]

In Detroit, UAW President Bob King said the union "deeply mourns the loss of Nelson Mandela, one of the most influential civil rights and social justice leaders of our time."

"Nelson Mandela demonstrated how commitment to core principles and social justice can change the world," King said in a statement. "His actions freed millions from the chains of racism. From his humble beginnings to his imprisonment for fighting against the apartheid system in South Africa, Nelson Mandela was an inspiration to the world.

"It was an incredible honor for the UAW . . . to play a role in supporting Mandela and other anti-apartheid activists" over the years of struggle, King said.

Despite massive coverage by the mainstream media of Mandela's life and death in December 2013, little attention was paid to the crucial role of independent black unions in the victory over apartheid.

Nor was there much coverage of the important support given them in their struggle by the UAW and many other unions throughout the world.

One of the very few writers who did take notice was a sports reporter, Sean Corp, who wrote on the SBNation.com website. He had seen a photo of Mandela in a Detroit Pistons jacket that he found "awesome."

The 1994 election went smoothly. These women waited in long lines to vote for the first time. Photo by Don Stillman.

"Originally, I set out to answer a simple question," he wrote. "Just how did Nelson Mandela get photographed in a Pistons hat and jacket . . . and why Detroit?"[26]

After researching those issues, he noted that Mandela said during his visit to the Ford Rouge plant that "in jail and behind the thick prison walls, we could hear loud and clear your voice calling for our release."

Sean Corp wrote that some of the loudest voices in America came from Detroit—more specifically they came from the UAW.

"The UAW and other powerful unions in the United States were the driving force" speaking out against the South African government and apartheid, he wrote.

"If that Pistons jacket reflects Detroit, then it surely reflects the union roots of the great American city," he noted.

Despite the current difficulties faced by the city and the union, Corp wrote, "it's important to remember the triumphant role unions played in applying the political and financial pressure to release Mandela, even when it wasn't popular to do so."

CHAPTER TWO

'Don't Let South Africa Hang This Labor Leader'
UAW Solidarity Helped Save Autoworker Moses Mayekiso

The South African embassy, then an outpost of apartheid, fronted on Massachusetts Avenue in Washington, D.C., just south of the official residence of the U.S. vice president on what is known as "Embassy Row."[1]

On a cool, cloudy late afternoon in the spring of 1988, security guards at the embassy scrambled to secure the doors of the Cape Dutch–style building made of Indiana limestone as if it were under attack.

Busload after busload of UAW health and safety reps pulled up in front of the embassy as D.C. police sirens drowned out all but the loudest conversations.

The reps disembarked from the buses and began marching up and down the sidewalk in front of the embassy, many of them carrying signs that read "UAW Demands Free Moses" above a photo of a black man wearing a cap and a union T-shirt, surrounded by young children.

Embassy guards, accustomed to smaller protests with pre-arranged arrests of celebrities there to publicize their opposition to apartheid, calmed down once they realized the UAW members conducted themselves peacefully. Soon they were asking just who this "Moses" was.

"We see some 'Free Mandela' demonstrations here from time to time, but this is the first 'Free Moses' protest we had," said one of the guards in a heavy Afrikaner accent. "Can you tell me who this Moses is?"

UAW President Owen Bieber addressed the more than 350 protesters a few moments later and provided an answer.

"Moses Mayekiso is the leader of the autoworkers union in South Africa, and he's rotting away in an apartheid jail," Bieber said. "Moses is on trial for applying trade union tactics in his township, and he's facing a hangman's noose if he's convicted. The UAW is committed to fight to keep that from happening."

Mayekiso led the Metal and Allied Workers Union (MAWU), one of the most important trade unions in South Africa in the 1980s when the independent black labor movement played a crucial role in the struggle to rid that country of its system of racial segregation known as apartheid. Arrested in 1986, Moses later was charged with treason, sedition, and subversion—if guilty, he faced death row at a time when someone was hanged every three days in South Africa.

The story of the white South African government's effort to repress union and township activists by targeting Moses Mayekiso reveals much about the darkest days of apartheid and about the UAW's important role in building international support aimed at winning not only his freedom, but that of all black South Africans.

In 1986, Moses Mayekiso had ample time on his flight home to South Africa to reflect on his trip to the United Kingdom and Sweden where he had talked with union members about the struggle of workers in the factories and black townships of South Africa.

The DC-10 from Stockholm to Johannesburg made its 14-hour journey as Moses thought about the small meetings he had with shop stewards and large, more boisterous rallies of anti-apartheid activists at which he described a South Africa where blacks had no political rights, where a white minority government dictated where blacks could live and work, and where blacks who resisted the virtual domination of their lives by whites were jailed or banned.

Mayekiso spoke of a country where repression of basic freedoms was the rule rather than an exception. As general secretary of MAWU, he outlined efforts to win a voice in the workplace, where blacks were stuck in the lowest-paying jobs with limited rights and benefits compared to their white counterparts.

A civic activist as well as a union leader, Mayekiso told of his own actions in the black townships, particularly Alexandra, where he lived with his wife and seven children. He had applied the skills and techniques of organizing learned in the union movement to the struggles for a better life in the townships. The emerging black labor movement had won victories in the workplaces, and, he argued, union tactics and strategies could be adapted to the townships where so many lived in squalor.

As the plane neared Johannesburg, Mayekiso thought about events that had occurred while he was out of his country. On June 12, 1986, two weeks earlier, the apartheid government had declared a state of emergency. P. W. Botha, the South African president, had responded to massive unrest in black townships and a nationwide "stayaway," a general strike by black workers.

The state of emergency gave the security forces the cloak of law to take actions that would otherwise have been illegal even under apartheid statutes. Now they had the ability to make arbitrary arrests and hold detainees without charging them with an offense or conducting a trial in a court of law. Authorities had the right to enter, search, and seize property without warrants and had broad indemnity for their actions.

Mayekiso believed these extreme measures had been imposed by an apartheid government that clearly saw the relationship between black protest in the workplace and similar actions in the townships. Each posed a threat to the minority government and the comfortable lives lived by many white South Africans, but together they meant insurrection.

Botha used the state's guns and tanks under the state of emergency. Thousands of blacks from Transvaal to the Cape and from Natal to the Orange Free State were being arrested. Apartheid's jails were packed with church and community activists, workers and union leaders, children and the elderly.

Many of these detentions made little sense. Workers who played no role in strikes or union actions nevertheless were picked up, while some top union leaders remained free. It was the same with church leaders and community activists. But the massive exercise in repression had an intimidating result.

As the plane landed, Mayekiso looked forward to seeing his wife, Khola, and his kids. He also felt a sense of urgency to see what could be done to free jailed members of his union and those from his township. He knew his leadership was needed more than ever.

But so did the burly members of the South African police force, who waited at Johannesburg's Jan Smuts Airport to meet Mayekiso as he departed the plane. He was arrested and taken to John Vorster Square prison to be placed in solitary confinement without charge or access to attorneys and family. Moses had been jailed on two previous occasions, but this time would prove different.

He would face the possibility of death by the hangman's noose.

Moses Mayekiso organized workers so effectively in part because, in his own youth, he confronted the same poverty and limits as those workers he sought to unionize. Born in Transkei, he could not finish school because of money problems faced by his father, a migrant laborer in Cape Town, about 1,000 miles away. Moses helped support his seven brothers and sisters by working in the mines, but he hated the crude, dangerous working conditions. In 1973 he moved to Alexandra township outside of Johannesburg, a move that was illegal under South Africa's influx control laws that required black workers to register both their residence and employment so authorities could track and control them.

Eventually, Mayekiso found work at a Toyota warehouse, and soon his fellow workers elected him to lead the shop stewards committee. Toyota had resisted recognition of the Metal and Allied Workers Union, but Moses took an organizing approach based on a steady, meticulous set of contacts from the bottom up. Each week he conducted general meetings of rank-and-file members and emphasized the importance of members controlling decisions and leaders obeying the mandates of the workers they represented.

Toyota management saw the threat posed by Mayekiso's tactics and fired him in 1979. He went on to organize in Wadeville, a large factory area on the Witwatersrand, the industrial heartland of the country. He started holding meetings in Katlehong, a black township, where he could reach workers from many different factories at once. MAWU's membership soared after Moses faced down the police who tried to disperse one such meeting.

Mayekiso's organizing success in Wadeville caught the attention of top leaders of the Federation of South African Trade Unions (FOSATU), a forerunner of what is today called the Congress of South African Trade Unions (COSATU).

"Moses had a phenomenal ability to persuade workers and great personal bravery," recalled Bernie Fanaroff, then an official of the union, who was close to the UAW. "He avoided rabble-rousing tactics. He always explained things to workers and made sure they understood. He [did] not believe in promising things which he [couldn't] deliver, or in 'triumphalism'—unrealistic optimism."

During this time, Mayekiso led an action that presaged the community activism he later employed in Alexandra. He worked with the shop stewards council on a successful campaign to stop the authorities from bulldozing squatters' shacks in another township. The effort was one of the earliest interventions by black unionists in community resistance and occurred

Moses Mayekiso, an autoworker, was elected general secretary of the National Union of Metalworkers of South Africa (NUMSA) while in prison on charges of treason, subversion, and sedition.

as they also focused on strengthening their base in the workplace following adoption of new labor laws.

Mayekiso excelled at confronting managers who were accustomed to exploiting the black workforce with impunity. That skill soon propelled him into the top leadership of MAWU, where he led a major strike in 1984 that got him arrested and jailed until the charges eventually were dropped. The same actions that caused apartheid leaders to attack him also sped Mayekiso's rise in the labor movement. He helped draft the constitution of COSATU in 1985. The formation of the new union federation quickly consolidated much of the progress made by the "emerging" independent unions. Soon those unions began the process of unifying into one union per industry in most cases.

But in Alexandra township, during this period of progress for labor, conditions deteriorated. Government authorities planned to destroy many homes of Alexandra residents and forcibly relocate them farther away from nearby Johannesburg. Over time, MAWU's shop stewards council had discussed township problems and decided to attempt to build a community organization based on trade union principles.

Thus the Alexandra Action Committee (AAC) was born. The activities of that organization led to Mayekiso's indictment on treason, subversion, and sedition charges by the apartheid government.

Mayekiso's arrest and subsequent trial proved so important largely because they represented such a frontal attack on the black trade union movement. What seemed to tip the apartheid government into this assault was the fear that union organizing skills and tactics that succeeded in the workplace would prove equally successful in the townships.

Alexandra township, almost completely surrounded by the wealthy white suburbs of Johannesburg, had no water-borne sewage disposal system for its then 100,000 residents. Waste was removed in buckets. I went there many times, and the overpowering stench remains powerfully in my memory.

Lacking storm drains, runoff water followed the terrain in open ditches down and eastward to the Jukskei River. The only drinking water in Alex, as it was known, came from standpipes

FREE MOSES MAYEKISO!

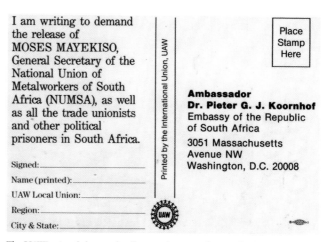

I am writing to demand the release of MOSES MAYEKISO, General Secretary of the National Union of Metalworkers of South Africa (NUMSA), as well as all the trade unionists and other political prisoners in South Africa.

Signed:_____

Name (printed):_____

UAW Local Union:_____

Region:_____

City & State:_____

Printed by the International Union, UAW

Place Stamp Here

Ambassador Dr. Pieter G. J. Koornhof Embassy of the Republic of South Africa 3051 Massachusetts Avenue NW Washington, D.C. 20008

The UAW printed thousands of postcards urging the apartheid government to release Moses Mayekiso, the autoworker put on trial for alleged treason in the mid-1980s.

with one tap for every four to six dwellings. Garbage piled up with putrefying effect along the unpaved roads of the township, because no refuse disposal existed.

Most Alex residents lived in shanties made of cardboard and plastic sheeting or in corrugated sheet metal shacks. Some occupied the shells of old buses long ago abandoned. The lucky few had real concrete-block houses but usually lived with other families in hopelessly overcrowded conditions.

The problems in Alex included not only the raw sewage and garbage strewn throughout, but also the lack of jobs, rampant crime, and a distinct sense of hopelessness that hung like a shroud over the township.

Alexandra, founded in the early 1900s, was not directly controlled by any municipality and thus had no funding for municipal services and township infrastructure. At the same time, the absence of governmental control attracted blacks who could not live elsewhere under South Africa's segregated system. In 1963, the apartheid government dictated that Alexandra become a hostel township in which single migrant workers would be housed near the mines, factories, and shops in the area. That plan failed by the mid-1970s, in part because of the death sentence it gave to family life.

As grievances in Alex worsened, so, too, did conditions in other black townships such as Soweto, where a famous uprising occurred in June 1976. Violence flared in Alex then as well, when residents burned stores and set fire to buses belonging to the Public Utility Corporation. A symbol of the hated "Bantu Education" system, Alexandra High School was torched, as were other schools throughout the country.

One government official promised that a new "master plan" for Alex launched in 1980 would transform the troubled township into a "Little Switzerland." This spurred high hopes for residents desperate for better housing and living conditions, but five years later only about 10 percent of the redevelopment had occurred.

As resistance grew in South Africa in the mid-1980s, the government essentially abandoned direct responsibility for the black townships. A black local authority was created in Alex with an elected town council. With no industrial tax base, the council turned to the residents for income, which came mainly from rent on the shacks and houses.

By 1986, Alexandra was a tinderbox due to sharp increases in rent and service charges, the failure of the redevelopment plan, the worsening of sanitation conditions, the increase in crime, and the prolonged lack of job opportunities. The members of the Alexandra town council, lacking popular support and under attack from residents, eventually resigned.

That collapse in governance at a time of broader unrest yielded a predictable response from the Botha government, which sent massive numbers of police and troops into the townships, including Alexandra.

Confronting turmoil and repression, residents of Alex turned to a trade union leader who lived on Seventh Avenue. His name: Moses Mayekiso.

In February 1986, prior to Mayekiso's arrest, the anger and despair in Alexandra ignited after a security guard at the Jazz Stores in nearby Wynburg shot and killed Michael Diradeng, a former member of the students' representative council at Alexandra High School.

At the request of the dead student's family, Mayekiso served as "master of ceremonies" at Diradeng's funeral in the township stadium, where about 13,000 people gathered to pay tribute to the youth leader and to express outrage at his killing. The South African government prohibited political demonstrations by blacks, so funerals frequently became not only vigils for the dead, but also opportunities to protest the repression of the apartheid system.

Diradeng's funeral ended without disruption by police and defense forces. But as mourners walked from the graveyard to the Diradeng home, tear gas canisters were fired into the crowd. As the confrontation escalated, troops shot down unarmed mourners.

Young friends of Diradeng barricaded streets with burning tires. When the apartheid troops finally pulled back, they left behind the body of 14-year-old Mono Lucy Ledwaba, a student at Minerva High School, shot while standing at the gate of her home.

Clouds of thick smoke from burning rubber hung over Alexandra the next day as angry residents attacked homes and businesses owned by blacks who had served on the town council as well as those of local police. Both were seen as collaborators—as agents of apartheid.

Thus began what came to be called the "Six Day War." When it abated, at least 19 people were dead and 30 or more wounded.

During that Six Day War, a group of Alex residents who had been talking about how to deal with the township's problems chose Mayekiso to lead the Alexandra Action Committee. They proclaimed the AAC would coordinate "all activities and problems in the township, such as education, unemployment, welfare, cultural unity, comradeship, and solidarity—political and social." The group was to represent the views of the residents to authorities and other "outside bodies." And the AAC described a goal of educating people about the "bad way of apartheid and the way people can stop this apartheid."

Over the Christmas holidays, Mayekiso's wife, Khola, had been in Queenstown in the Cape Province. She observed a system of street committees in that township that had helped residents cope with problems similar to those in Alex. Khola urged the AAC to adopt such a system. Moses liked that idea, in part because his trade union work was based on a system of accountability starting with mass meetings of workers up through shop stewards councils and finally to the union executive committee. He saw a similar system of yard, block, and street committees as

a workable method of organizing the community.

While that strategy developed, the Right Reverend Desmond Tutu, then Anglican bishop of Johannesburg, appealed to residents of Alex to halt the Six Day War. A mass funeral for 17 of the dead followed on March 5 with 60,000 mourners attending. The victims were laid to rest in coffins draped in the banned African National Congress (ANC) colors of black, green, and gold.

Mayekiso missed that funeral. He had been arrested on February 18 and not released until March 7. This proved to be crucial in his treason trial.

The AAC held meetings with residents in the weeks that followed. A consumer boycott began, targeting local businesses owned by whites and those owned by town councilors and police. The boycott demands included the return of missing corpses of those killed in earlier confrontations, withdrawal of troops from the township, release of all political prisoners, and removing the bans on political organizations. In addition, activists sought affordable rents, better housing, and the installation of adequate electricity in Alex.

On the evening of April 22, three days after the boycott began, a large group of armed vigilantes dressed in powder blue shirts and blue pants—clothing typically worn by the South African police—attacked homes of activists in Alex, burning some to the ground. Heavily armored police vehicles called "casspirs" trailed the vigilantes, but instead of intervening to stop the carnage, police did nothing. At least three Alex residents died from the attacks, and many more were beaten.

Mayekiso returned home from a shop stewards meeting that night to find an unexploded gasoline bomb had been thrown through his window. According to his neighbors, suspicious people had come to his house earlier, asking about his whereabouts. Henceforward, he and Khola no longer slept at home out of fear for their lives.

South African metalworkers led the campaign to free Moses Mayekiso. These workers demonstrated near the courthouse in Johannesburg on January 26, 1987.

The next day, police held a press conference in Alex and told reporters the vigilante attacks occurred because a collapse of authority and governance in the township had led to anarchy. Mayekiso responded with his own media event. He drew attention to the role of the police in the vigilante attacks. He received numerous questions about whether or not the Alexandra Action Committee was in de facto control of the township. With the town council having resigned, Mayekiso did not deny that his group was in control of Alex—both to protect the AAC's leadership role and to project legitimacy for the organization still new and facing pressures from young "comrades" talking about making Alex "ungovernable."

Mayekiso's group shunned that approach because of the anarchy it implied. Instead, the AAC continued to pursue bottom-up organizing that emphasized its role as a negotiating force on behalf of Alex residents, rather than taking on functions of local government directly.

In the aftermath of the vigilante attack, Mayekiso met with the administrator appointed to oversee Alex, given that the town council structure had collapsed. He also met with officials of neighboring white communities and repeatedly stressed the AAC's desire to restore "normalcy" by having troops withdrawn and by upgrading the minimal services in the township.

Shortly after those meetings, Mayekiso departed for the United Kingdom and Sweden to brief trade unions there on the repression happening in South Africa's workplaces and townships. He sought international solidarity for the efforts of his

DON'T
LET SOUTH AFRICA
HANG
THIS
LABOR
LEADER.

Moses Mayekiso
General Secretary
National Union of
Metalworkers of
South Africa

The UAW produced this brochure to provide union members with details on the Mayekiso case.

country's independent black trade unions and support for residents of townships such as Alexandra who bore the brunt of apartheid violence.

Mayekiso's European meetings were to be his last days of freedom for nearly two-and-a-half years.

The food in solitary confinement was almost inedible. The Bible was the only book allowed in his cell. No attorneys were allowed to see him. No visitors, either. Not even Khola or his children.

Having been jailed on two previous occasions and then released, Mayekiso initially expected to walk free relatively quickly. But then he learned he was being held under Section 29 of the Internal Security Act, rather than under the state of emergency regulations. That meant the apartheid government planned serious charges against him.

Six months after his arrest at the airport, Moses appeared in court for the first time. His brother, Mzwanele, and three other activists he worked with in the Alexandra Action Committee heard a prosecutor tell the court all five could be charged with sedition and subversion. Bail was denied.

On April 15, 1987, the formal indictment was handed down. The State charged Mayekiso and the four others with a main count of treason, in addition to alternative counts of sedition and subversion.

Treason meant Moses faced death by hanging under South African law. As noted, that penalty was imposed roughly every three days on someone convicted in apartheid courts, so no one doubted the severity of the government's charges against the group, which became known as the "Alexandra Five."

COSATU, the labor federation to which Mayekiso's union was affiliated, was named as a co-conspirator in the indictment, as was the banned African National Congress.

Some 16 months after the initial arrest, the treason trial commenced on October 19, 1987. While he languished in prison, Mayekiso's union colleagues evidenced their strong support by electing him general secretary of the National Union of Metalworkers of South Africa. NUMSA was a new union created by merging several large metalworkers' unions, including MAWU, as part of COSATU's "one industry, one union" drive.

At NUMSA's founding convention, union activists proclaimed that Mayekiso's arrest and treason indictment were intended by apartheid leaders to serve as a warning to other unionists to stick to "bread and butter" issues and not attempt to extend their organizing from the workplace into the community.

The union responded by calling strikes timed to his court appearances to underscore the view of workers that the attack on Mayekiso was an attack on the black trade unions.

M oses Mayekiso was no stranger to the UAW. Despite the 8,463 miles between Detroit and Johannesburg, the South African union leader sitting in solitary confinement in John Vorster Square prison knew he had friends at Solidarity House.

The first time apartheid authorities arrested Moses in 1984, UAW President Owen Bieber sent an angry telex to South African President P. W. Botha urging his release. In the era preceding fax machines and e-mail, telexes commonly were used to communicate quickly and reliably around the world. I followed up by contacting the South African ambassador in Washington, D.C., to demand Mayekiso's freedom. We had learned about the arrest through the International Metalworkers' Federation (IMF), the Geneva-based trade union organization with which the UAW and Mayekiso's union both were affiliated.

The UAW also rallied on his behalf in February 1986 after he was arrested in Alexandra during the turmoil of the Six Day War.

I met Mayekiso for the first time in April 1986, several months before his most serious arrest, when I attended a meeting of the IMF South African Council in Johannesburg. Along with Herman Rebhan, a UAW member who served as general secretary of the IMF, we set out a day later to attend the funeral of a member of Mayekiso's union killed by police in Tembisa township. As our vans approached Tembisa, we were halted by a phalanx of armored vehicles blocking the road. Security forces with automatic weapons and truncheons ordered us out of our vans and detained us.

While they sought orders from higher authorities after determining that some of us were foreigners, we waited. Moses and I passed the time chatting. I joked that "we could paper the walls of my office with all the telexes and letters sent to Botha demanding he let you out of jail."

We shared a laugh, and then he said: "Don't get rusty, man, I may need some more of them before long." Looking back, Mayekiso's comment, while light-hearted, was prophetic.

When the security forces got word that we were to be released, they also denied us entry to Tembisa, thus preventing Mayekiso from presiding at the funeral. An ABC television correspondent, Jim Hickey, had been on his way to Tembisa for the funeral and stopped when he saw all the commotion.

Hickey had covered the UAW negotiations with General Motors and Ford in 1982. Because I had been the union's public relations director during those talks, the ABC-TV reporter and I had logged many hours in the bargaining press rooms and occasionally had ventured to various watering holes near the GM Building and Ford World Headquarters.

When we were released, I steered the reporter to Mayekiso, and together we moved a half-mile down the road so the interview could be framed with the backdrop of the military vehicles called "hippos" and "casspirs." Hickey finished with Moses and turned to me to ask about what the UAW had been doing to aid the black unions in South Africa.

As I held forth, the ABC correspondent noticed two of the "hippos" loaded with troops coming full speed down the road toward us. We beat a hasty retreat, and the security forces trailed us for some distance before dropping off.

Hickey's report aired on ABC-TV back in the U.S., and soon a friend called my wife to say he'd seen me on TV under arrest by South African soldiers—a development that necessitated several trans-Atlantic phone calls before some calm could be restored in my household.

Mayekiso later took me into Alexandra so I could see firsthand the conditions in the township. We visited his home, the clinic, and the sites of the recent killings during the Six Day War. A few days after my visit, the vigilante raids occurred with police support, resulting in more killings and homes burned down.

On May Day, workers conducted a stayaway that shut down the entire country. Township unrest continued to worsen. Unions and anti-apartheid forces began building momentum for another general strike to commemorate the 10th anniversary of the Soweto massacre of 1976.

The Botha government responded to all this by imposing a new and far more draconian state of emergency in June. Two weeks later, Mayekiso was arrested.

The apartheid government's crackdown in mid-1986 resulted in many workers and union leaders being jailed along with community and church activists. UAW President Bieber and I flew to South Africa in mid-August at the invitation of the National Automobile and Allied Workers Union (NAAWU), which later merged with Mayekiso's union and one other to form the National Union of Metalworkers of South Africa (NUMSA).

The UAW had a long history of supporting South African autoworkers, in part because both General Motors and Ford had major auto-producing operations in South Africa (see Chapter 1). Many U.S. auto parts companies also had factories there. On many occasions, NAAWU asked the UAW for help,

and we did our best to provide it. Sometimes we succeeded in our interventions with GM and Ford. Other times we did not, but we always tried.

Because of Bieber's role on the State Department's Advisory Committee on South Africa, he could not be denied a visa by South Africa. During his visit, a number of high-ranking officials of the apartheid government agreed to meet with him. He also went to auto plants and talked with shop stewards and workers.

When we visited the union office, Bieber met with Khola Mayekiso, who described her husband's plight and made a moving appeal for UAW help. Bieber immediately fired off a telex to the commissioner of police in Pretoria protesting Mayekiso's detention and demanding a visit so that he could make an independent assessment of his condition.

Three days later, a "Brigadier Gloy" responded by rejecting Bieber's request. We were not surprised, but union activists thanked the UAW president, telling him that the demand to see Mayekiso could only help because authorities had great sensitivity to foreign pressure.

Bieber and I went on to Cape Town, where we met with Kobie Coetsee, the minister of justice. He directed the country's prison system, among other responsibilities. Because Bieber had interviewed a number of union detainees, he outlined some of their stories to the crusty Afrikaner, including accounts of torture and inhumane treatment while jailed.

The minister responded angrily and claimed South Africa's prisons were a model to the world that exceeded the Geneva protocols and other international standards. Coetsee had been briefed thoroughly on Bieber's very full schedule for the days ahead, which included meetings with other high government officials and leaders of parliament. So he issued a challenge the UAW president likely would be unable to accept.

"Come with me tomorrow morning, and we'll visit any prison you choose in the entire country unannounced, and

you'll be able to see that conditions are more than adequate," the justice minister told Bieber.

Years of give-and-take across the bargaining table had made the UAW president well-skilled at such gambits, and he immediately seized the opportunity.

"I accept," he said. "We'll go to John Vorster Square prison, where I want to see my good friend Moses Mayekiso from MAWU, who's been held there since June without being able to see his lawyers or his family."

"What time shall we leave?" Bieber asked. Coetsee turned ashen at this unexpected response. He began sputtering about how that could not be done; it would be out of order and would require other approvals he could not give.

Bieber and I left the meeting after a bit more heated discussion, and both of us felt a strong message had been sent about Mayekiso to the highest levels of the apartheid government.

The day Bieber was to depart from South Africa, Khola Mayekiso arranged for him to visit Alexandra. We had planned to go there at the beginning of the trip, but gunfire in the township caused our hosts to cancel that visit.

We walked through the cardboard shanties and watched children playing a few feet from raw sewage and garbage. Bieber choked up.

"On the farms around Grand Rapids where I grew up, the animals lived in better conditions than this," he told me. "I can see why Moses wants to do something about it. I would, too, if I lived here."

The UAW launched its solidarity campaign demanding freedom for Moses Mayekiso in the months that followed.

After talking with Herman Rebhan and Denis MacShane of the International Metalworkers' Federation, we decided to focus first on a postcard campaign that would involve UAW members across the United States. On one side, the postcards

had a photo of Mayekiso surrounded by a group of laughing children in Alexandra. On the other, text called for Mayekiso and other political prisoners to be set free immediately.

The IMF did its own cards, which were addressed to South African President Botha. We decided to address the UAW cards to the South African ambassador in Washington, D.C. Our concern was that rank-and-file members might fill out the cards but never mail them, given the difficulty of determining what the postage would be to send a card to South Africa.

At the UAW Community Action Program (CAP) conference in Washington, D.C., in February 1987, we launched the Free Mayekiso postcard campaign. About 2,000 local union political activists attended the meetings, nearly all of them seasoned political pros adept at the nuts and bolts of motivating their members back home.

Every delegate got a letter from Bieber describing Mayekiso's imprisonment, a copy of his telex demanding to be able to visit Moses, the rejection in reply, and a batch of postcards to take back to the local union. Bieber made clear in his keynote that the Mayekiso campaign had great importance to the UAW.

Soon bulk orders for the Free Mayekiso postcards began flooding in, and by the time of Mayekiso's treason indictment

In 1986, UAW President Owen Bieber visited Alexandra township near Johannesburg where Mayekiso lived.

in April 1987, more than 100,000 had been circulated. Cards would be distributed at a variety of union meetings: bargaining council sessions, health and safety seminars, civil rights committee gatherings, and union bowling tournaments.

I decided we should have our reps collect the cards at such meetings and then ship them to the UAW Washington office. Then we would mail about 30 or so cards each day to the South African embassy, each with the signature of a UAW member and his or her mailing address along with local union number. Each card was in its own unique handwriting, so its legitimacy was clear. The steady flow of cards to the embassy kept Mayekiso's name in front of the officials there.

Any global labor solidarity effort confronts the question of how to involve local union leadership and rank-and-file members. To build momentum, vehicles must be found for them to take action, even if it is, as in this case, relatively modest.

With the treason indictment handed down and Mayekiso facing a possible death sentence, the stakes had gone up. We decided to produce a brochure describing the trial with a cover that said: "Don't Let South Africa Hang This Labor Leader." Above Mayekiso's photo was a die-cut through to an inside page that showed a hangman's noose. When the brochure opened, you could see the noose was set in white over a map of South Africa.

Graphic? Yes, but our main goal was to hook the reader; to get the piece picked up and read. A long polemic about the evils of apartheid would not do the job. Here the focus was the human story of one man, a black trade union leader in South Africa facing the gallows because he tried to make his township a better place to live.

But the publication also made clear the South African government had targeted Mayekiso as part of a broader attempt to weaken the black trade unions, which had emerged as the leading force in the anti-apartheid struggle, particularly after the repression against church and political activists.

The UAW convened a committee of prominent American judges and lawyers to monitor the Mayekiso treason trial. The goal was to make the apartheid government and courts know their conduct was being watched carefully by global experts.

The UAW spent the money necessary to print this piece with very high production values. We intended to circulate it to officials of the South African government and our message was clear: the Mayekiso solidarity campaign was well-financed and professionally run. Back then, we were announcing that this was not a campaign slapped together by a couple of ideologues in a garage with a mimeograph machine.

Sorel, the French philosopher, once argued that what is important is not whether a myth is *true*, but whether it is *believed*. While the Mayekiso campaign remained deeply rooted in truth, we sought to have the South African government believe its parameters were much larger than, at least initially, they were. The forces of apartheid had not confronted a union-initiated solidarity campaign of this magnitude before. They were in for a real fight.

The UAW also pushed out a range of stories in union publications, some in those with national circulation and others prepared for reproduction in local union papers. Few had heard of the Internet then, so print played a larger role than it would today. The union's award-winning magazine, *UAW Solidarity*, edited by David Elsila, had a circulation then of more than 2 million readers. It kept them informed of the campaign.

Mayekiso's story, and the possibility he could face hanging, resonated at a grassroots level, in part because the UAW had such a skilled group of local union editors and writers. The union's African American leaders and members particularly took up the fight and saw lessons from America's own history.

The case became a component in union education classes as well. At the UAW's Walter and May Reuther Family Education Center in Black Lake, Michigan, thousands of workers attending sessions learned about Mayekiso, and more broadly

Bob King, then president of Local 600, hosted Khola Mayekiso, wife of the imprisoned South African union leader, in Detroit. U.S. Court of Appeals Judge Damon Keith (left) and UAW President Owen Bieber also spoke at the event.

about the repression of South Africa's black majority. Regional summer schools put on by the union also made the campaign part of their curricula.

The UAW's extensive effort to inform its local union leaders and members about Mayekiso's plight and the broader struggle of labor in South Africa led to the demonstration by 350 health and safety reps in front of the South African embassy. Dr. Frank Mirer, the union's director of occupational safety and health, had spent two weeks in South Africa running training classes for the metalworkers' unions as part of the UAW's ongoing support of labor there. With health and safety reps in Washington for a conference, Mirer and I hatched plans for the protest.

He kept urging me to charter enough buses to transport 300 people, but privately I expected only 100 or so to show up and had initially resisted. Mirer finally prevailed and, to my surprise and joy, every bus was packed.

I sat on my back porch in the humidity of Washington, D.C., in the summer of 1987 and talked with Halton Cheadle, whose Johannesburg law firm represented Mayekiso. A brilliant and combative lawyer, Cheadle might have won Olympic gold as a swimmer, but never got the chance because the apartheid government had been denied participation in the games due to its racist policies.

Cheadle had a year's sabbatical at Yale Law School and spent a few days with me talking about strategies for the Mayekiso campaign. He helped educate me on the role of the judiciary in the South African system. Until then, I had made little distinction between branches of government, assuming pretty much that the courts were about as repugnant as the executive and legislative branches were.

Listening to him describe some of the legal initiatives and strategies taken by labor and human rights advocates there, I began to see that some degree of independence existed in the South African judicial community.

On occasion, a judge would find on behalf of unions or detainees or others who fought the apartheid system, Cheadle said. True, those decisions often would result in quick revisions of laws or regulations by the parliament or state president, but the decisions occurred nevertheless.

Out of those discussions with Cheadle, I began to raise with Owen Bieber the idea of broadening the UAW campaign to include a focus on the South African judiciary. Cheadle had talked about the powerful impact several U.S. judges had when they came to South Africa to observe several of the major trials of anti-apartheid political figures.

The American judges looked on in the courtrooms, and a sort of peer pressure developed. It became a bit harder for the South African judges to rule on points of law and fact that flew in the face of international law. Some did, of course, but others seemed aware that the outside world was watching.

Cheadle also challenged us. Other anti-apartheid activists put on trial in South Africa, ranging from Nelson Mandela in the 1960s to the defendants in the Delmas treason trial in the 1980s, had received worldwide attention. Given the crucial role played by black trade unions, Cheadle asked, shouldn't labor leaders such as Mayekiso be entitled to similar international concern and support?

I flew to Detroit and met with Bieber to propose a new element of the Mayekiso campaign: an effort focused on the judiciary that would shine the spotlight of international opinion on the judge and the conduct of the trial itself.

Bieber sent out letters to 13 prominent American judges and lawyers asking them to serve on an independent ad hoc committee to monitor the Mayekiso treason trial. They included jurists such as Arthur J. Goldberg, who had served on the U.S. Supreme Court; Griffin Bell, the former U.S. attorney general; William Coleman, chair of the NAACP Legal Defense and Education Fund and former U.S. secretary of transportation; and Elizabeth Holtzman, then district attorney in Brooklyn, all of whom accepted the invitation. Three highly respected judges of U.S. Courts of Appeals, the second highest court level in the United States, also accepted, as did the president of Yale University.

Earlier, we had an internal debate over whom to invite on the jurists' committee. Some had argued for a group that had lesser stature, but greater "political reliability."

I believed the group needed to be made up of major establishment legal figures for it to have the credibility needed in South Africa. If the committee was seen merely as a "puppet" of the UAW, it would have little impact. That view prevailed.

Bieber and Eleanor Holmes Norton, then a law professor and former head of the Equal Employment Opportunity Commission, launched the American Committee of Jurists Monitoring the Case of Moses Mayekiso at a well-attended press conference in Washington in front of large illustrations of the Alexandra Five behind bars. *The New York Times* carried a long story on the committee and the UAW campaign along with photos of Bieber and Mayekiso. So did other major U.S. papers.

More important, the South African press ran with the story as well. As with the judiciary, some media outlets there operated with a degree of independence and covered stories adverse to the government. That declined somewhat when press censorship regulations under the state of emergency took effect

UAW President Owen Bieber and Eleanor Holmes Norton, former head of the Equal Employment Opportunity Commission, launched the American Committee of Jurists that monitored the trial of Moses Mayekiso in South Africa. Prominent judges and lawyers joined the UAW in pressing for justice. Photo by Earl Dotter.

in 1986, but there was greater freedom of the press than one might have expected.

The UAW produced a glossy brochure containing photos and bios of the members of the jurists committee, along with a description of its mission of monitoring the conduct of the Mayekiso trial. We circulated it widely, particularly to opinion-maker groups in the United States and Europe, including lawyers and legislators concerned about human rights.

Before launching the monitoring efforts, detailed discussions occurred with those directly involved in South Africa, including Mayekiso and his co-accused and the lawyers involved in the defense. They had green-lighted our effort and seemed very happy with the seriousness with which the jurists committee would be regarded within South Africa, in part because of the prestigious nature of its members.

Some of our momentum did diminish, however, as the prosecution sought and received long delays in Mayekiso's trial.

In April 1988, the UAW decided to return the case to the public eye by running a series of full-page ads in the major newspapers in South Africa, such as the *Star* in Johannesburg and the *Cape Times* in Cape Town. Both papers initially rejected the ads, which described the American Committee of Jurists and why it was monitoring the Mayekiso trial. After some weeks of negotiating, they agreed to carry the ads.

"The [Mayekiso] case is an unparalleled test for South Africa's legal system beneath the spotlight of international opinion," the ad stated. "The Committee believes the trial of Mayekiso and his four co-defendants raises critical questions about the fundamental issues of justice and due process under the law."

The ads generated a whole new round of discussion in South Africa about the trial and reached a broader audience there that expanded the profile of the Mayekiso case.

As the trial progressed, we received regular reports from our union allies and from Mayekiso's lawyers, Norman Manoim and Amanda Armstrong. We kept a stream of information flowing to the jurists committee, UAW locals, and our allies in the labor and human rights communities.

We began producing a newsletter, *Mayekiso Trial Update*, which we sent to all UAW locals and to friends in other unions in the United States and abroad. The UAW had long-standing ties to U.S. anti-apartheid groups, such as TransAfrica and the American Committee on Africa. They provided us with mailing lists of their supporters, and we sent the Mayekiso newsletters to them as well.

Under apartheid, South African officials had no obligation to provide Mayekiso with a prompt and speedy trial. But 16 months after his arrest, the trial opened and Judge P. J. van der Walt, who had a reputation as tough but competent, began with some good news for the defendants. He had decided not to hear the case with "assessors," which effectively ruled out the possibility of death sentences for the defendants, including Moses.

Although relieved, they nevertheless confronted the prospect of very long prison sentences. Still, the hangman's noose had been put aside, and that gave all those working on the defense a boost.

The trial proceeded slowly, largely because state prosecutors frequently came to court unprepared and sought numerous postponements that the judge granted. The delays had two very negative impacts.

First, the apartheid government had blocked the ability of Mayekiso and his co-accused to get a bail hearing that could have led to their release during the trial, so delays meant they continued to be imprisoned. And second, the longer the trial, the higher the legal costs to provide a defense. (The UAW contributed financial support to cover a portion of those legal expenses, as did the IMF.)

The prosecution presented a good portion of its evidence in closed court. The judge agreed to the private sessions to hear testimony from residents of Alexandra about the turmoil in the first six months of 1986 as well as the rent and consumer boycotts. Testimony also was taken on the efforts to get state troops withdrawn from the township.

But even with many months to prepare, the prosecution could not provide any witnesses who could present direct evidence against Mayekiso. They could describe what occurred in Alex, but no one provided details linking Moses to those events.

Finally, the state presented a witness in closed court who described an inflammatory speech given by Mayekiso at the mass funeral on March 5, 1986, for 17 of those killed during the Six Day War. It was powerful testimony that appeared to damage Mayekiso's case.

But on cross-examination, defense lawyers pointed out that Mayekiso was jailed in John Vorster Square prison on March 5, making it impossible for him to have incited the mourners as the prosecution witness claimed.

A major element of the prosecution case involved documents found in Mayekiso's possession. He had brought back union newspapers from his trip to Great Britain and Sweden, as well as pamphlets from a wide range of groups and individuals he had met during that visit.

A prosecutor singled out letters of support from different organizations for a major strike by South African metalworkers at BTR Sarmcol. He read one stating that "the CPSA has encouraged its members to support the BTR Sarmcol strike and to give money to MAWU [the union]."

The abbreviation CPSA, said the prosecutor, stood for the Communist Party of South Africa. The judge asked to see the letter, read it, and then noted for the record that the first page spelled out that CPSA actually was the Civil and Public Services Association, another union.

The focus on the union materials provided Mayekiso with an opportunity to testify at length about the history of the labor movement around the world, and particularly in South Africa. He described how workplace unrest in the 1970s led to the creation of the Wiehan Commission appointed by the government to recommend changes in labor law.

He told the court that those reforms, perhaps surprising under apartheid, led to an expanded role for independent black unions, which gained the power to sit across the bargaining table from powerful companies and negotiate for workers. The reforms grew out of the government's desire to quell unrest, but they had the impact of making unions one of the only sectors in apartheid society where blacks could wield real power.

In February 1989, Yale President Benno Schmidt Jr. and I went to South Africa to observe the Mayekiso trial on behalf of the American Committee of Jurists. Schmidt was a legal scholar specializing in constitutional law and had served as dean of Columbia University Law School before moving to Yale.

Many of us had been disappointed that Schmidt had not supported the total divestment of Yale's investments in companies doing business in South Africa. Yet his stand did serve to enhance his credibility with the South Africans we sought to influence.

Getting Schmidt a visa to allow his entrance into South Africa proved difficult. A common tactic of the apartheid government was to delay issuing a visa until after the conclusion of the event you had hoped to attend. Or they would delay visa issuance so long that trips would be canceled because appointments and travel arrangements couldn't be made at the last moment.

Both Schmidt and I waited more than a month without getting visas. Finally, I sought and received letters to the South African ambassador from Senator George Mitchell, the Senate majority leader; Paul Simon, chair of the Senate Africa subcommittee; Nancy Kassebaum, the ranking Republican on that subcommittee; and Howard Wolpe, chair of the House Africa subcommittee. All urged that South Africa grant the visas.

The author and Benno Schmidt Jr., president of Yale University, talk with the Alexandra Five defendants during a break in their trial that was monitored closely by a committee of prominent American jurists.

This bipartisan intervention underscored to South Africa that leading members of Congress with the power to shape sanctions legislation had a strong interest in the Mayekiso case.

South African Ambassador Piet Koornhof, to whom our "Free Mayekiso" postcards were sent each day, finally approved the visas for Schmidt and me at 6 p.m. on February 3, the day before our scheduled departure. In a letter, Koornhof said he wished us well on our journey, but he also expressed his "extreme displeasure" about remarks made by UAW President Bieber that Mayekiso was on trial for his efforts "to weaken the apartheid system" or because black trade unions "have emerged as the key force opposing apartheid."

In the weeks before our departure, I had briefing materials prepared for Schmidt on the South African laws on treason, subversion, and sedition, as well as other subjects, such as facts about Alexandra township.

I also sought help from the human rights project at Harvard Law School run by Henry Steiner, who arranged for me to work with Professor Jack Tobin and a law student named Carl Landauer, who had taught history at Stanford before enrolling in law school.

One advantage to my not being a lawyer was that I brought a layman's sense to the analysis of Mayekiso's plight. It seemed to me that, even if the facts about Mayekiso's conduct were true, they hardly constituted the crime of treason. How could consumer and rent boycotts in a single black township be treason?

Tobin and Landauer helped to develop the legal underpinnings for this argument. They provided a brilliant analysis that argued that the paradigm of treason "involves either a direct attack on the State or an act which in some way aids an external enemy." For it to be treason, there must be a link "to a violent attack on the State from within or without."

Having examined the treason laws of various nations, they concluded that "the acts of Mayekiso and the others in the present South African case do not fall under the definition of treason elsewhere."

Schmidt took all of our prep materials and hit the ground running. He spent many hours with the advocates and attorneys representing the five accused and then met with Witwatersrand's attorney general, Klaus von Lieres, who was responsible for prosecuting the case in the courtroom. Schmidt spent an afternoon in Alexandra to see conditions there, and he met with officials of the U.S. embassy as well as Kobus Meiring, South Africa's deputy minister for foreign affairs.

Next came the observation of the trial itself in Courtroom 2C of the Witwatersrand Supreme Court in Johannesburg. Schmidt then had his most important meeting: a private, one-hour session with the presiding judge of the Mayekiso trial, Judge P. J. van der Walt.

The Yale president was very careful to avoid any statement that could be construed in any way as an attempt to influence the judge, but he did describe who the members of the jurists committee were and why they had an interest in the issues raised by the trial.

Judge van der Walt asked how the committee planned to

follow the trial from America. Schmidt said that appeals court judges are not physically present for a trial, but they pass judgment based on the court record. With the ability to do likewise, he said he was confident the committee formed by the UAW would be fair and objective.

Before departing South Africa, Schmidt held a press conference where he said there was concern in America about the use of treason indictments against opponents of apartheid, particularly in cases such as Mayekiso's in which defendants were engaged in peaceful, nonviolent activity.

"Our jurists committee is asking, as I did in meetings here, where the line is between acceptable political dissent and treasonous activity," the Yale president said. "That is an extremely important question in a country where some 70 percent of the population is excluded from the political and legislative process, lacking voting rights and other rights taken for granted in democratic countries.

"Is the South African government, through these treason prosecutions and convictions, criminalizing what would be considered legitimate political dissent in the context of international legal norms?"

The American legal scholar also raised the subversion and sedition charges faced by the Alexandra Five, asking if their broad application turned what in America would be clearly legitimate political action into unlawful conduct. And Schmidt took note of due process questions involving Mayekiso's case, such as the lengthy detention without charge or access to attorneys and the failure to hear the bail application for nearly two years.

Schmidt told reporters there was great interest in the Mayekiso trial in many other countries. "It is being watched closely in legal circles, in trade unions, church groups, the human rights community, and by the public," he said.

The UAW solidarity campaign on behalf of Moses Mayekiso occurred in tandem with a broad international out-

SEPTEMBER 1988

MAYEKISO TRIAL UPDATE

JUSTICE FOR MAYEKISO

South African Unionist Faces Treason Charge

Defense Case Opens in Mayekiso Trial

The treason trial of black South African trade unionist Moses Mayekiso resumed in August in Johannesburg under an increasingly intense spotlight of international attention.

The Mayekiso trial deservedly has received widespread scrutiny in various legal, labor, human rights and anti-apartheid circles. It appears to signal the apartheid government's strategy for the future prosecution of local anti-apartheid activists—and the trial advances the government's desperate efforts to curtail the political and economic force of South Africa's independent black trade unions.

Moses Mayekiso is the General Secretary of the increasingly influential National Union of Metalworkers of South Africa (NUMSA). The serious charges of treason, sedition and subversion relate to the organization of rent and consumer boycotts in the black township of Alexandra, near Johannesburg.

DEFENSE ARGUMENTS OUTLINED

As the trial resumed August 1st after a two-month re-

Throughout the Mayekiso trial, the UAW produced a regular newsletter to keep members and union allies informed of what was happening in court proceedings and on the solidarity campaign.

pouring of concern.

At the International Metalworkers' Federation, Herman Rebhan and Denis MacShane worked tirelessly on Mayekiso's behalf. The British Trades Union Congress sent Tony Shaw to monitor the trial, and observers from what is now the International Trade Union Confederation also attended.

The German metalworkers' union, IG Metall, demanded Mayekiso's freedom in full-page ads in German newspapers. Germany was one of the apartheid government's most important trading partners.

The Swedish metalworkers' union, led by Leif Blomberg, had a long history of support for the anti-apartheid movement and felt a special responsibility because Mayekiso had been arrested after getting off his flight from Stockholm in 1986. Blomberg took out ads on May Day 1988 addressed to Mayekiso that said: "Your demands are our demands. Your words are our words. Your goal is our goal. We celebrate May Day in freedom. You do not. Why?"

The Swedish metalworkers also took the UAW brochure with the noose and the headline "Don't Let South Africa Hang This Labor Leader" and reprinted it in Swedish for distribution throughout that country.

While solidarity efforts abroad added to the pressure, so did campaigns in the United States by a number of informal coalitions of labor at the local and state level. Various labor committees against apartheid played an important role in moving the Mayekiso campaign forward and carrying our message to a broader network of union activists.

Two of the most effective were the Illinois Labor Network Against Apartheid and the New York Labor Committee Against Apartheid. Both groups developed as local and regional union activists came together around the desire to support the black union movement in South Africa.

UAW Local 259, District 65, AFSCME's District Council 37, and Amalgamated Clothing and Textile Workers (ACT-WU) joint boards and locals worked hard to educate members on the issues of the Mayekiso case. Kate Pfordresher, a talented organizer, staffed the New York committee, and the Communications Workers of America provided office space.

In Illinois, UAW leaders ranging from Bill Stewart to Dennis Williams supported the labor effort against apartheid. The Illinois Labor Network Against Apartheid, coordinated by Kathy Devine and Harold Rogers, took up the UAW postcard campaign and held rallies calling for Mayekiso to be freed.

Similar groups formed around the country. The Service Employees International Union (SEIU) and ACTWU launched the Labor Committee Against Apartheid in Philadelphia, while in San Francisco a group called the "Committee to Free Moses Mayekiso" conducted a petition drive among Bay Area unionists. That committee held a benefit at the Ashkenaz Music and Dance Café in Berkeley featuring the "Looters" and

the "Beat Freaks," which we took to indicate the campaign had begun to reach younger workers.

As the trial progressed in Courtroom 2C in Johannesburg, the prosecution sought to link Mayekiso and his co-accused to the then-outlawed African National Congress (ANC). But there was little evidence of any involvement by Mayekiso with the ANC that amounted to a conspiracy. Instead, testimony underscored that the accused themselves, not outside forces, charted the course within Alex.

The State finally concluded its case, and the defense moved to have the treason count dismissed because, under South African law, an element of violence normally was necessary to prove treason.

But in a major setback for the defense, the judge ruled that violence need not to have occurred for treason still to have been committed. That ruling raised the stakes, because the outcome could have set a precedent that substantially broadened what constituted treasonous activity.

The question those in South Africa soon raised was whether or not involvement with a rent or consumer boycott or the organizing of community residents could constitute treason. What room could remain for peaceful opposition by those excluded from political participation in the governmental system?

As the defense presented its case, it clearly was far better prepared than the prosecution. Over the weeks that followed, the State's case appeared to collapse under the weight of contrary evidence. Still, the nature of the apartheid system and its version of justice caused few to be optimistic.

Set to adjourn for the holidays in late 1988, the court heard yet another motion from the defense seeking a bail hearing. Mayekiso and his co-defendants were stunned as the attorney general agreed and the judge ordered the Alexandra Five released on bail.

The judge imposed stiff conditions, such as requiring the

five defendants to report daily to a police station and barring them from attending gatherings of 10 or more. But Mayekiso and his colleagues enjoyed their first taste of freedom in 901 days.

The granting of bail signaled to shrewd legal observers that the apartheid government knew its prosecution of Mayekiso was in trouble.

The trial resumed in February 1989. As final arguments approached in late March, a bombshell hit. Prosecutors announced the State would drop the treason charge against Mayekiso and his co-accused.

They argued that sufficient evidence existed to prove treason, but they had been unable to make that case for various reasons, such as witnesses from Alexandra being intimidated.

That left charges of sedition and subversion. Sedition is a common law crime like treason, while subversion was a statutory crime under South Africa's far-reaching Internal Security Act of 1982.

That law defined subversion as any attempt to bring about social, economic, or political change. And it also stated that it is subversion to commit any act that "demoralizes" the public or that seeks to force the government to act, or to refrain from acting.

Those of us in the UAW found the South African definition of subversion to be ludicrous. We get up every day and try to pressure the government we elect to act. It's the essence of democracy and civil society. But not in apartheid South Africa.

Finally, on April 24, 1989, Judge van der Walt entered a courtroom packed with NUMSA and COSATU members and Alex residents and began to read his verdict (South Africa did not have jury trials).

The first 20 minutes or so gave few hints as to the white-haired Afrikaner's decision. But then the defendants' hopes rose as he noted that "while white South African citizens may have a democracy, black South African citizens certainly have no share in it." He called that fact "notorious."

And he spoke positively about the black trade unions and their role, which "served to organize black workers and also to give expression to their demands in the workplace, as well as their political aspirations."

That morning, when the judge entered the courtroom, nearly all of the blacks there had refused to heed the summons to "rise in court." By the lunch break, it seemed clear where the verdict was headed. And when court reconvened, most of those in the courtroom rose to their feet when the judge entered and took the bench.

In the afternoon session, van der Walt continued to read his 57-page decision to the tense crowd.

He found that Mayekiso's effort to form yard, block, and street committees as well as the staging of rent and consumer boycotts in Alexandra were a reasonable response to primarily justifiable grievances and aspirations. Such activities were intended to improve township conditions, not to make the whole

Moses Mayekiso and his wife, Khola, celebrate after leaving the courthouse in South Africa. He won acquittal in April 1989 and went on to lead the metalworkers' union. In 1994, Mayekiso won election to South Africa's parliament.

UAW President Owen Bieber welcomes Moses Mayekiso to the union's 1992 convention where delegates gave him a standing ovation.

country ungovernable, he said.

Judge van der Walt blasted the government for having brought the treason charges and said Mayekiso and the four co-defendants "are just striving for a better South Africa."

Union members in the courtroom began to shout "Amandla" (power) as the judge finished by announcing that Mayekiso and the other defendants had been acquitted on all counts and were free to go.

Outside, on the steps of the courthouse, workers danced and hoisted Mayekiso to their shoulders. Riot police with guns and truncheons ordered them to disperse.

They moved on to a victory rally at a Methodist church hall. Mayekiso spoke there: "It is a big victory for the working class of South Africa, because the aim of the working class is to end apartheid. We built democratic structures that can assure accountability, democracy, and that leaders can't go loose from the masses."

Now free and ready to turn to his job as the top official of the National Union of Metalworkers of South Africa, Mayekiso credited international solidarity for the acquittals.

"As far as we are concerned—myself, my family, the co-accused, the NUMSA members, and COSATU in particular—we believe that if it was not for the international solidarity, we would have faced serious convictions.

"The judge was aware of the international focus on the case, so the judge and the white community had to look for justice and had to acquit us."

Mayekiso then joined the others and hopped into vans for a symbolic trip back to Alexandra township, where the struggle remained far from over.

FREE
BURMA'S
UNION
LEADERS

CHAPTER THREE

UAW Campaign Helps Free Unionist In Burma
Military Regime Jailed And Tortured Myo Aung Thant

Maung Maung, the exiled leader of the Burmese labor movement, took the stage in a union hall in Fort Wayne, Indiana, in 2000 and looked out at an audience of nonunion workers from nearby auto parts plants.

The UAW had sought Maung Maung's help in building support among the large group of refugees from strife-torn Burma who had been relocated to northeastern Indiana. Some had fled after a bloody crackdown on pro-democracy groups in 1988 by the military regime that ruled Burma.[1] Others gained refugee status as the repression continued.

Maung Maung himself had to seek exile in Thailand with other labor activists and had become the general secretary of the Federation of Trade Unions–Burma (FTUB), working from the Thai-Burmese border.

"One of the unions that has provided the workers of Burma with strong support is the UAW," Maung Maung told the crowd. "The UAW has been at our side in the struggle for democracy in Burma, and it will be at your side in the factories here in Indiana as you seek a better life."

Maung Maung, who distributed materials in Burmese describing the UAW and how it helps workers, knew the tough odds facing the refugees who hoped to organize their plants, a number of which were owned by Japanese companies with staunch anti-union policies. But he also understood that many of them had fought for democracy from Burma's jungles and jails, and he believed they would fight for democracy in the workplaces of Indiana.

The UAW's outreach to the Burmese workers in the Fort Wayne area included inviting them to the huge Labor Day picnics where, in addition to hot dogs and hamburgers, Burmese food would be served.

"We would open up the old Local 57 recreation center to them, and they would hold various Burmese festivals and celebrations there," recalled Dick Merren, a UAW Community Action Program area chair. "And the UAW would help the Burmese refugees get connected with the United Way so their families could get various services they needed."

Merren cited several successful organizing drives that were a result in part of the UAW's careful outreach to the Burmese refugees. "You had to respect their culture," he said. Himself an immigrant from Honduras, the UAW CAP activist could identify with their struggles.

Aung Myint Soe, a former professor, sounded a similar theme when he pointed out that the Burmese can face employment discrimination in America because of language and cultural barriers.

"There is a lack of democracy in Burma," he said in 2001, "but in the U.S. it flourishes . . . because of the right to establish unions." At nonunion American workplaces, however, workers' rights often are trampled, he noted, "and it is no different than in Burma."[2]

The efforts of exiled Burmese union leaders to support UAW organizing occurred in part because the union had fought vigorously over the years for human and labor rights as well as democracy in Burma.

As in the apartheid period in South Africa, workers fared very badly under Burma's military regime. Once ruled by Great

Britain, Burma suffered a military coup in 1962. The military nationalized its commerce and industry and isolated the country from the rest of the world for years.

In 1974 angry workers, tired of food shortages and inflation, launched a series of strikes. The army crushed the strikes by opening fire on workers at the Simmalaik dockyard and the Thamaing textile mill and arresting those on strike at the Insein railway yard.[3] More protests occurred later that year when former United Nations Secretary-General U Thant died. He was respected throughout the world as a global leader. In Burma he was a symbol of opposition to the military government, which denied him a state funeral and sparked more protests.

A major uprising occurred in 1988 as Burma suffered an economic downturn. The de facto ruler, U Ne Win, suddenly revoked much of the currency with which workers had been paid. Obsessively superstitious, U Ne Win declared Burma's currency should only include bills that were divisible by nine, which he believed to be his lucky number.

On August 8, 1988—which came to be known as "8-8-88"—hundreds of thousands of citizens began a general strike and other protests demanding democracy. Students, often at the forefront of protest movements around the world, marched with their symbol of the fighting peacock, while monks carried their alms bowls upside down to show they would not accept handouts from the military regime.[4]

The daughter of the famous independence hero Aung San had returned to Burma in 1988 to care for her sick mother. Aung San Suu Kyi spoke at the famous Shwedagon Pagoda where she rallied the people with a call for a democratic government. She soon became the figure around which the Burmese democracy movement coalesced.

By mid-September, the regime was cracking down on the protests. Troops fired into crowds, killing more than 3,000 people, and they hauled away thousands more in trucks, most of whom were never seen again.

Myo Aung Thant, shown here as a young worker, was imprisoned in 1997 by Burma's military regime. He served as a leader of the All Burma Petro-Chemical Corporations Union before his arrest.

In 1990 the military agreed to elections for a new parliament, and Aung San Suu Kyi's National League for Democracy won about 80 percent of the seats and more than 60 percent of the popular vote. The regime quickly made the elections meaningless by setting up a national convention to approve a new constitution that gave a dominant role to the armed forces.[5]

In addition, Burma's ruling junta more than doubled the size of the military, from about 175,000 in 1988 to over 400,000. Those forces and others imposed massive restrictions on the people of Burma.

"Members of the security forces committed numerous, serious human rights abuses," the U.S. State Department found, including killings, rape, and torture. "Disappearances continued, and members of the security forces tortured, beat, and otherwise abused prisoners and detainees," State's Bureau of Democracy, Human Rights, and Labor reported in 2001.[6]

Myo Aung Thant, a leader of the All Burma Petro-Chemical Corporations Union, experienced such abuse first-hand after he returned to Burma from a meeting in Thailand. The Federation of Trade Unions–Burma had chosen him as a Central Executive Committee member in 1995 because of his strong leadership in the oil and chemical union.

Security forces arrested him when he arrived at Mingaladon Airport in Rangoon on June 13, 1997. Initially, they said he had been detained for operating a nonregistered satellite phone used to relay information to the exiled leaders of the FTUB in Thailand, as well as other democracy movement groups the regime considered illegal.

General Khin Nyunt, the head of military intelligence, held a press conference after the arrest and accused Thant of "terrorist activities," saying he had maintained contact with the political party led by Aung San Suu Kyi, who had won the Nobel Peace Prize in 1991, the year after her party won the election.

Perhaps most telling, Myo Aung Thant was accused of recruiting new members for unions. A second "harmful" action was his assistance to international trade unionists during their visits to Burma. And he was charged with writing reports on the plight of "low-income earners" and "grievances and complaints on the high cost of living."[7]

Two months after his arrest, a special military court conducted a show trial, but denied Myo Aung Thant the right to his own lawyer. The government lawyer provided for him refused to offer any defense at the trial because, he said, he believed the verdict was a foregone conclusion. During the trial, which lasted three days, a newspaper controlled by the military carried a photo of Thant taken in detention that showed him with signs of swelling consistent with physical beatings.

As expected, the military court found Myo Aung Thant guilty and based its verdict on a "confession" that later was confirmed to have been extracted by torture—both physical and psychological. The sentence on the treason charge was life, plus seven years.

Even worse, his wife, Aye Ma Gyi, also was arrested. She had gone to the airport to pick him up and got a tap on the shoulder. It was military intelligence, she recalls, and "that [was] it."[8]

The same military court tried and convicted Aye Ma Gyi as an accomplice, alleging she had assisted her husband in his labor-organizing activities. She also was accused of providing lists of fax numbers of Burmese government ministries to exiled pro-democracy groups.

Aye Ma Gyi received a sentence of 10 years in prison. She and her husband had two young daughters, whom relatives took in after their parents had been detained.

Both Myo Aung Thant and Aye Ma Gyi were held in Insein prison near Rangoon, but he later was moved to Myitkyina prison in Kachin state in the far north, an isolated location that meant very infrequent visits from his brothers and other family members. His wife stayed in Insein, but in a tiny cell where she spent all but one half-hour a day.

The situation deteriorated further when the regime announced a new claim that Myo Aung Thant had tried to smuggle explosives into Burma. The military government clearly had manufactured the allegation, and no proof was presented to sustain the claim. Indeed, Thant had been arrested in Rangoon, and security forces had seized explosives in Kawthaung, hundreds of miles south of Rangoon.

It appeared the initial charges of trying to organize workers into unions and writing reports on low-wage workers had not seemed like crimes to the international community. Burma had just been admitted as a member of the Association of Southeast Asian Nations (ASEAN), which hoped this might moderate Burma's behavior. Some thought the explosives charge against Myo Aung Thant might have been an attempt to justify the harsh prison term he was serving.

Bill Jordan, a long-time ally of the UAW who had participated in programs at the union's Black Lake education center, denounced the verdicts. As general secretary of the International Confederation of Free Trade Unions (ICFTU), he was the highest-ranking union leader on the global scene.

"The arrest of trade union activists in retaliation for the exercise of legitimate trade union activities is a violation of internationally guaranteed rights to freedom of association," Jordan said in a letter to General Than Shwe, who ran Burma's military regime. "I would once again urge you to recommend the unconditional release of Myo Aung Thant from prison . . . the denial of basic trade union and other human rights carries a heavy price."

Jordan told the general that "international condemnation and economic sanctions continue to grow. To promote stability and social justice in your country, trade unionists such as Myo Aung Thant must not be persecuted, but (rather) be permitted to conduct their legitimate activities."[9]

The UAW learned details of Myo Aung Thant's arrest and prison sentence more than a year afterward. I had gone to Thailand to hold some initial meetings with Thai autoworkers

The UAW and its allies campaigned to win the release of Khin Kyaw (second from left), president of the All Burma Workers' Union. He was sentenced to a 17-year prison term, but won freedom after 10 years.

who hoped to unionize major Ford and General Motors factories in an industrial center called Rayong.

Phil Robertson, who now serves as Human Rights Watch's deputy director for Asia, arranged for me to meet with Maung Maung, the exiled leader of Burma's labor movement, while I was in Bangkok.

Maung Maung gave me a detailed briefing on the workers' movement in Burma, the repression of virtually all union rights there, the massive human rights violations by the military regime including killings and torture, and the jailing of top members of the FTUB's Central Executive Committee, including Myo Aung Thant.

He also described the arrest and imprisonment of another Burmese union leader, Khin Kyaw, who had been a radio officer for the state-owned Myanmar Five Star Shipping Enterprise Co.

When the 1988 popular uprising had occurred, Khin Kyaw was elected president of the newly organized All Burma Workers' Union at a labor meeting held at Htan Ta Bin High School. As a result of his efforts to organize the union, the military regime forced him to resign from his job at the shipping company.

Khin Kyaw's arrest occurred in 1997, as did that of Myo Aung Thant. But Khin Kyaw's case did not go to trial, and for a year there was no word on where he was being held or on what charges. Eventually, news surfaced that he had received a 17-year prison sentence. Speculation was that he had been found guilty of treason for operation of a nonregistered satellite phone.

I came away from my discussions with Maung Maung believing UAW President Steve Yokich and the International Executive Board should know what union activists in Burma were up against.

The union's earlier success in campaigning for freedom for Moses Mayekiso, the South African autoworker who had been imprisoned on treason charges, was very fresh in our minds.

While the issues and conditions were quite different in Burma, some of the experience we had gained in mounting the South African campaign seemed likely to be helpful.

Soon Kristyne Peter, who worked in the UAW International Affairs Department (and now heads it), had produced campaign materials based on those used in the Mayekiso campaign.

The UAW materials included a postcard that had photos of both Myo Aung Thant and Khin Kyaw and provided many details of the repression in Burma of both democracy and labor rights. It highlighted the jailing of Thant's wife, Aye Ma Gyi, and urged freedom for all jailed worker activists in Burma.

"Burma has one of the world's most horrendous labor rights records," the card stated. "Freedom of association, the right to organize, and collective bargaining are met with violent opposition by the Burmese government, while forced labor is commonly imposed on its citizens."

"Multinational corporations increasingly are relocating production to countries such as Burma, where repression of unions is widespread," the UAW card said. "The denial of union representation and worker rights in Burma undermines the livelihoods of workers throughout the world."

Our success in the Mayekiso campaign led us to print thousands of the cards, and soon they were being passed out at UAW meetings on bargaining, health and safety, political action, and so on. We also sent them to the Black Lake education center, where they were used in the two-week summer sessions and other programs.

The response was good from rank-and-file workers and local union leadership, but we got slightly less participation than with the South Africa campaign. The UAW's substantial African American membership had provided strong leadership in the fight against apartheid. In addition, South Africa was covered prominently in the news media, while Burma press coverage was less frequent. Nevertheless, thousands of UAW members sent protest messages to the Burmese embassy in Washington, D.C.

UAW President Steve Yokich raised the campaign's profile with a strong denunciation of Than Shwe, the general in charge of Burma. In a letter to him, Yokich stated:

"The international labor movement will not sit idly by while our fellow trade unionists and their families in Burma are under the constant threat of violence, arrest, or worse for exercising their right to organize unions and protect worker interests. We will continue to fight until brothers Khin Kyaw, Myo Aung Thant, and all other union detainees are freed, and labor and human rights are respected in Burma."

The UAW has taken on campaigns of global solidarity, such as the fight to free imprisoned labor activists in Burma, because it is the right thing to do. And while the jailed individuals are the focus, the union's campaigns seek more broadly to rally our members and others to demand basic norms for worker rights.

In the case of Burma, we were fighting not only to win release of Myo Aung Thant, his wife, and other jailed unionists, but also to support Burmese workers in the struggle to achieve internationally recognized labor rights and a political/economic system based on democratic norms.

In addition to the AFL-CIO and its Solidarity Center, we worked closely with the International Confederation of Free Trade Unions and the International Labor Organization on our Burma campaign. The ICFTU, now known as the International Trade Union Confederation (ITUC), is a global confederation of national labor centers, such as the AFL-CIO. The International Labor Organization, based in Geneva, Switzerland, is a specialized agency of the United Nations that aims to promote labor rights.

Each year, the ITUC issues an annual survey of violations of trade union rights that examines individual countries throughout the world and holds them accountable for worker repression. When the UAW has had information relevant to those reports, the union has worked closely with the ITUC/ICFTU.

In 2003, as Myo Aung Thant suffered horrible conditions in Myitkyina prison, the ICFTU Annual Survey of Violations of Trade Union Rights found the following about worker rights in Burma:

- Trade unions are forbidden by law and no collective bargaining exists.
- Abuse of workers' rights is rampant, especially in export-oriented industries.
- Any attempt to protest leads to dismissal, detention, and sometimes torture at the hands of the ruling military.
- Independent unions must work underground, and their leaders, when captured, are given severe prison sentences.
- Forced labor has continued on a massive scale.[10]

"Trade union groups became the focus of violent army attacks," the ICFTU said. "Foreign multinational investment helped to keep the junta afloat as the world's governments looked on. An estimated one million Burmese have fled to Thailand and Bangladesh because of forced labor, forced displacement, and fear of the military regime."

The report noted the FTUB had been forced to operate clandestinely, but still maintained structures, organized migrant workers, and ran worker training activities inside Burma, as well as in countries bordering it. In 2003 the FTUB facilities were attacked by the military, which burned down the Kawthoolei Education Workers' Union office in the Papun district after FTUB union members celebrated May Day there.

An FTUB member, Saw Mya Than, who had been trained as a human and trade union rights specialist by the exiled union federation, was shot dead by soldiers on August 4, 2003. He had been forcibly recruited as a porter and "human shield." The military frequently made forced laborers march at the front of

battalions to "protect" the soldiers against ambushes by supporters of the ethnic independence movements.

The UAW also met a number of times with experts at the International Labor Organization (ILO) to urge tough action on Burma. The union had close ties to the ILO in part because former UAW General Counsel Steve Schlossberg had served as director of the ILO's Washington, D.C., office from 1987 to 1994.

Two years after the jailing of Myo Aung Thant, Aye Ma Gyi, and Khin Kyaw, the ILO found violations by Burma's military regime.

The ILO had established a Commission of Inquiry to examine whether or not the country was complying with its obligations to prevent forced labor. The United Nations body found massive use of forced labor, and, as time went on, it also strongly criticized Burma's prosecution of those who alerted the outside world to the abuses.

On numerous occasions, the ILO called for the release of Myo Aung Thant and other jailed union activists. It also demanded an independent inquiry into the murder of Saw Mya Than.

Because Burma had signed ILO conventions prohibiting forced labor and agreeing to respect freedom of association under which workers could form trade unions, the regular monitoring of the massive violations of those commitments carried great weight in the broader global community. In addition, the ILO is a tripartite body that has participation not only by labor and government, but also by business.

AFL-CIO International Affairs Director Barbara Shailor and staff members of her department consulted the UAW going into the annual ILO meetings held each year in June. Shailor, who had worked at the International Association of Machinists, pressed the U.S. delegation to the ILO to focus on Burma's labor abuses and the imprisonment of the leaders for whom we sought freedom.

Throughout the Burma campaign, we worked closely with

Earl Brown, a lawyer at the AFL-CIO's Solidarity Center, who fought tirelessly on behalf of Burmese unionists and workers. Phil Robertson, who then directed that region for the Solidarity Center, played a crucial role in winning freedom for Burma's jailed union activists and repeatedly helped the UAW in our campaign.

The UAW also lobbied in Washington, D.C., for strong sanctions to be imposed on Burma by the U.S. government.

Our experience in fighting together with allies to win sanctions against South Africa's apartheid government in the 1980s helped as we sought to ratchet up pressure on the regime in Burma.

President Bill Clinton issued an executive order in 1997 banning all new investments in Burma as required by Section 570 of the Appropriation Act that year. In 2003, the Burmese Freedom and Democracy Act required President George W. Bush to impose a ban on the import of products from Burma;

FREE BURMESE UNIONISTS
Jailed, Beaten and Tortured for Labor Activism

Left: Khin Kyaw, President of the All Burma Workers' Union, sentenced to 17 years for organizing workers.

Above: Myo Aung Thant, Executive Officer of the Federation of Trade Unions---Burma (FTUB), serving a life sentence for relaying information to union and pro-democracy organizations in exile.

The UAW produced this brochure for local unions. It explained the repression of labor in Burma under the military government and contained a tear-out postcard UAW members could mail to the Burmese embassy urging freedom for Myo Aung Thant and Khin Kyaw.

After another brutal crackdown in Burma that killed hundreds in 2007, UAW members joined protesters near the Burmese embassy in Washington, D.C. Photo by Don Stillman.

freeze assets of certain Burmese officials; block U.S. support for loans from international financial institutions; and ban visas for certain Burmese officials. Additional sanctions were passed in 2008, adding to the economic pressures on the military regime in Burma.[11]

The International Metalworkers' Federation also launched a campaign to "name and shame" corporations that still invested in Burma.

The first good news after many months of campaigning came in 2002 when Burma freed Aye Ma Gyi, who had been jailed in 1997. The military regime gave no public explanation, but the UAW campaign appeared to have contributed to her release. After many months of trying to pressure the regime and feeling like we were not having an impact, the release of Myo Aung Thant's wife gave new energy to our efforts.

As we had on other labor rights campaigns, the UAW decided to produce a poster that could go on local union and plant bulletin boards and also be distributed to the broader human rights community to build support.

I had recently visited the Rubin Museum of Art, which had just opened in New York City in what had been a Barneys department store. The museum specialized in Himalayan art and contained some beautiful Buddhist art tapestries depicting handprints and footprints, some of which were objects of worship and others historical in nature.

We used several images from that Buddhist school of art and created our own poster based on elements in those works. Our goal, as with other posters we produced to highlight labor rights campaigns, was to create something that made our political point while still being beautiful enough that the posters would end up on the walls of diverse organizations ranging from human rights groups to members of Congress to other unions and labor coalitions.

The poster demanded in large type "Free Burma's Union Leaders" and had text blocks describing how one could seek freedom for Myo Aung Thant, Khin Kyaw, and others in Burma. It was a huge hit and soon was in great demand after it was posted on the website of Labor Rights Now.

In 2005, I received news of a second important development: the release of Khin Kyaw, founder of the All Burma Workers' Union and a member of the Seafarers Union of Burma. He gained his freedom seven years before his 17-year sentence was up.

"With the release of Khin Kyaw in Burma, we know that pressures from [the campaign] can similarly help Myo Aung Thant," I said in a statement after we learned of the release. "We are in regular touch with his family, which has asked that we redouble our efforts now that Khin Kyaw's freedom raises the prospect for further releases."[12]

By then the UAW campaign was being run by Steve Beckman, who had become the union's International Affairs director when I retired after 28 years at the union. I continued to work closely with the UAW in my new role as president of Labor Rights Now, which had become an independent human rights organization. Kristyne Peter, who had worked so hard on the Burma campaign, also left the UAW. She became the director of trade union rights and campaigns at the International Metalworkers' Federation in Geneva.

During the mid-2000s, the Service Employees International Union (SEIU) greatly expanded its global programs. SEIU began working closely with the UAW and with Maung Maung and the FTUB, eventually providing the exiled Burmese federation with an office in the SEIU headquarters in Washington, D.C.

SEIU President Andy Stern and Secretary-Treasurer Anna Burger met with Aye Ma Gyi, who after her release from prison was living in Thailand pending relocation to the United States. She filled them in on her husband's case, and FTUB leaders added additional information.

With 2.1 million members, SEIU added a powerful voice to the campaign to win freedom for Myo Aung Thant and other jailed Burmese worker activists. Stern commanded a great deal of media attention and offered a strong critique of the military regime in Burma.

During the eight years George W. Bush served as president, the wars in Iraq and Afghanistan overshadowed all other international issues. The abuses at Abu Ghraib prison, the treatment of prisoners at Guantanamo, revelations of secret prisons and widespread torture, and other human rights violations dominated the news, and rightly so.

In the midst of the "war on terror," the UAW's efforts to raise labor rights issues involving Burma, China, Zimbabwe, and other countries became extremely difficult. Because human/labor rights work largely invokes moral suasion, America had lost the "high ground" we once had in the world community. Many countries had become highly critical of Bush and the swagger with which he discarded democratic ideals that had long set the United States apart.

In 2007 Burma saw a new round of major protests that thrust the country back into the news. The military regime cut fuel subsidies, and the price of gasoline and diesel fuel skyrocketed. The cost of basic commodities, such as rice, eggs, and cooking oil, had jumped 30 percent to 40 percent.

Meanwhile, the generals, who had become extremely wealthy through control of state corporations that dominated the economy, often flaunted their wealth. The top general, Than Shwe, angered Burmese citizens when a video of his daughter's wedding showed her wearing millions of dollars worth of diamonds.

Students and pro-democracy workers led protests over the fuel and other price increases during 2007. In mid-September, they were joined by thousands of Buddhist monks, who demonstrated in the streets and brought a huge boost to the protests.

Soon demonstrations had spread across Burma, and many thousands of workers, students, and monks took to the streets in a major challenge to the military, which had moved army trucks into strategic positions and tried to impose dusk-to-dawn curfews. But rank-and-file soldiers, many of them deeply religious, seemed reluctant to employ the same brutal tactics used against workers and students in the past.

General Than Shwe then brought in new regiments of elite troops loyal to the regime. He also cut Internet access to Burma and unleashed soldiers who were told to target the news media in an effort to reduce visual images of the crackdown ahead. Many world leaders urged Burma to seek a peaceful end to the conflict, and the UN sent special envoys.

But soon the blood flowed. The army and police cleared protesters, raided monasteries, and arrested monks. The UN Human Rights Council later reported that 30 to 40 monks had been killed along with about 50 to 70 civilians. Some 200 were brutally beaten. Other sources put the death toll in the thousands.

Throughout the world, people saw photographs of dead monks with the maroon of their robes blending with blood in the streets of Rangoon and other cities.

A massive wave of arrests followed with workers, students, and monks hauled off to interrogation cells and prisons.

President Bush announced a new round of sanctions against Burma, as did other countries where staunch conservatives were in power, including Australia, where the Howard government issued its own sanctions.

The slaughter of the monks in particular seemed to ener-

gize protests around the world. UAW members demonstrated at the Burmese embassy in Washington, D.C., and other groups such as the U.S. Campaign for Burma and the Burma Campaign U.K. expanded their own efforts.

Online petitions developed to demand an end to the military regime and restoration of Aung San Suu Kyi to power. On October 4, bloggers throughout the world were asked to focus on Burma for the entire day.

Some of the protests took surprising directions, such as a "Panties for Peace" campaign that began October 16. It sought to capitalize on the superstitions of Burma's generals, particularly Than Shwe. They viewed contact with any item of women's wear as depriving them of their power. Soon women activists were sending packages containing underwear to Burmese embassies in Australia, Europe, Singapore, and Thailand.

In the aftermath of the repression, a number of worker activists had been jailed, and a broader crackdown once again targeted unionists. Su Su Nway, a labor activist who had filed a forced labor complaint at the ILO, had helped organize protests. She was held in Insein prison on sedition charges. Lay Lay Mon, a labor activist and former political prisoner, organized workers to support the protesting monks, and she, too, ended up in jail.

U Tin Hla, a member of the Burma Railway Union, got seven years in prison. He had organized railway workers to support the uprising. The regime charged him with possession of explosives, but the ITUC reported that, in fact, he possessed electrical wires and tools in his electrician's toolbox.

This new round of highly publicized repression in Burma gave a fresh impetus to the UAW campaign.

A year after the crackdown, I received an e-mail from allies in Thailand working on the campaign that said Myo Aung Thant was about to be released. I was ecstatic, thinking that our hard work, and that of many other groups, finally would end with his freedom.

someone whose name I did not recognize. The e-mail said Myo Aung Thant had died in prison and the campaign for his freedom was over. They thanked me for the support but proclaimed the effort ended by virtue of his death.

That was crushing news, if true. But it did not sound right to me. And shortly thereafter, the FTUB and Phil Robertson, who had become deputy director for Asia at Human Rights Watch, both cast doubt on the claim. I had thought about contacting Myo Aung Thant's wife, who by then had been relocated to the Tri-Cities area in eastern Washington. But I worried about the traumatizing impact it might have on her and her two daughters to get such a call, so I held off.

In the end, it appears to have been perhaps a clumsy effort by someone in the Burmese regime to dampen the UAW's Free Myo Aung Thant campaign.

On a beautiful fall day, October 12, 2011, the news came from Maung Maung and our allies at the FTUB that Myo Aung Thant had been released from prison as part of an ongoing shift in Burma that reduced repression and expanded some freedoms there.

Six other jailed trade unionists also were released that day, and more won their freedom in the weeks and months that followed.

I e-mailed Myo Aung Thant's wife and daughter, May Cho, proclaiming, "It's a very happy day for you and your family and for all of us who campaigned for nearly 10 years now for his release. I only wish we could have done even more and helped win his freedom earlier."

After a devastating cyclone struck Burma in June of that year, I had been in contact with the family to see if any damage had occurred in the area of the prison. Now the discussions were on a much happier note.

But in the months after his release, our allies at the FTUB cautioned that Myo Aung Thant's torture and harsh imprison-

A number of other political prisoners, some with high profiles, had been released in the months after the 2007 crackdown. I e-mailed the FTUB in Bangkok seeking more information on Myo Aung Thant's possible release, but soon they were downplaying the possibility. They proved right. He continued to be imprisoned in the far north of Burma, where he went to sleep each night without blankets in the harsh cold.

Some weeks later I received an e-mail from Burma from

ment for more than 14 years had taken a toll. He suffered both physically and psychologically. Word was he would be "taking it slow."

In 2012, however, Myo Aung Thant had begun participating in FTUB activities. By midsummer, I heard from Phil Robertson of Human Rights Watch that he hoped to reunite with his family in the United States. Robertson asked me to get involved in the process.

Myo Aung Thant's family had been relocated from Thailand to Kennewick, Washington, seven years earlier by World Relief, a nonprofit church organization with great expertise in refugee resettlement. I called Karolyn Hopper in World Relief's Tri-Cities office and offered my help.

Soon I drafted a letter to the U.S. Citizenship and Immigration Services (USCIS), the agency that handles petitions for refugee status. The goal was simple. Normally, it might take two years or more for a petition for refugee status on humanitarian grounds to be considered. Given the horrors experienced by Myo Aung Thant, we hoped to speed up that process.

My March 28, 2012, letter to USCIS, which was cleared with his family and also World Relief, stated:

"As you consider Myo Aung Thant's initial refugee petition and request for the exception on humanitarian grounds, I respectfully ask that you reflect on what it means:

- to wake every day in horrible conditions in a Burmese prison for 14 years;
- to be denied your freedom and to be tortured instead;
- to miss the chance to watch your children grow up;
- to freeze in your cold cell wondering if you will ever see your wife again; and

Myo Aung Thant laughs with grandson Daniel Thant and his wife the day he arrived in the United States. He had not seen his family for more than 16 years after being imprisoned in Burma for his union activity. Photo by Kai-Huei Yau.

- to know that you are an innocent man imprisoned because you wanted to help your fellow workers have a better life."

On June 21, 2012, I got word from Karolyn Hopper at World Relief that Myo Aung Thant had been granted refugee status. "I have never seen a case like this in my work here in 10 years and I really feel that [UAW/Labor Rights Now] support played a huge role in pulling on the heart strings of the adjudicators and getting his case approved," she wrote.

On Friday evening, May 24, 2013, Myo Aung Thant walked off a plane at the Tri-Cities Airport in Pasco, Washington.

He hadn't seen his wife and family since 1997. The 57-year-old union activist and political prisoner saw his oldest daughter, May Cho, rushing toward him.

She embraced him tightly just past the security gate, while his wife and youngest daughter, Mabel Thant, waited in turn to greet him.[13]

And for the first time he met his three grandchildren, ages 3 to 11—all born while he was imprisoned.

"What can I say? [I'm] really happy," Thant told reporters. "Really happy."

He thanked the UAW, World Relief and other groups, and the United States.

Then, for the first time in 16 years, he went off to dinner with his family to begin a life far from Myitkyina prison in Burma.

CHAPTER FOUR

Close Ties To German Union Bring Victory
How Solidarity Helped UAW Win At Freightliner

The snow started to fall in the northern suburbs by mid-morning and began to pelt Chicago soon after. President Obama's top political strategists gathered later that day in the Prudential Building where the 2012 presidential campaign had its headquarters. They looked out at lake-effect snow—nearly 20 inches of it—that had closed O'Hare Airport, canceling more than 300 flights. But Obama's campaign staff thought little about the storm.

Their discussion, cramped around a small conference table, focused instead on a relatively warmer locale: North Carolina and exactly where in the Tarheel State the president should go on his upcoming campaign trip.

Some had argued for the so-called Research Triangle in the Piedmont near the cities of Raleigh, Durham, and Chapel Hill, where Obama could meet with high-tech business leaders. Others pushed for a small town on the Catawba River called Mount Holly, home to about 14,000 people in an old mill and textile area of North Carolina.

Mount Holly also was home to a Freightliner Truck Manufacturing plant that employed about 1,500 UAW Local 5285 members. The more they discussed it, the better it seemed for President Obama to travel to Freightliner in Mount Holly, where he could focus on a bright spot in North Carolina's hard-hit economy, which at the end of 2011 had the fourth-highest unemployment level in the country.

Freightliner's parent company, Daimler Trucks North America (DTNA), had recently announced that it would add a combined 700 jobs to the Mount Holly plant and to a parts plant in Gastonia that employed about 780 workers belonging to UAW Local 5286. It would be a chance for Obama to talk about how and why the economic recovery was working and the additional steps needed to create more good-paying jobs.

The president's political staff settled on the Freightliner plant for a March 7, 2012, campaign stop.

"The economic recovery is not only working in the domestic auto industry, but in other areas as well, such as heavy truck assembly and parts," the union said in a statement reacting to Obama's decision to visit Mount Holly rather than one of North Carolina's larger cities. "President Obama cares about middle America."

The decision that snowy day in Chicago to have the president visit a unionized heavy truck plant in the South proved helpful in highlighting the jobs message during a difficult economic recovery. And it was that message that prevailed on November 6, 2012, when American voters gave President Obama a second term.

If you were going to pick a state where unions face a particularly uphill struggle to organize, it would be North Carolina. According to the Bureau of Labor Statistics, North Carolina in 2012 had the lowest union-member rate in the entire country: just 2.9 percent of the workforce in the Tarheel State belonged to unions.[1] The story of how workers at Freightliner's plant in Mount Holly came to belong to the UAW—despite the staunch anti-unionism of many of North Carolina's politicians and corporations—is one of courage and perseverance.

And it is also one of global solidarity.

For Stanley Roseboro, that story began some 10 years after he began working at Freightliner. The 32-year-old truck assembler had had stomach surgery, and the doctor had ordered "light duty" for a few weeks until he had recovered. But the company had him working a regular shift, high up on a ladder, often straining unsuccessfully to attach a grab handle before the truck pulled away.

It was not the first time he had been forced to work in an unsafe situation as he helped build the giant, custom-designed trucks sold to Ryder Trucks, Builder Transport, Roger Penske Co., and other customers.

"I had no one to turn to," he told *UAW Solidarity* magazine in 1992. "It seemed that if you had 10 or more years' seniority, like me, the company just targeted you for discipline. I felt I couldn't just go to my co-workers and say, 'Let's start a union.'

"Then someone asked me about signing up with the UAW. I thought it was the best thing that could happen to us."[2]

Lila White had 12 years seniority at Freightliner and, like Roseboro, had never really thought about joining a union. But in early 1989, she and several other workers contacted the UAW.

"Wages weren't the real issue—it was the way we were being treated," White said. "You were moved from one job to another, you were told you're either going to work 10 hours a day, six days a week, or be without a job. They'd got to the point where you had to put your job before your family, your children, or anything else. If they wanted you in on Saturday, you had to be there."[3] White, Roseboro, and others soon began asking their fellow workers to sign cards seeking a union representation election—a secret ballot vote to determine if a majority favored the UAW to bargain for them.

Freightliner executives in North Carolina, a "right-to-work" state with an incredibly strong anti-union history, unsurprisingly greeted the workers' desire to join together in a union with deep hostility.

Here's how Dean Eason, a UAW supporter, described it in 1991:

"The company hired an anti-union firm. We heard rumors about the plant's closing. They threatened people for passing out union checkoff cards, and the plant manager intimated that he'd see the names of everyone who signed and would check them off on a roster in his office.

"They also gave away free T-shirts, free coffee, and free doughnuts. They had captive audience meetings in the plant, and made a rock-and-roll video telling us we didn't need a union. They made fun of the people who were trying to get the union in by accusing them of being the kind of people who'd sell out their mother.

"One of management's films had an old 'Grandpa Walton' kind of guy saying that anyone who'd vote for a union is the kind of person who'd hold a loaded gun to the head of a friend."[4]

Eason said that all through 1989 and the early part of 1990, supporters of the union really struggled during this harsh anti-union onslaught from the company. "We started off with a lot of support in the plant, but the company's campaign got some people scared," he recalled.

On April 6, 1990, Freightliner workers at the Mount Holly plant had their say. They voted for the UAW by a 652–606 margin. UAW Local 5285 soon was certified.

Eason, Roseboro, White, and other workers expected the company would bargain hard and the two sides would come together in an agreement both could live with. That's how labor-management relations are supposed to work, they believed.

But Freightliner execs, stunned and stung by their loss, had just begun to fight. They refused to even come to the bargaining table for more than a year. Local 5285 leadership got a strong vote of confidence from the Mount Holly workers in April 1991 when 92 percent voted to authorize a strike.[5] When management finally showed up at the bargaining table in August, their tactic soon was obvious: stall, and then stall some more. "They'd come in, sit down for three days, fly out of town for a week," Eason recalled.

Then, in a blatant violation of federal law, a notice went up on the bulletin board stating that everyone but UAW-represented workers would get an annual wage increase of 5 percent. UAW leaders immediately filed charges with the National Labor Relations Board on Freightliner's unfair labor practice.

The company fired Roseboro and three other pro-union workers. The UAW challenged those dismissals. The union also took on Freightliner's unsafe working conditions that had led Roseboro and others to seek union representation. The UAW's Health and Safety Department performed an inspection of the Mount Holly plant, and it took 23 pages to write up all the health and safety violations.

"But we couldn't get management to talk about health and safety," said Eason, a leader of the new local union, "so we eventually called in North Carolina's OSHA Department for a full-scale inspection." That put additional pressure on management when initial findings of about 170 violations meant the company might have to pay more than $200,000 in fines.[6]

By November 1991, UAW members at the Mount Holly plant were frustrated that Freightliner seemed to care little about reaching a contract. Bill Casstevens, then UAW secretary-treasurer, flew to North Carolina to meet with the workers and raise the possibility that a strike might be necessary to get Freightliner to take their negotiating responsibilities seriously.

"The company is insisting that we accept wages and benefits inferior to what they pay Freightliner workers in Portland, Oregon," Casstevens told Local 5285 members. "We refuse to accept second-class status.

"Freightliner charges the same prices for the trucks it produces in North Carolina as the ones it builds in Portland. They should also pay their North Carolina workers the same wages and benefits as they pay Portland workers."[7]

As he met with the Freightliner workers, Casstevens knew the UAW still had a very important card to play. While local management hewed carefully to the North Carolina anti-union agenda, Freightliner was owned by the German vehicle manufacturer Daimler-Benz, best known for producing Mercedes-Benz luxury cars.

In Germany, Daimler-Benz had excellent labor relations with the union representing workers at all its car and truck operations. The German metalworkers' union, known as IG Metall, then had about 3.6 million workers and was a powerful force in the German economic and political world. Their contracts covering Daimler-Benz workers were among the best achieved by labor anywhere.

The UAW and the German union had enjoyed close ties for many years. The father of long-time UAW President Walter Reuther was a brewery worker who had immigrated from Germany, and Reuther had known IG Metall leaders such as Hans Brummer and Otto Brenner very well.

Reuther's successors in UAW leadership built even stronger ties to the German union. Owen Bieber, who led the UAW during the Freightliner Mount Holly organizing drive, also had a father of German ancestry, and he developed close relationships with Hans Mayr and his IG Metall successor, Franz Steinkuehler.

During a meeting of the International Metalworkers' Federation in Denmark in 1989, I had breakfast with Albert Schunk, my counterpart at the German metalworkers' union, and told him the UAW had an organizing drive at Freightliner.

Schunk initially expressed optimism but became concerned as I described the long history of anti-unionism in North Carolina. He said he would update the leadership of the German metalworkers' union about the Freightliner campaign.

As the union representation election approached at Freightliner in 1990, UAW President Bieber asked IG Metall President Steinkuehler to give us a letter urging the North Carolina workers to vote for the UAW.

"He sent that letter, which noted that he sits on the supervisory board of Daimler-Benz under Germany's worker participation laws and that he would use that position to be of assistance to the UAW when asked," Bieber noted in his report to the UAW convention in 1992.[8] Given the union's narrow 46-vote margin, it is not inconceivable the German union leader's pledge to use his power on behalf of UAW members in Mount Holly helped to tip the balance.

After more than 19 months had gone by without a contract in Mount Holly, Bieber asked me if I thought the Germans could help. I said yes, but urged him to send Casstevens to meet personally with the IG Metall leadership and the Daimler-Benz Works Council. If we were going to win real German union support, we needed to dispatch a top UAW leader there to fully brief them. Just sending faxes or telexes wouldn't convey the seriousness of the Freightliner situation.

Casstevens, who now led the Freightliner bargaining, flew to Frankfurt on Thanksgiving Day with John Christensen of the UAW international affairs staff, who had been to Germany many times and knew IG Metall officials very well. Bieber asked Steinkuehler to meet Casstevens and Christensen, which he did.

After hearing their story of Freightliner's anti-union behavior, the German union leader promised full support for the UAW's effort to get a contract in Mount Holly. He then called officials of the Daimler-Benz Works Council and set up meetings in Stuttgart, Germany, for the UAW.

Works councils in Germany have real power. They represent all company workers—union members as well as non-union employees, including lower-level managers. In addition to union contracts, company officials must reach agreement with the works council on a wide range of local issues.

Casstevens presented the Daimler Works Council with a Freightliner memo berating a foreman for not getting "112 percent" out of his workers. With Germany's social protections

for labor, the memo offended works council members, who saw it as condoning the exploitation of the Freightliner workforce. The members became even angrier when the UAW secretary-treasurer outlined the unfair labor practice charges, including the health and safety firings and the illegal withholding of the annual wage increases due union members.

Karl Feuerstein, an IG Metall official who also led the Central Works Council at Daimler-Benz, told company executives that if Freightliner hired strikebreakers in the United States, the parent company would face major turmoil from its German workers.[9] Casstevens and Christensen flew home with a strong sense the UAW's bargaining position had just been strengthened immeasurably.

But still negotiations didn't progress in North Carolina. After discussions with Bieber and local union leaders, Casstevens set a deadline. If Freightliner failed to send a top company official to the negotiating table by 11 a.m., December 4, the UAW would go on strike.

Freightliner management ignored the deadline, and 850 Mount Holly workers walked off the job.

Dean Eason was still at the bargaining table when the strike began. "I'm told the plant suddenly looked like a ghost town," he said. "Brothers and sisters told me it brought tears to their eyes to see so many workers leaving the plant."

Soon Stanley Roseboro, Lila White, Eason, and hundreds of others walked the picket lines carrying signs. Some were in English and said: "UAW Protests Unfair Labor Practices." Other signs carried by strikers were in German and provided a visual message that soon got the strike attention in German media.

Very quickly, the North Carolina Chamber of Commerce demanded that Freightliner hire permanent replacements. It feared a successful strike would encourage workers elsewhere in the state to begin their own organizing drives that could lead to union contracts and higher wages.

Management set a deadline of its own: show up for work by December 9 or lose your job. That ultimatum was sent to workers' homes in hopes that family members might pressure them to go back to work and end the strike. The UAW countered to its members that the company could face millions of dollars in back pay if it called in permanent replacements prohibited by law in an unfair labor practice strike.

The strike got a boost from a huge rally in a local high school auditorium. Workers set up a 12-foot Christmas tree as a symbol they planned to stay out through the holidays. They carried placards in English and German and sang songs of solidarity from the UAW songbook. The speeches really came from the heart. Some at the rally seemed surprised that the company they worked so hard for did not want to play by the rules.

Many children of the strikers were there. Some carried strike signs, and others belted out "Solidarity Forever" from the song sheets. The scene no doubt left the company spies and chamber of commerce representatives on the fringes of the crowd looking like they'd just eaten some bad meatloaf.

Freightliner production had dropped sharply at a time of year-end high demand for heavy-duty trucks that normally enriched the company's bottom line.

A vital element of the strike was close communication with the German metalworkers' union in Frankfurt and with the Daimler-Benz Works Council in Stuttgart. We had set up a direct phone link from the UAW local in Mount Holly to both IG Metall and the works council. John Christensen was there to facilitate contact with Germany.

Each day the UAW sent strike reports, copies of union leaflets, stories from North Carolina newspapers, and other information to our allies in Germany, who felt a sense of detailed involvement in the struggle as a result. We faxed the company letter demanding that workers return by December 9 or risk losing their jobs, and that further angered IG Metall President

Steinkuehler and Central Works Council leader Karl Feuerstein. Both reacted to the letter as if Freightliner/Daimler had snubbed them personally.

UAW President Bieber continued to urge Steinkuehler to intervene at the top executive ranks of Daimler-Benz and get them to force Freightliner's American bosses to return to the table and reach an agreement. Bieber said Casstevens believed that if a deal was not reached before the Christmas holiday, the strike would last a very long time and could end in disaster.

A few days later, the negotiations got serious. Management suddenly sent executives to the table who had the power to make a deal. Led by Casstevens, the Local 5285 rank-and-file bargaining team had plenty of backup. International Union staff, from Research Department economists to Social Security Department actuaries to Legal Department lawyers, all were in Mount Holly working round the clock.

Five days before Christmas, Freightliner finally gave in and agreed to a contract for the Mount Holly workers who had joined together under the UAW banner 19 months earlier.

For Stanley Roseboro, not only did he get his job back, but the new agreement also provided a range of health and safety victories, including in-plant medical services, medical treatment for plant injuries, no-cost work-related physical exams, an ergonomics program, and other improvements.

For Lila White, contract provisions put tough limits on overtime so workers could have more flexibility to be with family. She and her fellow workers won an upfront across-the-board wage increase of 8.7 percent as well as a cost-of-living allowance and a retroactive lump sum payment of $2,300.

Casstevens proudly told Local 5285 members that "workers will get wage parity with workers at Freightliner's Portland, Oregon, truck plant."

The UAW also won a seniority-based layoff and recall program, 37 paid holidays over three years, a prompt grievance procedure including strong union representation, a no-cost prescription drug program, and improvements in pensions, sick leave, and healthcare. The contract also guaranteed that if Freightliner ever sold the plant, the new owner must honor the workers' UAW rights.

Union members at Mount Holly ratified their first contract by a 99 percent majority vote.

UAW Solidarity analyzed the significance of the Freightliner victory:

"For workers throughout the South—particularly those in the younger generations—the victory means more than just specific contract gains. It's a recognition that if workers want a union and fight for it, they can add immeasurable security and dignity to their lives."[10]

Tommy Elmore, a production worker at Freightliner, put the victory this way: "We didn't just take a company contract. We won a UAW contract."

And it was a victory for the German metalworkers and works council members, who showed global solidarity with the UAW.

"They put pressure on the German management and that, combined with the courage and tenacity of the Freightliner strikers and their families, helped us win an excellent settlement," UAW President Bieber reported at the union's next convention.

The old saying goes something like, "Tall oaks from little acorns grow." Looking back on the UAW's Freightliner victory in 1991, it is clear how pivotal that success was.

Mount Holly workers won six successive UAW contracts—each with major economic and workplace improvements—without having to resort to a strike. Instead, with some ups and downs, the union built a good relationship with management there.

Local 5285's membership actually doubled from 1990 to 2000. In 2012, Freightliner employed about 1,500 UAW workers in Mount Holly who produced 108 trucks a day. And, in a "right-to-work" state, 98.5 percent of the workers there chose to belong to the UAW.

The Mount Holly success spurred more UAW organizing in North Carolina. Workers at the Gastonia Parts Manufacturing plant began a union drive in April 1999, which stalled after Freightliner's parent Daimler Trucks North America (DTNA) arranged for anti-UAW literature to be distributed. The organizing drive, marred by threats and violence against union supporters, ended with the UAW losing by 24 votes.

"The company's conduct in the final 48 hours before the vote not only violated the law and neutrality protections that DaimlerChrysler agreed to and reaffirmed in writing," said Bob King, then a UAW vice president and director of the union's National Organizing Department. "It also stole from these workers the union rights and recognition they deserve."[11]

Faced with a company that engaged in a range of illegal activities, such as threatening to close the plant if the union succeeded, the UAW went on to reach an enforceable neutrality agreement. Under it, Daimler Trucks North America agreed to recognize the union with proof of majority status.

In January 2003, the UAW and DTNA officials addressed workers at Gastonia as well as in Cleveland, North Carolina, where Freightliner also has a plant, and at High Point, where DTNA's Thomas Built Bus plant is located. Those meetings occurred on nonwork time and allowed workers to hear about the company's neutrality.

Very quickly the UAW won strong majority support at each of the three Freightliner plants in Gastonia (parts), Cleveland (assembly), and High Point (Thomas Built Bus).

"We know that when workers are given a free, democratic choice to vote on union representation in an atmosphere without intimidation and threats, they almost always choose to be represented," said Gary Casteel, then director of UAW Region 8, where all the UAW-represented plants are located. "It isn't

UAW Contracts Pay Off

The UAW's organizing and contract success at Freightliner's Mount Holly, North Carolina, plant in the 1989–1991 period led to new agreements with the company that proved crucial in the economic downturn.

Heavy truck industry production in the United States nosedived in 2008 when the economy collapsed. In addition, some truck purchasers had moved up fleet purchases to beat new federal emissions-control requirements.

Freightliner responded by shipping thousands of jobs to Mexico in violation of the UAW contract. Union negotiators had won job protection language in 2003 that required 70 percent of the M2 business-class truck line to be built in Mount Holly, and similar provisions were included in the agreement at the Cleveland plant.

By April 2009, however, there were just 120 workers building four trucks a day in Mount Holly, in large part because Freightliner had shifted production to Mexico. The UAW filed a grievance over the contract violation. In January 2010, an arbitrator ordered the production returned to the Carolinas and that back wages be paid to UAW members negatively affected by Freightliner's violation.

Workers at Freightliner's Thomas Built Bus plant in High Point also benefited from being in the UAW. North Carolina school officials several years ago ignored the fact the school buses built there created thousands of jobs in the state. Instead, they set up a bid process that called for a specific engine type that would have shut out Thomas Built buses in favor of an out-of-state nonunion bus maker.

UAW Region 8 officials quickly contacted then Governor Beverly Perdue, a Democrat, and explained the true costs of the school bus specifications that would prevent union workers in High Point from having a shot at the bus contracts. The specs were changed, and new work building those big yellow school buses came to UAW Local 5287.[13]

---

rocket science. Workers know they come out ahead when they have a say in their wages, benefits, healthcare, health and safety, and other workplace issues.

"Being able to decide in an atmosphere that is calm and free of threats is critical, and that's what those neutrality agreements are all about."[12]

By December 2003, UAW Local 5286 members in Gastonia and Local 3520 members in Cleveland, North Carolina, won their first-ever contracts. They included provisions for plant-closing moratoriums. At the Thomas Built Bus plant, an NLRB-supervised election occurred in July 2005 with workers voting by a 59 percent majority for the UAW. A first contract followed in October.

The UAW agreements at all these Freightliner plants grew out of the 1991 victory in Mount Holly in which global solidarity from the German union and works council helped so much.

When President Obama chose to visit UAW workers at Freightliner in Mount Holly on March 7, 2012, as the presidential campaign heated up, he affirmed the importance of union manufacturing in a "right-to-work" state.

He also paid tribute, whether or not he knew the history there, to the power of global solidarity to improve workers' lives.

Dita Sari —
jailed for her
union organizing
in Indonesia.

FREE Dita

CHAPTER FIVE

Woman Organizer In Indonesia Wins Freedom
UAW Campaign For Labor Activist Dita Sari Succeeds

About 300 women trade unionists from 130 countries listened intently as Kristyne Peter, a UAW activist in her late 20s, described the plight of another young woman about her age who languished in an Indonesian prison.

When Peter finished, a hush fell over the hall in Rio de Janeiro, Brazil. Delegates to the Seventh World Women's Conference of the International Confederation of Free Trade Unions (ICFTU) considered the plight of Dita Sari, who had been imprisoned for nearly three years. Then a Malaysian delegate proposed a resolution calling on the Indonesian government to release Sari; a second came from a British delegate.

The vote in favor of a campaign to seek freedom for the young Indonesian labor activist carried unanimously and energized a broad international effort demanding Dita Sari's release. The activists at the ICFTU women's conference in Brazil returned to their home countries in late May 1999 armed with materials prepared by the UAW on the case.

Nearly three years earlier, on July 8, 1996, Dita Sari had led a march of about 20,000 workers from 11 different factories in Indonesia protesting low wages and unsafe working conditions in the Tandes industrial area of southern Surabaya. At the rally, Sari called for a wage hike to the equivalent of about $1.25 from the $1 per hour workers had been receiving in the textile and garment factories in that locale.

At age 25, Sari had become a leader of the Center for Indonesian Labor Struggle, known there as the PPBI. The workers she organized—about 70 percent of whom were women—had to work 12–14-hour days without overtime pay. They lived in overcrowded dormitories with unsanitary conditions and often faced sexual harassment on the job.

"Dita led strikes, and after she was captured by security forces, she was beaten and interrogated for hours," Peter told the delegates to the ICFTU women's conference. "She was thrown into solitary confinement, where she stayed for months. We are told she remains in a horrendous jail cell and has been severely beaten by the military agents holding her.

"My union, the UAW, is working closely with the AFL-CIO and its Solidarity Center to rally support for Dita in hopes the government of Indonesia will release her and other labor activists still held in prison there."

Just as strong women helped organize and build the UAW from the union's earliest days, so, too, have women in many countries endangered their livelihoods and lives to create workers' movements in the face of employer and government repression.

Dita Sari took daring risks on behalf of Indonesian workers, who joined together despite the fact that organizing truly independent unions had been illegal there since 1975. The military dictatorship allowed only a government-controlled "union" federation called the SPSI.[1]

The UAW worked hard on her case as part of its broader support of workers in Indonesia, which is the world's fourth-most-populous country with some 240 million people, about 90 percent of them Muslim.

During the time Sari and other labor activists were jailed, Indonesia was ruled by General Suharto, a dictator who committed massive human rights violations, including the killings of more than one million political opponents and innocent civilians in the wake of a 1965 coup attempt.

Here's how Human Rights Watch assessed Suharto's regime:

"Suharto presided over more than three decades of military dictatorship and systematic human rights abuses, including media censorship, tight restrictions on freedom of association and assembly, a highly politicized and controlled judiciary, widespread torture, attacks on the rights of minorities, massacres of alleged communists, and numerous war crimes committed in East Timor. . . .

"He also presided over a famously corrupt regime in which he, his family, and his cronies amassed billions of dollars in illegal wealth—funds which could have addressed Indonesia's widespread poverty and social problems."[2]

Sari herself had studied law at the University of Indonesia in the early 1990s and came from a middle-class family. She joined study groups that talked about radical philosophy and theory and began organizing students to press for human rights.

"As students, we recognized the need to connect with workers in order to bring about democratic change," she later told Dan La Botz, who wrote an excellent book on the Indonesian labor movement after Suharto. She spent some time living in workers' quarters, dropped out of law school, and started organizing textile and garment workers.[3] "We began with those purely economic issues, such as meal and transportation allowances," she recalled, "but from the economic issues, we tried to show the connection between the bosses and the Ministry of Manpower: between the bosses and the state. . . ."[4]

Needless to say, General Suharto and the military strongmen of his regime had little interest in the organization of independent unions that empowered workers to be strong in dealing with his government and multinational employers.

Dita's imprisonment underscored the tough odds facing workers who sought to organize to win a better way of life. But labor experts such as La Botz noted that Dita might have been

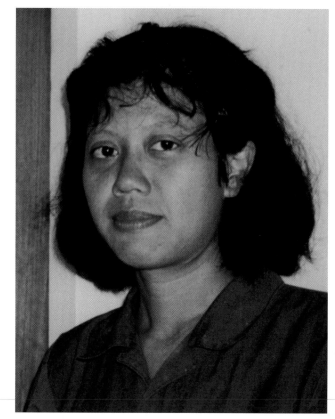

Dita Sari, a young union leader in Indonesia, was jailed by the Indonesian dictatorship in 1996. She led a strike of 20,000 workers from 11 factories demanding better working conditions and a living wage. The UAW responded with a campaign to win her freedom from prison.

fortunate to have been jailed rather than "disappeared."

Three years before Dita's imprisonment, another young woman activist named Marsinah, a 25-year-old who worked at a factory in East Java, led strikes for higher wages. Workers at the plant, which produced watches for export, were in negotiations with the company when military leaders began sitting in on the talks. On May 2, 1993, the military took on the role of employer and fired 12 workers.

Marsinah spoke out strongly against the dismissals. Then, three days later, she disappeared.

Her body was found about 60 miles from her home on

May 8, and an examination revealed she had been tortured and raped before being murdered.

"Her throat had marks showing that she had been strangled, and some instrument had horribly damaged her vagina," La Botz wrote. "The military was put in charge of investigating her murder, though human rights organizations suspected that it was the Army itself that had murdered Marsinah because of her labor union activities."[5]

Initially, Sari faced charges that she had insulted the government and officials of the Suharto regime. But later she was charged with violating the Anti-Subversion Law, a far more serious allegation that grew out of the burning of the offices of the Indonesian Democratic Party (PDI). Many believed the military arranged for the torching as a pretext to crack down on opposition forces. Indeed, Dita was in jail when the fires occurred and had no connection to them.

She was a founder of a political group growing out of her student activity called the People's Democratic Party (PRD), and it supported the labor organizing of the Center for Indonesian Labor Struggle (PPBI). The PRD supported repeal of the Suharto regime's repressive "five laws" dealing with political parties, mass organizations, elections, parliament, and the process through which to amend the constitution.

The effort to change those laws, according to the dictatorship, made one guilty of subversion.

During the trial, "we tried to talk about workers' rights and conditions, such as the right to freedom of association," Dita later told La Botz. "We argued we shouldn't be tried because of our thoughts."[6]

Predictably, the Surabaya District Court found Sari guilty[7] and sentenced her to six years in prison (later reduced to five). She served her first months in Surabaya, where she organized a demonstration of women prisoners who protested the prison's conditions and corruption.[8] Authorities then transferred her to a prison in Melang.

While the UAW and the AFL-CIO campaigned for her release, Dita's day-to-day conditions worsened. Here's how she described them to La Botz:

"(Prison officials) started a smear campaign against me among the other prisoners and guards. . . . They created a space of hate and suspicion between the other prisoners and me. This put me in a corner, and I was not able to relate to anyone in a normal way. . . .

"The conditions were very bad during the seven months when I was in Melang Prison. My access to visitors was restricted. All my reading material was censored, and worst of all, I was very isolated from all of the other women prisoners. This was psychologically very tiring."[9] Eventually, with the help of the AFL-CIO Solidarity Center, Sari was moved to Tangerang Prison, where conditions improved. That shift to West Java also put her closer to her family and friends, who soon were allowed occasional visits.

During this time, UAW President Steve Yokich raised Dita Sari's plight in many of his speeches to union meetings and in public forums. He admired her courage as a woman in her

Dita Sari (left), who organized workers and led strikes, is shown here during her trial in Indonesia. Her labor activism led to her conviction by the Suharto dictatorship and a sentence of five years.

20s willing to organize strikes and challenge a military strong-man who had ordered the deaths of hundreds of thousands of opponents.

"The UAW is committed to fighting as long as it takes until Dita Sari wins her freedom," Yokich said at the time. "She is in prison because she fought to improve the lives of Indonesian workers.

"UAW members believe in solidarity with our sisters and brothers struggling to build unions in Indonesia and around the world. We call on Indonesia's ruling elite to release Dita and halt their repression of labor and human rights."[10]

One way she kept her spirits up was to write letters to famous world figures, such as then First Lady Hillary Clinton, asking for help in winning her release. Here is an excerpt from a letter she wrote to Nelson Mandela on April 17, 1999:

"It is only two years left, then my punishment will be over. But for my people, for my workers, it's a long way to freedom. Freedom from fear, freedom from poverty, and freedom from repression. . . . Whenever the hard times come in this prison, I try to think about the harder times that you have been through. It does help me. My friends always tell me we should create new Mandelas; not in South Africa, but here in Indonesia. . . .

"I am 26 years old, and most of the activists in my union are young people. The waves of mass struggle will shape us, fill our minds with new ideas and opinions, and somehow strengthen us. It's a long way to go, Sir, and life in the struggle does not always treat us kindly. But anyhow, I sincerely pray for your strength and health to take care of the people, the children of South Africa who love and admire you."[11]

During Sari's time in prison, the political turmoil in Indonesia escalated due in large part to severe economic conditions growing out of the broader Asian economic crisis in 1998. Indonesia's crony capitalism with its high debt levels and bad financial management brought rising levels of unemployment and outflows of capital.

General Suharto dispatched other generals and top military officials to stand in shopping malls and markets with reassuring words about how the economy would soon improve. The Indonesian currency, the rupiah, lost much of its value, despite Suharto's "I Love the Rupiah" campaign. Banks began to collapse, and Suharto himself fell from public view (perhaps because of a stroke).

Widespread rioting and political demonstrations occurred, often led by students and some by workers. Human rights groups believed the military was behind other disturbances targeting Chinese-Indonesians as a way to divert attention from core economic failures as well as to divide the political opposition.

On May 21, 1998, the military forced Suharto to resign, and B. J. Habibie, his vice president, replaced him. After more than 30 years in power, Suharto had lost support from the military from which he came, and they acted to restore some semblance of order.

One result was that many political prisoners soon were released from Indonesian prisons. But the new regime refused to free Dita Sari.

The military controlled many important posts in Habibie's new government. The home affairs minister, for example, previously had been the force behind the campaign against the PRD and strongly opposed Dita's release.

Given its economic difficulties, the Indonesian government needed various forms of international financial assistance. Habibie soon sought a huge rescue package from the International Monetary Fund and the World Bank. Inflation was rising at 80 percent a year, productivity had plummeted, and the price of rice had tripled.[12]

The UAW and the entire American labor movement had some difficulties with the Clinton administration in this period, including bitter fights over NAFTA and other important trade issues. However, we continued to have good ties to Secretary of State Madeleine Albright.

Working with the AFL-CIO, we sought in 1997–98 to leverage Indonesia's hope to get international economic aid as a way to increase the pressure on Habibie to release Dita. I asked UAW President Yokich to call AFL-CIO President John Sweeney to urge the federation to escalate the pressure for both Dita's release and a broader agenda of labor reforms in Indonesia. Barbara Shailor, the AFL-CIO's international affairs director, was deeply involved in this effort and with positive effect.

We knew we were making progress when Indonesia agreed to sign the Freedom of Association convention of the International Labor Organization in June 1998. The ILO had pressured Indonesia on Dita's case, but the signing of Convention 87 gave new protection to Indonesian workers seeking to band together to form independent unions. While some countries fail to abide by their commitments to the ILO, global labor is able to pressure them more effectively if they have signed the conventions.

In addition, we learned that officials of the U.S. embassy in Indonesia visited Sari in the fall of 1998, several months after Habibie took power. Soon after, the regime offered Dita a deal to get out of prison if she agreed to do no union organizing or political work and to refrain from traveling to other countries where she could highlight her mistreatment.

Despite her weariness after nearly three years in prison,

Indonesian troops beat demonstrators in Bandung who protested the labor and human rights abuses and failing economy under the dictatorship in that nation, which is the world's fourth-most-populous country.

Sari said no to the deal. Upon her release, she fully intended to rejoin the labor/political struggle.

In early 1999, Barbara Shailor visited Dita in prison and told her the American unions would continue to push for her release.

Several months later, Kristyne Peter of the UAW's International Affairs Department flew to Indonesia in an attempt to meet with Dita and discuss details of the union's global solidarity effort on her behalf, including the union's pressure on Habibie to agree to further reforms of labor laws.

Because of the UAW's high-profile campaign demanding labor and human rights in Indonesia, authorities refused to allow Sari to meet with Peter, who waited outside the prison for three days. Dita was able to have a message of thanks to the UAW smuggled out of the prison by her father.

Shortly thereafter, the UAW rallied delegates to the ICFTU's women's conference in Brazil to support Dita's release and the broader labor reform agenda in Indonesia. During this time, a group of workers met in West Java to found a new union, the National Front of Indonesian Labor Struggle (FNPBI). Although Sari remained in Tangerang Women's Prison, the FNPBI delegates chose to elect her their leader. The old labor group, PPBI, had been made illegal in 1996, and their efforts had moved underground until the formation of the FNPBI.

The Habibie government found itself pressured on the broad global front by the "Free Dita" campaign and also saw protests within Indonesia, including some in front of the prison, pressing for her release. Even a group from the old government-controlled union federation demonstrated at the prison and also at the Ministry of Justice.[13]

Fahmi Idris, the minister of manpower who had handled the signing of the ILO convention on freedom of association in early June 1999, visited Dita in prison at the end of that

After the UAW and its allies helped win her release, Dita Sari walked through these gates at Tangerang Women's Prison on July 5, 1999. Photo by Kristyne Peter.

month. He asked about her views on unions, the ILO action, and other changes in labor regulations.

Afterward Dita said the issue of her release had sparked arguments among government officials, according to the minister, with the military not wanting to see her freed. "If I'm released, they fear fresh labor rallies which, they think, would threaten national stability," she said.[14]

On July 5, 1999, the Indonesian regime yielded to the internal unrest and the broad global campaign of the UAW, the AFL-CIO, and other labor and human rights organizations.

Dita Sari finally was a free woman.

She left the penitentiary at 12:30 p.m., accompanied by her father, Adjidar Ascha.

"I was released because of international pressure," she said. "Unions, women's organizations, and human rights organizations carried out campaigns . . . demanding my release. This international solidarity, combined with campaigns by workers' and students' groups and political parties in Indonesia, was the main reason for my release."[15]

Dita and her father departed Tangerang Women's Prison in a Honda Civic and headed to Menteng Pulo cemetery in central Jakarta.[16] Sari's mother had died while she was in prison, and the Indonesian regime had refused to allow her to attend the funeral and burial.

The day of Dita's release, she went directly to the gravesite and used her prison uniform to clean her mother's headstone.[17]

Then she returned to her union to begin once again the job of organizing workers and fighting on behalf of the Indonesian labor movement. She now holds a seat in the legislature in Indonesia.

Global Solidarity Won Release Of Pakpahan

The UAW's success in helping win freedom for Dita Sari was not the only time the union worked on behalf of Indonesian workers and unionists seeking a better life.

In 1994, Muchtar Pakpahan, a father of three and leader of Indonesia's then only independent union, sat in solitary confinement after leading strikes and protests in Medan, North Sumatra. A court there increased his sentence from three years to four, but the Indonesian Supreme Court freed Pakpahan for lack of evidence in 1995.

After leaving prison, he told reporters international pressure had been crucial in winning his release. And the head of the Supreme Court was quoted in the newsweekly *Gatra* as stating: "If we had extended (Pakpahan's) stay in jail, we'd have never seen the end of attacks on us from overseas."

A party to welcome Pakpahan's release in Jakarta signaled that his plight was not over when it had to be aborted due to the large number of plainclothes intelligence agents who showed up at the event.[18]

In part because of UAW efforts on his behalf, Pakpahan came to the United States in 1996, where UAW President Steve Yokich hosted a reception for him at the union's Washington, D.C., office.

But just two weeks later, the Indonesian dictatorship arrested Pakpahan again after unrest in Jakarta followed a police-supported violent raid on the headquarters of a legally recognized opposition party.

"In the dead of night, security agents raided his home and jailed him," Yokich told delegates to the union's 1998 convention. "As we have seen in other countries, Indonesia's goal has been to maintain low wages for its workers in order to give companies a competitive advantage for their products.

"Key to their strategy is to prevent independent unions from aggressively pushing for improved wages and working conditions," Yokich said. "The UAW and our allies are waging a campaign seeking Pakpahan's unconditional release. Our Labor Rights Now project, coordinated by the International Affairs Department, has produced materials aimed at building awareness and support for the Free Pakpahan effort."[19]

Many UAW members had taken up Pakpahan's cause. One example: Shirley Luczyk, a member of Local 19 from Rockford, Michigan, sent a letter to the editor of *UAW Solidarity* on Indonesia.[20]

"I wrote the Indonesian ambassador to protest the jailing of union leader Muchtar Pakpahan as you asked," Luczyk reported. "I'm pleased to see UAW join the fight for human rights in Indonesia."

Labor Rights Now produced materials on the Pakpahan case noting the new charges he faced included subversion, punishable in the worst case by the death penalty.

In a two-page spread, *UAW Solidarity* said Pakpahan "could face the firing squad."

"We can't let M.P. [as he was known] die. If his struggle fails, Asian workers will find it harder to win the labor rights and better wages they need for a higher standard of living. Meanwhile our corporations will keep blaming us for not being 'competitive,' as they pack up and move their production to low-wage places like Indonesia."[21]

The International Confederation of Free Trade Unions (ICFTU) wrote to the International Labor Organization (ILO) detailing the "significant new violations of trade union rights" involving Pakpahan. About 30 trade unionists from his SBSI union had been jailed throughout Indonesia.

In February 1997, the ICFTU referred his case to the United Nations, and in July of that year, the SBSI offered new evidence that Pakpahan had not been involved in the Medan protests in April 1994, the earlier case for which his quashed sentence had now been reinstated.

Working closely with the new leadership of the AFL-CIO, the UAW organized a number of rallies and events demanding Indonesia free Pakpahan and other trade union prisoners, including Dita Sari. That work escalated after a tumor was found in Pakpahan's right lung, resulting in his admission to Cikini hospital in central Jakarta for treatment.

Many rank-and-file UAW members took up Muchtar Pakpahan's cause. The leader of Indonesia's only independent union at that time ended up on trial twice for leading strikes and protests in the 1990s.

Doctors went on to find a blockage in an artery in his brain. They also urged that Pakpahan have a lung imagery fluorescence endoscopy, an examination not available in Indonesia because the country lacked the necessary medical technology.

The UAW offered to join with other allies to fly Pakpahan to the United States for medical treatment, but the Suharto regime had little interest in the union leader's health problems.

Instead, his trial in South Jakarta District Court resumed in September 1997, although each session was limited to three hours due to his poor health.

The UAW expanded the campaign by opposing the request by the International Monetary Fund for an additional $18 billion in funds for Indonesian activities. "In Indonesia, independent union leader Muchtar Pakpahan remains on trial for his life for his union activity. Yet the International Monetary Fund has made no effort to use its leverage to free him," a UAW International Executive Board resolution stated.

Two months later, Pakpahan was convicted and sentenced to three years in prison. The prosecution appealed, and Pakpahan then was resentenced to seven years.

It was the economic crisis that ultimately would bring Pakpahan his freedom. As the Indonesian economy worsened, the military removed Suharto and replaced him with B.J. Habibie, who freed Pakpahan on May 25, 1998.

For more than a decade, Muchtar Pakpahan—who could have been executed by firing squad—instead went on to serve Indonesian workers as leader of his union and later as a political activist who formed a labor party modeled after those of Europe.

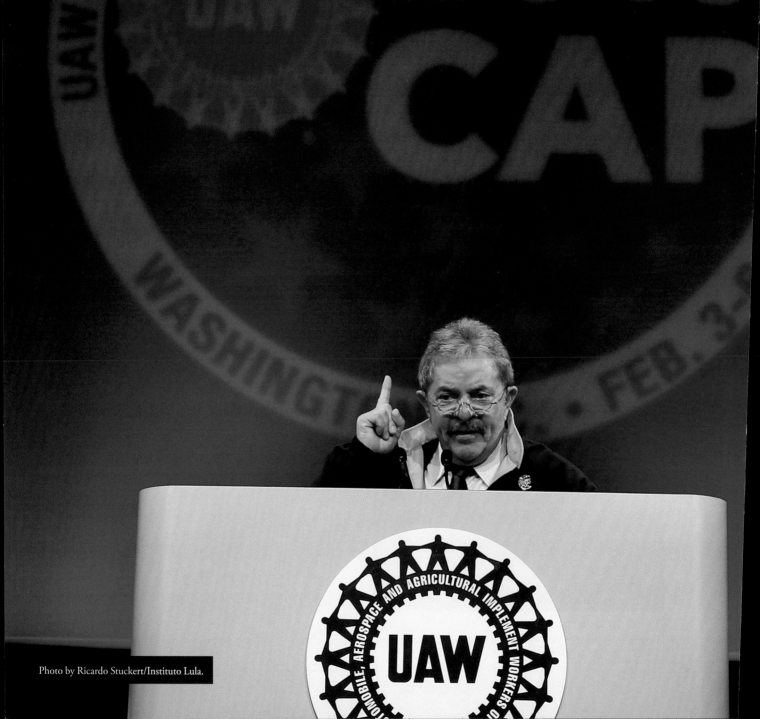

Photo by Ricardo Stuckert/Instituto Lula.

CHAPTER SIX

Brazil's President Backs UAW Organizing Efforts
Union Stood With Lula When Military Jailed Him

Jeff Moore, a quality-control body shop worker for Nissan in Canton, Mississippi, does not impress easily.

But after listening to an hour-long speech by Luiz Inacio Lula da Silva, the former president of Brazil, Moore was blown away.

"Lula's speech was powerful for me," Moore said in February 2013 at the UAW Community Action Program conference in Washington, D.C.

"When he stuck his neck out for workers in Brazil, it made me realize he really cares about the labor movement," said Moore, one of many Nissan workers who want to be represented by the UAW. "I think it's going to move my co-workers to get motivated toward a vote for the union.

"It will make everyone want to step off the curb and be braver and bolder in our effort to organize and fight for the rights we deserve."

The strong support for the UAW by the former two-term president of Brazil, a country of more than 190 million people living in the world's seventh-largest economy, put Nissan on notice that the Canton workers had powerful allies. Indeed, Nissan's CEO, Carlos Ghosn, is a Brazilian, and Nissan sought to triple its market share in Brazil.

How did a world leader of such stature come to be at a union gathering in America pledging all-out support for a UAW organizing drive?

The story goes back more than 30 years to a time when a very young lathe operator at an auto parts factory in Brazil rose to lead strikes during a period when the country was ruled by a repressive military regime.

That youthful union leader then found himself in prison and later on trial facing a long sentence. At a time when Lula and the workers' movement in Brazil needed help, the UAW was there.

John Christensen grew up in Racine, Wisconsin, and worked at Massey Ferguson, Inc. He became chief steward of UAW Local 244 and rose to president there in 1972. Shortly after UAW President Doug Fraser was elected in 1977, he appointed Christensen to the staff of the union's International Affairs Department in Washington, D.C.

One of Christensen's assignments from Fraser was to go to Brazil in February 1981 to be in the courtroom as a very direct, on-the-scene act of solidarity by the UAW in support of 11 metalworkers, including Lula, who faced trial by Brazil's military regime for violations of the National Security Law.

Lula and the other union activists had been involved in a strike in the auto and metal trades industries that occurred in and near São Paulo in April 1980. Rather than charge them with violations of the labor code, the regime used the National Security Law, under which "acts of collective disobedience," "subversive propaganda," and "subversive" rallies and demonstrations all could subject unionists to prosecution.[1]

The regime argued that Lula and his colleagues had committed "collective disobedience." But the evidence amassed by prosecutors failed to indicate the labor leaders had ordered the metalworkers to strike. Indeed, the facts showed that a majority vote of the workers had favored continuing the general strike, and the leaders simply followed along.

The day before that trial was to begin, the only civilian member of the five-person military tribunal, Nelson Guimaraes, told Lula, the other defendants, and their lawyers that he had already reached a guilty verdict. With a conviction guaranteed, the defendants boycotted the two-day trial. The military tribunal unsurprisingly convicted them.

But a higher court reversed the conviction on September 2, 1981. It held that the lower tribunal acted unlawfully by proceeding without the defendants and their counsel.

Two months later, with the UAW in the courtroom again at the São Paulo Council of Justice, Lula and the 10 others went on trial a second time.

In addition to the UAW's John Christensen at the first trial, there were several other foreign trial observers, including Stanley A. Gacek from the United Food and Commercial Workers (UFCW), who was a lawyer. A representative of the German labor federation DGB also attended.

Christensen particularly hit it off with Lula. They would tell stories and laugh together during breaks. At the November trial, the two shared the bond of factory and union work and neither opposed raising a glass or two on occasion.

"When you're looking at a long prison sentence, that's a moment when you appreciate people who came from far away to stand at your side," recalled Gacek. "Over the years, the UAW really stood with the Brazilian workers, and that flowed from the unique chemistry that developed between Christensen and Lula during the trial."

On November 19, 1981, the Brazilian army's justice council once again convicted Lula and his co-defendants. Lula was sentenced to three and a half years in prison along with several others. The remainder got two to two and a half years.

UAW President Doug Fraser condemned the conviction and sentence, as did Bob White, director of the UAW's Canadian region, who said that Lula's "crime" was to lead a strike that aimed solely to improve workers' living standards.

Herman Rebhan, a UAW member who had become general secretary of the International Metalworkers' Federation in Geneva, Switzerland, a global union federation with which the UAW was affiliated, also blasted the verdict.

"This puts Brazil into the camp of the worst kind of authoritarian state and makes nonsense of [Brazilian President] Figueiredo's claims that the country is moving to democracy," Rebhan said.[2]

Lula was the seventh of eight children and did not learn to read until he was 10. He quit school after fourth grade to help his family survive. He worked shining shoes and as a street vendor at age 12. When he was 14, Lula got his first formal job, working as a lathe operator in a copper-processing factory.

He worked at the Fabrica de Parafusos Marte, but quit when management refused to pay him the same wages as older men even though he had worked there as long, according to Richard Bourne's history, *Lula of Brazil: The Story So Far*, on which this section is based.[3] During this time, João Goulart gained broad powers in Brazil after a referendum in which citizens voted by a margin of 5 to 1 to return to an executive presidency. In 1963, he called for land reform, taxing the wealthy, and nationalization of certain foreign-owned utilities. Goulart, while a big landowner, pushed a populist program that included support and benefits for organized labor.

The next year he expropriated private oil refineries, and almost immediately the military revolted. A three-day military coup ousted the populist Goulart with the active support of the U.S. government, which remained worried about the spread of Cuban-style revolution elsewhere in Latin America.[4]

Lula spent about eight months of 1965 without a job, and his brothers were unemployed as well. He would leave home every morning at 6 a.m. to search for work, starting at the bigger automakers and moving on to smaller metal shops.

The experience of being out of work was something he

never forgot. He and his extended family couldn't afford chicken or meat and got by on a diet of rice and potatoes cooked in oil, according to Bourne.[5]

Eventually, he was hired by Fábrica Independência as a lathe turner. At age 19, he lost a finger on his left hand working the graveyard shift as a press operator at the plant. A heavy metal press fell on his hand after a screw broke.[6] He had to go from hospital to hospital before finally getting medical attention—an experience that increased his interest in unions.

Lula moved to a new job at Fris-Moldu-Car, but didn't last long.

"The boss there wanted him to work on a Saturday," Bourne wrote in his excellent biography of Lula. "But he wanted to go on a picnic to Santos with his brothers. So Lula refused to work that Saturday, went on the picnic, and lost his job."

He then got a job at Acos Villares, a large engineering firm, where his brother, Frei Chico, also was employed. Inspired by his brother, he joined the metalworkers' union and rose quickly through the ranks due to his skills, toughness, and charisma. He had signed on as a member of the Sindicato dos Metalúrgicos de São Bernardo in September 1968 in what is known as the ABC area of industrial suburbs around São Paulo.[7] That area was home to Ford, Volkswagen, and other auto companies in Brazil.

In 1968, Lula was elected to the union leadership at Villares, and by 1972 he had risen to be a full-time official.[8] When the union's presidency came open in 1975, Lula won with 92 percent of the vote.

The International Metalworkers' Federation held a Toyota workers meeting a few months after Lula's union election. While in Japan, Lula got word that his brother, Frei Chico, had been eating lunch in a bar when he was arrested by military intelligence as part of a broader sweep throughout Brazil.[9] Some of those arrested died in the military regime's custody. Lula's brother was tortured and beaten, and his interrogators faked a confession that stated Lula had been a messenger for communists. Frei Chico was released after 78 days.

Lula came away from the incident radicalized on several levels. He had difficulty grasping how a worker and unionist like his brother could be a target of the government. Rather than being cowed by the arrest, Lula began to push the union to be more aggressive.[10] His approach was to focus on improving wages and working conditions instead of pursuing the more ideological approach favored by some.

For its own reasons, the military regime was touting an "economic miracle" that occurred with tight limits on wages. The Brazilian growth rate had averaged about 11 percent in the five preceding years, and inflation was at its lowest level since the 1950s.[11]

"Some of the union leaders had become soft with comfortable careers in the labor bureaucracy and generally tried to restrain the workers," wrote Ted Goertzel in his book titled *Brazil's Lula: The Most Popular Politician on Earth*.[12] "Lula's sympathies were with younger, more militant leaders who wanted to push the limits of what was allowed, mostly by calling strikes."

Goertzel argues that the labor activism of this period evolved not out of desperation and misery, but instead was "born of hope caused by things getting better—the belief that they could work together to make their lives better."[13] Indeed, the skilled workers at the big automakers in the ABC area around São Paulo had both secure employment and the highest wages in the country.

In addition to becoming more militant during this time, Lula pushed labor in the ABC region to stay independent of other movements that also opposed Brazil's military government. Various factions of students and intellectuals made up vital elements of the opposition, but Lula believed it was important for labor to remain an independent force that had its own popularity among the broader public.

Brazilian members of the UGT gathered at a Nissan dealership in Belo Horizonte to show their solidarity with workers in Canton, Mississippi, who had been threatened by Nissan during the UAW organizing drive.

Malcom Sutton
Nissan Technician, Mississippi
Threatened by Nissan.

Robin Moore
Nissan Technician, Mississippi
Threatened by Nissan.

SINDICATO DOS COMERCIÁRIOS D
DIREITOS DOS TRABALHADORES DA

SINDICATO DOS COMERCIÁ
www.comerciari

Lee Ruffin
Nissan Technician, Mississippi
Threatened by Nissan.

UNIDOS NA LUTA
PELA LIBERDADE
SINDICAL NA NISSAN

UNIDOS NA LUTA
PELA LIBERDADE
SINDICAL NA NISSAN

O PAULO NA LUTA PELOS
SSAN EM TODO O MUNDO

E SÃO PAULO
br

UGT
UNIÃO GERAL DOS
TRABALHADORES

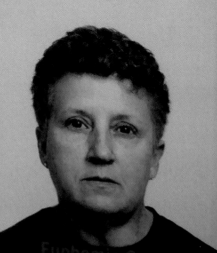

Euphemia Coats
Nissan Technician, Mississippi
Threatened by Nissan.

During this period, Lula regularly had to lead negotiations to adjust wages to compensate for inflation. As a result, he appeared frequently on television news programs and in the newspapers.

"Bearded, often carrying a few extra pounds and a bit disheveled, he became a media icon of the São Paulo industrial worker," Goertzel wrote.

Lula truly became a national figure when he commissioned a study on the inflation figures being used in the wage negotiations. Building on an analysis by DIEESE, the primary research arm of the Brazilian union movement, Lula argued that Brazilian workers had lost more than a third of the value of the minimum salary because the government manipulated the inflation numbers to show a far lower rate than that actually occurring.

Lula ran for president of the São Bernardo metalworkers in 1978 on this platform and got 97.3 percent of the vote. At the congress of the Confederação Nacional dos Trabalhadores da Industria in July of that year, he played a central role in rallying other labor leaders in a drive to build a free union movement that could bring democracy to Brazil.[14] That congress adopted a program that called for:

- a secret, free, and direct vote for the country's top political posts;
- a new constitution for Brazil;
- the right to strike;
- the right to have union representatives and works committees inside factories, and
- guarantees of human rights.[15]

During this time of rising expectations, strikes by metalworkers in the ABC region spread. They began at Saab Scania on May 12 and soon were breaking out all over. Usually, the work stoppages weren't called by Lula or the union leadership, but occurred spontaneously as worker grievances and anger spread.

Brazilian members of the CUT metalworkers protested in front of a Nissan dealership there to show support for workers at Nissan in Mississippi who are seeking UAW representation despite the Japanese automaker's anti-union campaign. The CNM-CUT workers held a poster with a photo of Calvin Moore, a pro-UAW activist unfairly fired by Nissan.

The workers were seeking higher wages, the right to have union stewards on the shop floor, job security after 90 days' work, employment rights after an accident, and other gains.[16] Because strikes were illegal, union leaders such as Lula were subject to arrest. But at the onset, even the military regime seemed to realize the leaders weren't driving the unrest but were responding to it.

"There was an informal, popular quality to these strikes," Bourne wrote in his Lula biography. "Lula and his colleagues made many of the decisions in a bar in São Bernardo run by Tia Rose—'Aunt' Rosa—who, like Lula, [came from the northeast of Brazil]. They were a group of friends, not union bureaucrats."[17]

By the end of 1978, about 539,000 workers had participated in 24 strikes. Because the core issue was economic, soon the multinational employers and those locally based began to fear their substantial profits under military rule might be in jeopardy.

"The fruits of growth had not been shared with labor because unions had been decapitated and strikes prohibited," Bourne wrote. Employers and the government had been caught off-guard by the sudden upsurge of labor unrest, and "they resolved to act differently in the future, mobilizing police and other agencies of force."[18]

The battle was joined in 1979 when more than 3.2 million workers participated in 113 strikes.[19] In March of that year, just as the Brazilian presidency was handed to another military figure, João Baptista de Oliveira Figueiredo, Lula had negotiated an agreement with the employers' federation that would have given 63 percent wage hikes to the lowest-paid metalworkers and 44 percent raises for the higher paid.

But when Lula presented the agreement to the workers in a soccer stadium, he got a chant of "Strike, Strike, Strike" in response. Standing on a table, there was little he could do. "So, we are on strike," he responded.[20] Things quickly deteriorated. The military government removed the elected union leaders, including Lula, and shut down the São Bernardo metalworkers' union.

UAW President Doug Fraser, who had asked the union's international affairs director, Leo Suslow, to keep him informed, was among the strongest critics of the military regime in Brazil.

"The 1.5 million members of the UAW, and trade unionists everywhere, will be closely watching Brazil during this period," warned Fraser in a telegram to Brazilian Labor Minister Murilo Macedo. "We hope your government will allow the workers to freely present their demands unhindered by the repression and intimidation so common in the past."

The generals, unfortunately, had other plans. When 20,000 strikers gathered in the Samuel Sabatini Square in São Bernardo, they were attacked by about 1,000 shock troops, more than 100 armored cars, and a vehicle firing sand and colored water.

"The workers sang the national anthem," said Bourne. "They called out Lula's name." The bishop of São Bernardo led the crowd in reciting the Lord's Prayer. In the face of the workers' solidarity, the military forces withdrew and the workers won a moral victory of sorts.

Lula and his colleagues learned lessons from the 1979 crackdown. They created more decentralized structures to deal with the military regime's attempts to disband unions and arrest labor leaders. The metalworkers moved to a pyramid organizational structure in which about 450 leaders were elected in factory meetings. They could continue a strike even after the top union officials had been jailed.

Strikes began again in the ABC region in April 1980. Legal maneuvering postponed an immediate crackdown. Lula had an opening to end the strikes, until a confrontation occurred at the Vila Euclides soccer stadium filled with thousands of workers and their families, according to Bourne.

Command of the Second Army had been seized by an old right-wing hard-liner who ordered up army helicopters that flew very low over the strikers, seeking to intimidate them. Instead, the move backfired, and the support for the strike strengthened. A few days later, the regional labor court declared the strike to be illegal.

The regime arrested Lula and 12 other union leaders on April 19, 1980. The Roman Catholic Church gave Lula and the strikers very strong support. The cardinal and a number of bishops spoke out on labor's side, and strikers' families would line up at churches each week where they received food and money.[21] Authorities did allow Lula to visit his mother, who suffered from cancer, and to attend her funeral when she died May 12 while he was still imprisoned.

When Lula finally was freed later that month, he returned home. His first act was to set free his caged birds—a symbolic statement that indicated his own relief at being released. One reason authorities let Lula out was that the strike had been ended by the workers.[22] Despite some in the military government believing the time had come to cede some power back to civilian control, the process of *abertura* (opening up) had not extended to labor issues. In an article in *Dissent*, UFCW lawyer Stanley Gacek outlined the restrictive nature of labor laws in this period:

- The government had the legal authority to intervene in any union and could remove union leaders from office by promulgating an ad hoc decree/law.
- The state established the jurisdictional boundaries of all trade unions. It determined which professions or crafts were included in a particular union and the geographic area where a union could operate.
- The government determined the entire trade union structure, including the vertical relations between the local unions and their national confederations and the lateral relations between the local organizations.
- The government held the purse strings to union budgets. Revenues from paychecks of all workers were pooled into a common, state-controlled fund and then allocated to the unions according to a formula.
- "Political expenditures," which were defined broadly in Brazil to include virtually all union-organizing activities, were prohibited.
- The government directed all of the bargaining sessions, which were limited primarily to the discussion of wage bonuses to somewhat balance the significant inflation that eroded workers' purchasing power.
- Restrictions had been imposed that left little room for "legal" strikes.[23]

Despite these harsh laws, workers continued to strike. The militancy shown by Lula also had spread to other sectors, and soon teachers had walked off the job. Peasants who wanted land reform began to occupy farms of wealthy landowners. In the *favelas*, or shantytowns, the poor demanded price freezes on basic food items, better sanitation, electricity, and schools for their children.

Hard-liners in the military regime sought to dampen the growing opposition by putting Lula and his union colleagues on trial in February 1981. As noted above, Lula and his co-defendants refused to participate in the trial, and their convictions later were overturned.

That led to the retrial where John Christensen of the UAW sat in the Brazilian courtroom every day with Lula and pledged the union's solidarity with the workers' struggle.

Lula's conviction and sentence of three and a half years in November 1981 appeared to sideline him at a critical moment. But by then, Lula had become a sort of folk hero—a Brazilian equivalent of Lech Wałęsa, who had been leading Polish workers at this very same time in their own struggle against another entrenched state willing to repress labor.

The parallels were interesting. The strikes in both Brazil and Poland had been illegal stoppages by workers seeking a better life through independent unions.

Both countries had populations that were heavily Roman Catholic, and the church leaders in Brazil and Poland stood with the workers against authoritarian states—one run by the military and the other by a communist government that had been a satellite state of the Soviet Union. In each case, there were powerful forces pushing for political democracy.

For Brazil, the military had held power since 1964. Some generals saw dangers in continued repression as the union movement had grown in sophistication, numbers, and power.

Within a few months, General Figueiredo, who held the presidency, continued some aspects of liberalization. For Lula, that meant an annulment of his conviction and a return to the struggle.

But by this time, Lula had handed off leadership of the metalworkers to Jair Meneghelli, a 34-year-old Ford worker who went on to be a close ally of the UAW.

Lula, whose focus had been on achieving gains for

workers, decided to make a shift into politics. There was a general feeling among unionists that none of the existing parties represented their interests, including those aligned with various left ideologies.

He believed it likely the government would move to allow the formation of new parties, and he saw the nearly 11 million workers in Brazilian industries as a base from which a workers party could make gains.

The Partido dos Trabalhadores, known as the PT, formed in 1980. Some two years later, the government permitted general elections for the first time since the mid-1960s. Lula ran for governor of São Paulo as the PT candidate. He was shocked to come in fourth—a major setback that indicated many Brazilians at that time seemed wary of a union-based party.

Shortly after this electoral failure, Lula shifted gears and began pushing for direct elections for the Brazilian presidency.

Dennis Williams, then UAW secretary-treasurer, was welcomed by Lula, Brazil's former president, at the CNM/CUT Congress in São Paulo, Brazil, in April 2011. Williams has played an important role in building global support for UAW organizing efforts at Nissan in Canton, Mississippi.

The move proved popular with the public, and soon Lula was addressing rallies of hundreds of thousands of supporters of direct elections.

After some political maneuvering, direct elections finally were achieved and Brazil faced a new political landscape. Lula ran for Congress in 1986 and won the most votes nationwide.[24] While a member of Congress, Lula ran for the presidency unsuccessfully in 1989, then lost again in 1994 and in 1998.

Each defeat taught him and the PT lessons. Finally, in 2002, Lula succeeded in being elected president of Brazil. A worker and trade unionist had risen to lead the country as a progressive democrat.

At the UAW Community Action Program (CAP) conference in Washington, D.C., in February 2013, Lula was the featured speaker. In introducing him, UAW President Bob King described some of the union leader–turned–president's achievements.

Lula showed his commitment to labor when he named his first cabinet to run Brazil, King said. Out of 28 cabinet appointments, seven were trade unionists—one quarter of the entire cabinet.

Under Lula's predecessor, Brazil's public debt had doubled, the trade deficit was twice the Latin American average, interest rates exceeded 20 percent, and the Brazilian currency had lost half of its value in the run-up to that election.

Lula went to work using the skills he had honed in the union movement. He publicly pushed for policies that created jobs and reduced inequality.

The average economic growth rate in Brazil during the 1990s was about 1.6 percent, but in Lula's first term, growth jumped to 4.3 percent. By the end of his second term, Brazil had a growth rate of more than 7 percent—and that meant jobs.

During Lula's administration, the unemployment rate

Women in Brazilian unions spoke out strongly on Nissan's violations of worker and human rights at its Canton, Mississippi, plant where their counterparts want to join the UAW.

dropped from 11 percent at the start of his term to 5.3 percent at the end. Brazil created at least 15 million new formal sector jobs while he served as president.

When he came to power, Lula mothballed the executive jets. He said no to the tradition of gourmet chefs for the president and ate in the cafeteria instead. He put a hold on his predecessor's plan to spend millions on new military fighter planes.

Instead, to set a tone, he led his entire cabinet on a "reality tour" of poor areas in northeastern Brazil, so they would see firsthand how those at the bottom of the economic ladder lived.

Lula, the lathe operator turned president, had many achievements, but five stand out, King told the CAP delegates:

- Under Lula the minimum wage in Brazil, which affects millions of workers, rose by 67 percent, more than 40 percent above the pace of inflation. Because social security benefits for retirement in Brazil rise along with the minimum wage, the impact has been huge.

- Lula's family assistance program, the Bolsa, has played a major role in reducing hunger and poverty. That program provides direct federal help for poor mothers, as long as they send their children to school and get their health checked regularly.

- Under Lula, Brazil withstood the global economic crisis better than almost any other nation. Tight regulation of banks and forced transparency meant that not a single Brazilian bank went under during the recent global crisis. Instead of worshiping the free market, Lula regulated it to everyone's benefit.

- Lula rejected the privatization of government services that turn over valuable public resources and functions to corporations. Instead, under his Growth Acceleration Program, Brazil invested $250 billion in its infrastructure so its economy could expand further and faster.

- Lula directly attacked Brazil's inequality. Before he took office, Brazil ranked fourth worst in the world in the gap between rich and poor. Once his policies had time to work, the poorest 10 percent of the population saw their incomes grow at nearly double the rate of the richest 10 percent.

In addition, during his second term, Lula was the principal advocate among the heads of state of the G-20 nations, the major industrial countries worldwide, to push for the inclusion of worker issues at summits and conferences. By including the International Labor Organization (ILO) at the G-20 table, Lula helped focus the most powerful nations to consider international labor standards and rights as part of their negotiations.

For his part, Lula always included trade unionists in the international missions he took as Brazil's president.

Lula served from 2003 through the end of 2010. In his second term, Lula had an approval rating of 80.5 percent from the Brazilian people. No American president since World War II has had an approval rating anywhere near that.

Time magazine in 2010 named Lula one of the 100 most influential people in the world, largely because he took Brazil from a struggling third-world country to a world superpower.

The Washington Post took note of Lula's achievements as he left office:

"Under Lula, Brazil became the world's seventh-largest economy, more than 20 million people rose out of acute poverty, and Rio de Janeiro was awarded the 2016 Summer Olympics—the first time the Games will be held in South America."[25]

Lula took the stage at the 2013 CAP conference after a long ovation. He presented the UAW president with an official jersey of Brazil's Corinthians soccer team. On it, in Portuguese, was a message: "To my good friend, Bob King. From Lula." The back of the jersey had King's name and the number 8.

"The UAW is an extraordinary union and plays a huge role," Lula said. "It is a great, quality union."

The former two-term president of Brazil told delegates that Brazilian workers were in complete solidarity with American workers at Nissan in Canton, Mississippi, who were campaigning for the right to organize free of intimidation and threats from the company.

"Labor cannot accept that Nissan comes to America and says workers can't organize," Lula said. "It's unimaginable."

In the week before Lula's address, leaders of Brazil's CUT labor federation went to Canton to meet with Nissan workers who sought to form a union and also with community leaders in Mississippi who backed the UAW drive. Those Brazilian unionists then joined Lula in Washington for the CAP meeting, where they introduced some Canton Nissan workers to the former Brazilian president.

"The Brazilian CUT leaders will return to send a strong message to Nissan that it needs to do better by the workers in Mississippi and learn from the Brazil example: Strong unions build strong communities, and strong communities build a strong economy, and a strong middle class," King told the CAP delegates.

"Lula and the Brazilian union movement's support shows how important global solidarity is," the UAW leader noted. "Year after year, the UAW stands with our sisters and brothers around the world who need our help.

"And they stand with us in our struggles here at home to organize and to rebuild the great American middle class."

**W SAMO POŁUDNIE
4 CZERWCA 1989**

This poster is captioned: "It's High Noon, June 4, 1989." That was the date of crucial elections in Poland in which voters effectively ended communist control of their country. Gary Cooper, the star of the Western film *High Noon*, is depicted as the sheriff with the Solidarity union logo and a folded ballot. He's come for the showdown with the communist "bad guys" in the election that propelled Lech Wałęsa, the leader of the Solidarity union, to power. Poster by Tomasz Sarnecki.

CHAPTER SEVEN

Solidarity Union In Poland Toppled Regime
UAW Gave Money, Equipment To Underground

The union revolt in Poland that toppled its communist government nearly three decades ago began with a case of indigestion.

It started after a plant manager fired a 51-year-old widow who had only five months to go before retirement.

Anna Walentynowicz, a crane operator at the state-owned Lenin Shipyard in Gdańsk on the Baltic coast, had worked there since 1950. She had often led small work stoppages in specific departments in the shipyard.

Management regarded Anna as a troublemaker and earlier had her declared "mentally ill" in an attempt to get rid of her. But she had won that battle in local court.[1]

Late in her shift on August 6, 1980, Anna had to go home because she felt ill. The next day, management fired her for "deserting her post."

Workers there were not fooled. They knew her dismissal was in reprisal for her union work. So, after a few days of discussion, they downed their tools, turned off their machines, and proclaimed the shipyard on strike.

The Gdańsk shipyard strike in 1980 led to the founding of the Solidarity union in Poland, known there as Solidarność. And it sparked events during the following decade that weakened, and then destroyed, the Communist Party's control of Poland.

The democratic elections that followed the martial law period saw Poles choose Lech Wałęsa, the independent union leader, as the country's president.

Throughout the struggle of the Polish workers, the UAW repeatedly stood with them. The union provided cash, food, and equipment that enabled Solidarity to continue fighting, even in the darkest days when many of its activists had been imprisoned and their families were left with few resources.

Like most of Poland and, indeed, of the world, the UAW did not know the significance of the Gdańsk strike immediately. There had been work stoppages throughout Poland off and on, and that summer became more unsettled after the government imposed big price increases on many items, particularly food.

Meat prices became unaffordable for most Poles. Many blamed the government because it was shipping meat to the Soviet Union to ensure ample supplies for the Summer Olympics in Moscow. Rolling strikes followed in various state-owned factories around the country in protest.

But the Gdańsk shipyard workers had not gone out. There was considerable unrest there in response to the deaths of eight men and injuries to 60 more in an explosion on the docks. Workers also held vigils for two activists who had been jailed for organizing a rally in May that called for the establishment of trade union rights. And there were job issues that fed anger, such as the continuing practice of sand-stripping paintwork on ships in the repair yard—an outmoded practice that caused serious health problems.[2]

The weekend after Anna's firing, workers met to develop a list of demands. At the top were her reinstatement and a rollback of the food price increases. But the Gdańsk shipyard workers also wanted the right to form their own union and elect its leaders.

On August 14, 1980, about 17,000 workers at the shipyard went on strike. A decade before, there had been a strike at Gdańsk that ended in failure after about 30 workers had been killed by the government. This time, workers decided to occupy the shipyard, much like workers in the auto plants in Flint, Michigan, and elsewhere had done in the mid-1930s.

Lech Wałęsa had been one of the strike leaders in 1970. He continued to work there as an electrician, which gave him free run of the entire shipyard and enabled him to get to know many of the workers personally. But his involvement in illegal unions and his campaign for a memorial to honor those slain in the 1970 strike eventually got him fired.

He remained jobless for long periods, interspersed with occasional work at small electrical companies.

Wałęsa had been "wolf-ticketed," the Polish term for blacklisted. As a result, when the strike began in 1980 at the shipyard, he was on the outside looking in.

Early on he had climbed over the railings and entered the shipyard, where he joined striking workers, many of whom knew him as a strong leader. They asked Wałęsa to speak to the crowd. Soon he was their lead negotiator.

"He was the perfect choice to go and present demands to management," wrote Denis MacShane in his excellent book on Solidarity published in 1981. "He could look after himself verbally. They would not pull the wool over his eyes.

"He was a worker, not an intellectual. He was a devout Catholic, a good family man. He had been arrested dozens of times. Best of all, he had nothing to lose. If it all went horribly wrong, he could not be sacked or demoted and another prison sentence held no fears. . . . He was in the right place, with the right ideas, at the right time."[3]

Initially, the workers had five demands:

- the right to form an independent union with the right to strike and to elect their own leaders;
- the reinstatement of Anna Walentynowicz and Lech Wałęsa;
- the erection of a monument to the workers killed at the shipyard in 1970;

- a wage increase of about $60 per month, with increases in pensions and family allowances as well; and
- cancellation of the meat price increase.

A few days into the strike, which had spread not only along the Baltic coast but also to other workplaces in Poland, management had conceded on the rehirings and the wage increase.

The government wanted to take up the other demands later. When that idea was rejected, authorities then proposed the negotiations occur in secret.

Instead, the workers not only insisted talks be in the open, they also used the shipyard public address system to broadcast them throughout the workplace, according to Lawrence Weschler, who covered the strife in Poland for *The New Yorker*.[4]

Wałęsa proved an effective bargainer, and some progress occurred in the negotiations.

"With his electrifying personality, quick wit, and gift of the gab, he was soon leading [the talks]," wrote Oxford historian Timothy Garton Ash. "He moved his fellow workers away from mere wage claims and toward a central, daringly political demand: free trade unions."[5]

While negotiations continued, communist authorities had arrested several important advisers to the workers, including Adam Michnik and Jacek Kuroń—intellectuals who had been involved with a group called the Workers' Defense Committee, known by its Polish initials, KOR.

Their release was added to the shipyard strikers' list of demands, as were other items—21 in all.

Families and local residents passed loaves of bread and vats of soup over the top of the shipyard wall, as well as blankets. One of the first acts of the strike committee had been to ban vodka to underscore the sober nature of the struggle.[6]

The gate into the shipyard had flowers tied to it and photos of the pope and crucifixes attached by tape and string.[7]

The strikers clearly had support that was broad and deep.

It rested not only on the 21 demands of the shipyard workers, but also on the strong nationalism in Poland that resented the government imposed by the Soviet Union after World War II, and on the social justice teachings of the Roman Catholic Church, now led by Pope John Paul II, a fellow Pole with strong feelings for his countrymen.

A week after the Gdańsk shipyard stoppage began, UAW President Doug Fraser sent the striking Polish workers a message of solidarity. He proclaimed the UAW's "admiration and moral support" for their struggle and urged Polish government officials to respond to their demands in negotiations.

As the talks went on in August, Mieczysław Jagielski, the wily government negotiator, tried to rush Wałęsa and his colleagues into signing a deal before several of the demands had been resolved, because of "time constraints."

"Time," Wałęsa responded. "Don't worry, we have time."[8]

The unity of the strikers and, indeed, of virtually the entire Polish citizenry could not be ignored, even by a government that repeatedly seemed to misread public opinion.[9]

One sign of how out of touch it was with the lives of Polish workers was that the government had aired the American film *Norma Rae* repeatedly on television shortly before the strike. The movie shows how textile workers formed a union in the face of an anti-union employer operating a mill in the South with harsh and unsafe conditions. The communist government thought it was educating the public on the evils of American capitalism, while Polish viewers seemed to focus on the message that workers needed a union to defend their interests, according to Weschler.[10]

The workers at the Gdańsk shipyard, and those on strike in the coal mines and factories in other parts of Poland, triumphed. On August 31, 1980, the government capitulated on the 21 demands and signed the "Gdańsk Agreement."

Here is what the striking shipyard workers forced the Polish government to agree to:

1. Acceptance of free trade unions independent of the Communist Party and of enterprises, in accordance with the International Labor Organization's Convention No. 87 concerning the right to form free trade unions, which was ratified by the communist government of Poland.

2. A guarantee of the right to strike and of the security of strikers and those aiding them.

The birth of Poland's Solidarity union was sparked when authorities fired Anna Walentynowicz, a union activist, at the Gdańsk shipyard. Walentynowicz here addresses striking workers in Gdańsk in August 1980. Photo by W. Gorka.

3. Compliance with the constitutional guarantee of freedom of speech, the press, and publication, including freedom for independent publishers, and the availability of the mass media to representatives of all faiths.

4. A return of former rights to: (a) people dismissed from work after the 1970 and 1976 strikes, and (b) students expelled from school because of their views; the release of all political prisoners, among them Edward Zadrozynski, Jan Kozlowski, and Marek Kozlowski; a halt in repression of the individual because of personal conviction.

5. Availability to the mass media of information about the formation of the Interfactory Strike Committee and publication of its demands.

6. The undertaking of actions aimed at bringing the country out of its crisis situation by the following means: (a) making public complete information about the socioeconomic situation; and (b) enabling all sectors and social classes to take part in discussion of the reform program.

7. Compensation of all workers taking part in the strike for the period of the strike, with vacation pay from the Central Council of Trade Unions.

8. An increase in the base pay of each worker by 2,000 złotys (the Polish currency) a month as compensation for the recent rise in prices.

9. Guaranteed automatic increases in pay on the basis of increases in prices and the decline in real income.

10. A full supply of food products for the domestic market, with exports limited to surpluses.

11. The abolition of "commercial" prices and of other sales for hard currency in special shops.

12. The selection of management personnel on the basis of qualifications, not party membership. Privileges of the secret police, regular police, and party apparatus were to be eliminated by equalizing family subsidies, abolishing special stores, etc.

13. The introduction of food coupons for meat and meat products (during the period in which control of the market situation was regained).

14. Reduction in the age for retirement for women to 50 and for men to 55, or after 30 years' employment in Poland for women and 35 years for men, regardless of age.

15. Conformity of old-age pensions and annuities with what has actually been paid in.

16. Improvements in the working conditions of the health service to insure full medical care for workers.

17. Assurances of a reasonable number of places in day-care centers and kindergartens for the children of working mothers.

18. Paid maternity leave for three years.

19. A decrease in the waiting period for apartments.

Lech Wałęsa speaks to striking shipyard workers in Gdańsk in August 1980. Workers won the right to form an independent trade union and the right to strike. Solidarity made many gains in the 16 months it was legal before the communist government declared martial law and jailed union activists. Photo by Erazm Ciolek.

20. An increase in the commuter's allowance to 100 złotys from 40, with a supplemental benefit on separation.

21. A day of rest on Saturday. Workers in the brigade system or round-the-clock jobs are to be compensated for the loss of free Saturdays with increased leave or other paid time off.[11]

Striking workers, led by Lech Wałęsa, won their 21 demands in the Gdańsk Agreement reached on August 31, 1980.

The workers' victory at Gdańsk in August 1980 resonated throughout the world. An independent trade union movement with the right to strike in Poland, an Eastern bloc country under the control of the Soviet Union, offered hope that even greater freedoms might be achieved.

It was viewed globally as a huge victory for workers at a time when labor had been challenged by multinational corporations and conservative governments in many countries.

Many political leaders and pundits had seen little possibility of success for the Polish workers and their union demands. But the UAW had been prescient in quietly forming ties with elements of civil society in Poland some years *before* the Gdańsk breakthrough.

On September 23, 1976, a group of Polish citizens including academics, artists, and lawyers formed a "Workers' Defense Committee." Its goal was to provide legal, medical, and financial assistance to workers who had suffered during and after the strikes and riots over food price increases in June of that year.

Immediately, the committee activists suffered harassment and intimidation from the police. The group still managed to provide help to about 300 families of those jailed or harmed during the food protests.

Leonard Woodcock, who was UAW president from shortly after Walter Reuther's death until mid-1977, read about the Workers' Defense Committee, or KOR. He had received a letter from a group of prominent citizens in the United States, United Kingdom, France, Italy, West Germany, Switzerland, and Poland asking for support.

Woodcock took the issue to his fellow UAW officers and the International Executive Board, which voted to support KOR and the Polish workers' struggle.

The UAW announced a $10,000 contribution in a press release on March 6, 1977.

"This contribution is in line with the UAW's long record of fostering international labor solidarity," Woodcock said in the statement.

"Wherever and whenever workers' freedom is under attack—whether it be in Chile, Argentina, South Africa, or Eastern Europe—the UAW speaks out and offers support. Workers and unions cannot be truly free anywhere unless they are free everywhere."

The UAW support for KOR received some media attention, and the union had a number of groups, particularly from Polish-American organizations in the United States, wanting more information.

Woodcock decided to put the UAW's muscle behind fundraising for KOR. He sent letters that spring to presidents of a number of other major U.S. unions. Most were affiliated with the AFL-CIO, from which the UAW had withdrawn in 1968, in part over foreign policy disagreements.

But a number of the more progressive AFL-CIO affiliates responded to Woodcock's call to support Polish workers financially. Most gave only $250, but their consideration and involvement raised the profile of the Polish struggle within the American labor movement. As time passed, the AFL-CIO became an extremely vigorous supporter of Solidarity in Poland.

KOR's initial support for workers imprisoned or otherwise targeted for their roles in the 1976 food price protests broadened the ties between intellectuals and workers in Poland. "Intellectuals" in Polish society was a much broader term than that normally used in the United States and included not only academics but also musicians, actors, lawyers, scientists, and others who felt marginalized by Poland's hard-line authorities.[12]

"The link-up with intellectuals after 1976 was the key that unlocked the frustration of the Polish working class," wrote Denis MacShane, then an official of the International Metalworkers' Federation, in 1981. "The help of intellectuals since August 1980 has contributed immeasurably to the success of Solidarity."[13]

KOR wrote to the UAW just before Woodcock retired as UAW president to thank the union and inform it that the Polish government had declared an amnesty for jailed strikers.

One of the important activities of the UAW-funded KOR was to publish a newspaper called *Robotnik* (The Worker). Although its press run was only 20,000 or so in the early days of Solidarity, the paper provided a forum for workers to debate ideas and strategies. It was passed hand-to-hand in plants and workplaces and soon had a strong following.

Robotnik also helped workers outside of Warsaw feel a part of the struggle and debate. It reduced their geographical isolation and gave them a way to participate in the discussion.

"By early 1980, the groups that helped distribute *Robotnik* in different towns formed a more coherent body that was seeking to raise specific workers' issues, using language that made sense on the shop floor," MacShane wrote.[14]

The close ties between KOR and the plant activists came to fruition when Gdańsk shipyard workers achieved their demands in August 1980 and began building Solidarity as an independent and legal trade union in Poland.

Workers throughout Poland soon learned what Wałęsa and the shipyard workers had won in Gdańsk. The 21 demands agreed to by the authorities had been published in the government-controlled press.

From the coal miners in Silesia to the autoworkers in Bielsko-Biała, Polish workers demanded the same. Strikes spread in many areas of the country as a result, even though the Gdańsk Agreement had not been applicable to all Polish workers.

The widespread negotiations and conflicts that followed meant large numbers of workplace activists got their own taste of the struggle. Nearly every town had its own group of Wałęsas fighting factory managers, forming ties to intellectuals and allies, organizing the workers, and so on.[15]

Edward Gierek, the Polish communist leader, resigned in September 1980. He claimed health problems, but clearly the hardcore party elements and the military disliked the concessions made to Solidarity.

The first task for the newly independent union was to draw up its formal statutes and file them with the courts in order to finalize its legal status. When it did so, the Warsaw court, obviously under government control, amended them to include a clause in which Solidarity specifically recognized the leading role of the Communist Party.

Union leaders privately understood they had not supplanted the party as the ultimate power in Poland, but they did not

CAL 259 REGION 9A·UAW

WE SUPPORT

SOLIDARITY

POLAND

want a statement to that effect in their governing document. They reacted angrily, perhaps also because there were many signs the authorities were slow-walking implementation of parts of the Gdańsk agreement, according to MacShane.

So Solidarity geared up for a general strike across Poland on November 12, 1980. To show they meant business, they conducted a warning strike in which tram drivers parked their trams in the center cities and halted transportation.[16]

The union prepared leaflets telling workers to occupy the plants, bring food and bedding, and prepare for a siege.

On the government side, the new Polish leader, Stanisław Kania, was called to Moscow. Other countries in the Warsaw Pact, including East Germany and Czechoslovakia, closed their borders to Poland. Journalists were denied entry, and Polish TV repeatedly aired clips of Soviet troops performing maneuvers.[17]

The message seemed to be: either Solidarity backed down, or there would be a Soviet invasion to reassert its control of Poland forcibly and harshly.

But Solidarity did not quit. And it was the communist government that blinked.

On November 10, two days before the general strike, the Polish Supreme Court reversed the lower court in Warsaw and struck out the offending paragraph about the leading role of the Communist Party in Solidarity's governing statute.

Once again, the union had won.

The victory really had less to do with the statute and more to do with the fact that the government had sought to reassert its authority and had failed.

While this high-stakes poker game was going on, Solidarity also was going about the business of establishing local offices around the country and doing the hard work of building locals that could function day to day.

In the aftermath of the Gdańsk strike, the UAW had established direct contact with Solidarity. The union's support for KOR had marked the UAW as a friend and ally that could be trusted.

We set out to provide Solidarity with materials that would help them build their union. Here's how that support was described in the UAW President's Report to the convention delegates three years later:

"Almost from its inception and the historic Gdańsk Agreement in August 1980, we established direct contact and developed steady exchanges of information and ideas.

"Polish workers were reading *UAW Solidarity* magazine, and their leaders the UAW *Washington Report*. We sent every available publication we've published, giving them our history of struggle of over 45 years and sharing with them some of our own growing pains they [also] were experiencing with the enormous tasks their union was undertaking."[18]

UAW President Doug Fraser had sent financial support to Solidarity in mid-September 1980 through the International Metalworkers' Federation, which was led by Herman Rebhan, a UAW member from Region 4.

That fall, Lech Wałęsa sent a broad appeal stating that Solidarity needed more than money.

"We need contacts with you, educational material, and technical equipment for the publication of our trade union journals," Wałęsa wrote. "It is particularly important that your assistance should come as quickly as possible."

His letter, sent to the International Confederation of Free Trade Unions in Belgium, ended:

"We need your solidarity and support. We are fighting for the common cause: the right to organize, the right to decide our destiny, the right to participate in the management of the economy, and the right to influence and control the results of our work."[19]

Fraser wanted to provide Solidarity some of the equipment requested. Leo Suslow, then the director of the union's International Affairs Department, researched the issue. After discussions with Rebhan at the International Metalworkers' Federation in Geneva and with Region 9 Director Ed Gray, the union decided to go forward.

Ultimately, the union dealt directly with IBM to arrange for delivery of electronic typewriters to Solidarity and with Xerox to facilitate the Polish union's receiving new copying machines. Both were sorely needed to outfit Solidarity's offices throughout Poland.[20]

While the UAW was aiding Solidarity in getting the equipment it needed to run its offices, a new conflict broke out. Workers at the Ursus tractor factory and those at the Huta Warszawa steel plant went on strike seeking to win the release of the union's chief printer in Warsaw, Jan Narożniak.

Solidarity's Warsaw leaders printed leaflets that said: "Today, Narożniak. Tomorrow, Wałęsa. The Day After, You."

But the Warsaw unionists not only demanded Narożniak's release. They also said the strikes would not end until there was an investigation of the militia, the secret police, and the Ministry of the Interior. In addition, they wanted reductions in the budgets of the militia and the security police.[21]

The government caved immediately on the demand to release Narożniak. But the strikes continued over the demands on Poland's security apparatus.

Wałęsa and Jacek Kuroń, a KOR member and close adviser to Solidarity, immediately went to Warsaw. They saw huge potential danger in strikes focused on investigating the state security forces and also were upset that the Warsaw locals had called strikes without approval from Solidarity in Gdańsk.

Wałęsa and Kuroń prevailed, and the workers at the tractor factory and steel mill near Warsaw returned to work. Some saw the outcome as a sign the union was maturing, while others grumbled about interference from Gdańsk and felt the union should have pressed on.[22]

A typical empty butcher shop in Poland today; why we must help

Help Poland now

Two million Polish children will suffer permanent damage to their health this winter—unless they get necessary food and medicine.

Many millions of older Poles face serious food shortages.

Workers—almost all of them members of the 10 million strong Solidarity workers movement—face terrible food shortages.

The UAW has set up a Polish Solidarity Fund to help meet some of these needs.

Poland is a special situation. Some 10 million Polish workers are in a struggle for worker rights which is a struggle for all workers no matter what their nationality or political belief.

As UAW Secretary Treasurer Ray Majerus said in a letter to all UAW locals: "The Polish trade unionists have been an inspiration to us. Now the time has come for us to do what we can to help them."

All money collected by the UAW will be used in the most effective way possible to meet immediate needs of the Polish people, mainly working through international religious groups on the spot in Poland, and through our own special contacts with the Solidarity movement.

The food is American food, stored in U.S. warehouses. It can be purchased at special below-market prices for needy people overseas,

and the distribution in Poland is made directly with families who need our help.

While we emphasize the winter needs facing the Polish people, the needs may stretch out longer than the return of warm weather. The Polish economy is in great disorder today, and workers in the cities—along with their families, and especially their children—are the most vulnerable. That is why we in the UAW feel a special responsibility.

The money we collect in the UAW goes directly to help people. There are no administrative costs. We are helping to add our money to a network of help inside Poland which is underway now.

Send your contributions to UAW Polish Solidarity Fund, Attention: UAW Secretary Treasurer Ray Majerus, Solidarity House, 8000 E. Jefferson Ave., Detroit, Michigan 48214. For further help and information contact either John Christensen or Frank Wallick in the UAW Washington Office, 1757 N St., NW, Washington, D.C. 20036

The UAW distributed this flyer at meetings and plant gates to raise money for the union's Polish Solidarity Fund. The funds went to buy food and medicine for working families hard hit by extreme food shortages and the loss of income resulting from the jailing of union members.

In November 1980, Solidarity ordered a halt to strikes over pay. Top union leaders worried about inflation, given the huge wage increases won throughout the country. They feared inflation would rob workers of gains in real purchasing power.[23]

And they recognized that "strike fatigue" had begun to set in. Here's how one worker at the Ursus tractor factory put it to Denis MacShane at the time:

"We have been on strike five times in five months: in July over food prices, in August over Gdańsk, in October over pay, and twice in November over the registration of Solidarity and the arrest of Narożniak. . . . Now we are tired of strikes. I think if I were asked to strike again, I wouldn't, unless it were of exceptional importance."[24]

The government continued to probe Solidarity, looking for areas of weakness.

The old official government unions technically still existed, and they took on the word "Independent" in their various names, which created confusion for a few in Poland and many outside the country.

In January 1981, the government proclaimed the agreement reached in Gdańsk four months earlier to make Saturday a day off would not be implemented. It hoped that Solidarity would give in, or else look responsible for the weak Polish economy by pushing for time off that reduced production.

The union challenged the government by asking workers not to work on a Saturday in January. The issue was resolved with authorities agreeing that three out of four Saturdays would be days off.[25]

Solidarity recognized the government repeatedly was reneging on the Gdańsk Agreement and forcing the union to strike to win what had already been agreed upon.

"Gradually, Solidarity was realizing that its most effective weapon—an all-out national strike—was rather like a nuclear bomb," MacShane wrote. "It could be used, but how many times?"[26]

Yet another conflict took place in March 1981, when Polish farmers demanded their own Rural Solidarity that would have bargaining rights just like Solidarity. The government said they were self-employed and could not have trade union status.

The farmers then occupied the headquarters of the peasant association set up by the Communist Party in Bydgoszcz. The regional Solidarity backed the farmers, and several union leaders were taken out by the militia and badly beaten. Posters and flyers of their bloody faces soon appeared throughout Poland.[27]

In the face of such violence, Solidarity called a general strike for March 31. A four-hour warm-up strike days earlier had seen the entire country briefly shut down.

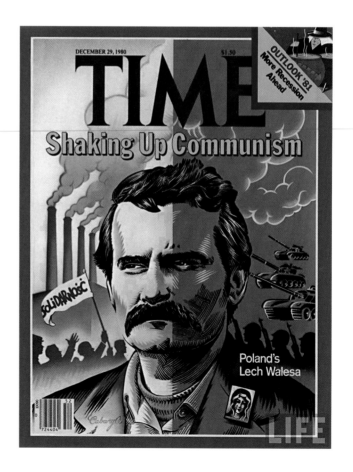

A new prime minister, General Wojciech Jaruzelski, knew he would have to confront the challenge of workers who were united across Poland. The first sign that he would yield came March 26, when the chair of the regional government council in Bydgoszcz resigned. Two days later, the government issued a report blaming party officials and the militia for the attacks.

Jaruzelski caved in the face of union pressure, because he knew the only way the party could defeat a general strike by Solidarity was to call in the military, perhaps even forces from the Soviet Union.[28]

Solidarity also continued to have powerful support from Pope John Paul II and the Catholic Church, as it did throughout the workers' struggle there.

As Solidarity moved through 1981, the union continued to gain strength, and everyone knew it.

In the summer of 1981, Solidarity responded to an invitation from UAW President Fraser to send a delegation to visit the UAW and exchange views.

The group included Julian Dziura, an autoworker from Lublin; Andrzej Kralczyński, an autoworker from Bielsko-Biała; Marek Dolat, an agricultural implement worker from Kutno; and Andrzej Czupryn, chair of the Research Center in Plock.

They came to the United States in August 1981 and visited Detroit, Chicago, Milwaukee, and the UAW's Black Lake education center in Onaway, Michigan. They met with UAW local union leaders, toured plants, and attended study sessions on the principles, strategies, and history of the UAW. They also visited the Canadian Auto Workers (CAW), which was a region of the UAW at the time.

The Solidarity leaders spent time with Fraser, Secretary-Treasurer Ray Majerus, and other top officers and regional directors. The Polish unionists made it clear to them that early support for KOR and then for the Gdańsk strike caused Soli-

darity to seek close ties to the UAW.

A similar message had been conveyed earlier by Mieczysław Gil, leader of Solidarity in Krakow and an important member of the union's national coordinating commission. He attended the International Metalworkers' Federation congress held in Washington, D.C., in May 1981. UAW President Fraser gave the keynote speech at that gathering of trade unionists and later spent time with Gil.

Lech Wałęsa invited Fraser and Majerus to attend Solidarity's First National Congress in September 1981. Fraser could not attend because of the deteriorating health of the U.S. auto industry, which ultimately led to the reopening of union contracts with the automakers. But Majerus did take a UAW delegation to Poland.

After attending the Solidarity congress, the UAW group visited Gdańsk, Warsaw, and Kutno.

A year earlier, one could see posters in major cities that said: "21 x TAK" (21 times YES). The slogan highlighted the Gdańsk victory when authorities were forced to say yes on the 21 demands of the shipyard workers.[29]

When the UAW delegation visited a year later, new posters had appeared, which translated said: "Still, After a Full Year, Only 2 x YES and 19 x NO." Solidarity believed the communist government had honored only two of the 21 commitments made in the Gdańsk Agreement: the right to form independent unions and the right to strike.

Solidarity's first congress came after a relentless attack on the union by party leaders in speeches and articles that summer.

As Weschler described the onslaught in *The New Yorker*, "The state media also took delight in pointing to the Reagan administration's handling of the air-traffic controllers' strike in America. In essence, the editorial line boiled down to: 'See, strikes by government employees are not allowed even in the United States! How dare all of you state-employed workers threaten to strike here!'"[30]

At the time of the congress, Solidarity had 10 million members. There had been a rigorous process of union democracy to choose delegates through grassroots balloting, local caucuses, and regional conventions. The congress met for six days, adjourned for two weeks so delegates could return home to receive instructions from the rank-and-file, and then resumed for 12 days. The UAW delegation witnessed some of that second session.

The union democracy on display was important, both on the merits and as a contrast to the top-down authoritarian nature of the ruling Communist Party in Poland. But 18 days of speeches took a toll on some, such as the delegate who told Weschler, "Boy, this democracy may be worth dying for, but it can kill you with boredom once you've got it."[31]

After debates over a wide range of issues, some delegates clearly were frustrated with Wałęsa. Toward the end of the congress when elections occurred, Wałęsa won Solidarity's top job with only 55 percent of the vote.

After the congress, the government seemed to take a harder line. General Jaruzelski began to test Solidarity with arrests of top leaders as well as new food-price increases. The union responded with wildcat strikes that, by the end of October, involved more than 300,000 workers.[32]

The most profound impression Majerus came away with from the UAW observer mission in the fall of 1981 was the food shortages experienced by the Polish people.

In the shops of Warsaw and Gdańsk, shelves were empty. When there was food to be had, long lines developed. Some farmers had stopped selling their produce altogether and begun to barter instead.

The government had implemented a system of ration cards with Solidarity support, but it did not work.

One of the jokes then making the rounds described how to make a Polish sandwich: take a ham ration card and place it between two bread ration cards.[33]

"I saw long lines of people waiting 10 hours or more with the hope of getting a few ounces of butter or meat to feed their families," Majerus said. "And I talked with union leaders who told me how bad they expect the food crisis to become as the cold weather begins."[34]

"The Polish unionists have been an inspiration to us," he said. "Now the time has come for us to do what we can to help them. That's what solidarity is all about."

The UAW launched a "Polish Solidarity Fund" in late 1981 aimed at raising money for food and medicine for workers and their families in Poland struggling in the midst of the terrible shortages.

The union began collections at plant gates, in local union halls, at education seminars, CAP meetings, and other gatherings. The UAW effort provided a vehicle through which members could help Solidarity and also feel a part of the struggle of Polish workers.

Detroit, Milwaukee, Cleveland, and other cities with

UAW locals also had substantial populations of Polish-Americans, many of them first-generation immigrants who had relatives still in Poland.

Polish-Americans had played important roles in the early days of the UAW. One example: the Detroit Polish Falcons Hall had been the headquarters for the Kelsey-Hayes sit-down strike in 1937.

UAW President Fraser, an immigrant from Scotland, worked as a young man at Chrysler's Dodge main assembly plant in Hamtramck, Michigan, which had large numbers of workers of Polish descent in the workforce going back to 1914.

The ties between Poland and the UAW were diverse and strong. They made the fundraising for food and medicine a top priority, even as the industrial states had suffered their own economic downturn in this same period.

The UAW worked through religious organizations, primarily Catholic relief groups. They could get the shipping containers with food and medicine from the union into Poland with virtually no interference from government authorities there. Because Solidarity effectively controlled the port at

The Polish regime declared martial law on December 13, 1981, and arrested many union activists. In some cities, T-55A tanks were deployed in a show of military force. Photo by Zolnierkiewicz.

Gdańsk and because the Roman Catholic Church played such a huge role in Poland, we believed the initial shipments from the UAW food drive would reach their destination.

Success was confirmed when the UAW started to receive letters from Poland. Fraser got one from Czesław Domin, a bishop and president of the Charity Commission of the Polish Episcopate in Katowice, Poland. He thanked the UAW for a shipment of eight containers of butter and 14 containers of cheese received through Catholic Relief Services.

Bishop Domin reported the food had been distributed through the dioceses, which then divided it among the parishes for delivery to the most needy families.[35]

On December 13, 1981, down came the hammer. General Jaruzelski declared martial law and suspended Solidarity. He put the country under a "state of war."

Thousands of union activists were jailed. Poland sealed its borders to other countries. Telephone lines were cut and airports closed. Roads into the main cities were blockaded, and military vehicles patrolled streets in a show of force.

Coal miners resisted, as did other workers. Jaruzelski's response was to send in the hated ZOMO paramilitary forces to the Wujek coal mine, where they killed nine miners. About 90 people were killed across the country in the first days of martial law.

The regime deployed 80,000 troops, 30,000 police, 1,750 tanks, and 1,900 armored vehicles to crush the Solidarity movement.[36] Jaruzelski later claimed he took such harsh action to forestall an invasion by the Soviet Union, which had been unhappy at the independent power gained by Solidarity during its 16 months of existence.

But documents obtained recently by the National Security Archive reveal the Polish leader had sought help from Soviet troops and other military aid. Jaruzelski called Marshal Kulikov, a top Soviet official, on December 11, 1981, two days

before the declaration of martial law, to ask for Soviet troops.

The response was conveyed through the Soviet ambassador to Poland: "Nyet."

Most people today think of President Reagan as one of the Solidarity union's strongest supporters. The Reagan administration, which had spoken out on behalf of Solidarity as part of its Cold War opposition to the Soviet Union and its satellite states, appeared surprised by the declaration of martial law.

At the time, the administration let it be known that it had been unprepared for the move.[37]

Years later, it was learned the Reagan administration in fact had been receiving secret information from a top military officer on the Polish General Staff, Colonel Ryszard Kukliński. He was involved in the preparations for martial law and passed on the crucial information to American operatives.[38]

The failure of the Reagan administration to warn Lech Wałęsa and the Solidarity leadership continues to raise questions about the president's motives and the degree to which he truly was committed to that movement. A warning would have allowed many of the union leaders to disappear underground, rather than being jailed immediately by the Polish regime.

Contrary to the Reagan administration's frequent public worrying about a Soviet invasion in response to Solidarity's militancy, the intelligence gathered by the CIA and other sources provided little support for such a possibility.

"The declassified intelligence materials also show that whatever the assertions and/or convictions about the 'inevitability' of a Soviet military intervention, no preparations were underway for even a minimal Soviet support force at the time martial law was imposed," wrote Douglas J. MacEachin in a monograph for the CIA.[39]

If the Reagan administration sent Solidarity no warning, someone else may have. The union in Wroclaw somehow managed to withdraw all of its local unions' money from local banks several weeks before martial law. It amounted to more than 80 million złotys available to help as Solidarity went underground.[40]

I was spending nearly every day that December with UAW President Fraser as union leaders worked through plans for the auto bargaining that would occur in 1982. Several days after Poland declared martial law, Fraser remained angry over the move. He also told me he was surprised it had not happened earlier, given the growing power Solidarity amassed and the union's willingness to challenge party rule there.

Fraser immediately had publicly condemned martial law and the imprisonment of thousands of Solidarity activists. He pledged the UAW's help to the union as well.

Herman Rebhan, general secretary of the International Metalworkers' Federation, joined the UAW in blasting Jaruzelski's crackdown:

"The military takeover in Poland solves nothing," he said. "The arrest of trade unionists . . . and the suspension of basic trade union rights will shock working people and all those who believe in freedom throughout the world."

The Polish regime would soon find "that bayonets cannot dig up coal and tanks cannot produce food."[41]

We got more bad news when we learned that Mieczysław Gil, the metalworker who led Solidarity's Krakow region, had been arrested. He initially had avoided capture and helped organize Solidarity's move to clandestine operations. But eventually Gil had been caught.

The Polish regime sentenced him to three and a half years in prison for leading a strike of 37,000 steelworkers at the Lenin Steelworks in Krakow. After Gil's sentencing, workers at the plant defied the security forces there and conducted a one-hour protest strike.

The UAW, the United Steelworkers of America, the IMF, and others waged a vigorous campaign urging freedom for Gil. In response, he was released for medical reasons involving a painful spinal condition. But authorities soon jailed him again.

Solidarity set out to establish support networks for the families of thousands of union activists who had been jailed and communications networks so those not imprisoned could wage their underground activities.

Some older Solidarity members had lived through the Nazi occupation of Poland in World War II. Others had learned of the underground that covertly resisted Hitler's occupying forces.

Since the Gdańsk strike, the publication of many newspapers, journals, and books had allowed Solidarity to hold vigorous debates over strategy. Because the state-controlled media often distorted or failed altogether to report on major issues, the publications supporting Solidarity found huge readerships. The papers contained not only daily news, but also analysis, history, sports, and practical items.

Because of the experience in World War II, Solidarity leaders had hidden away printing equipment to be available in the event of a Soviet invasion or a crackdown by the regime.

"It's very well-organized," one activist told *The New Yorker*'s Lawrence Weschler in 1983. "This is one field in which Solidarity was prepared for the coup. For 16 months, for example, printing equipment was being hidden away, and although [printing] plants are regularly seized, we still have plenty of machines in storage and more being smuggled in."[42]

The UAW indeed had undertaken to help smuggle printing equipment into Poland, starting in 1982.

We had learned important lessons in the previous 16 months when Solidarity had asked for equipment for their local union and regional offices. Some supporters during that period had shipped typewriters and copiers to Poland, only to find they were incompatible with Polish electrical current or that ink, paper, and parts for the machines could not be procured.

The UAW knew that Solidarity under martial law needed printing equipment the underground could operate and repair.

We worked with the union's exiled activists in Brussels, Belgium, where Solidarity had set up an office to deal with the outside world.

We also were in regular contact with the International Metalworkers' Federation in Geneva and the Swedish metalworkers' union, Svenska Metall, in Stockholm. The basic strategy was to source the printing equipment from Europe, particularly West Germany.

It then was shipped to Sweden, where union truck drivers hid the equipment and parts amidst their legitimate cargo. The trucks then went to Malmö, in the far south of Sweden, and then to Polish ports, including Gdańsk and Gdynia. Stevedores and longshoremen loyal to Solidarity would remove the presses, stenciling machines, copiers, etc. and move them covertly into the hands of activists nearby who coordinated dispersal throughout the Solidarity underground.

The AFL-CIO ran its own very effective effort to get material to Solidarity. The UAW had rejoined the AFL-CIO during 1981, but we continued to operate totally independently of the federation on international affairs issues.

Some of the AFL-CIO's assistance went to Solidarity exiles in London, who arranged for tour bus drivers to carry in equipment during trips to Poland with elderly Poles returning to their homeland for visits.

"We figure the life expectancy of a clandestine [printing] plant to be four months," an activist told Weschler. "In a well-run police state, once a plant starts up it shouldn't take more than two months to expose it, but the authorities here are still a bit slow. During the Nazi times, I'm told, the life expectancy was six months, so (we're) better than that.

"If we're lucky, when a plant falls our people have time to escape and all that's lost is the machinery. Then within a few days the same people can start up again somewhere else. But we're not always lucky, and the minimum sentence is three years."[43]

The printing equipment the UAW helped get into Poland, and from other allies, enabled Solidarity to keep distributing news and reaction to events. It gave workers throughout Poland a sense the movement, while underground, was still alive and fighting.

Some years later, when Lech Wałęsa visited the United States, he thanked UAW President Owen Bieber profusely for the financial aid and equipment provided to Solidarity during its darkest moments.

During the months that followed the imposition of martial law, thousands remained imprisoned. Jaruzelski "suspended" martial law in late 1982, but that did not result in meaningful changes to the repression.

The government-controlled unions that attempted to replace Solidarity received little real support from workers, but Jaruzelski shrewdly had certain resources distributed through them, such as hard-to-get children's shoes. So Solidarity chose not to boycott the replacement unions, but rather it generally ignored them.[44]

The UAW not only provided financial aid to the Solidarity union in Poland, but also arranged for printing presses and duplicating equipment to be smuggled into the country when communist authorities imposed martial law. Solidarity published newsletters and newspapers during its underground period that kept members informed and involved. Collage courtesy of the Walter P. Reuther Library, Wayne State University.

Solidarity went underground during martial law, but strikes and protests occurred as the economy worsened.

The regime tried to drive wedges between important Solidarity leaders. It eventually released Lech Wałęsa, but continued to jail the three activists who had run against him at the Solidarity congress in 1981.

The government continued to blame Solidarity for the weak Polish economy, price increases of food, and other woes felt by the public.

It also accused the union of violence, but the top leadership of Solidarity, both in prison and underground, had made a clear decision against violence. Terrorist tactics, they believed, would only bring more repression and, conceivably, a Soviet response.

Authorities who had initially suspended Solidarity chose to delegalize the union in October 1982. Soon after, the regime began requiring workers who had supported Solidarity to sign loyalty oaths renouncing that allegiance, according to Weschler.

They also were subjected to "reaccreditation hearings" at which their loyalty to the new order was assessed. Any hint of residual fondness for Solidarity meant the loss of a worker's job as well as housing and other necessities in that harsh economy, Weschler reported.[45]

Another tactic was the forced conscription into the military of workers with loyalties to Solidarity. They soon found themselves in remote military encampments doing hard labor in what amounted to a form of imprisonment.

Conditions for union members in prison varied, but many came down with serious illnesses, such as tuberculosis. Others suffered beatings and torture.

The *Uncensored Polish News Bulletin*, a publication based in London, described the case of Jerzy Mnich, a coal miner who had organized a strike at the Manifest Lipcoy coal mine shortly after martial law had been imposed. He suffered a heart attack during the strike and almost died.

It took police a while to track him down. But they found him on an IV in a hospital on January 13, 1982, and, after detaching him, dragged him off to a police station, where he was badly beaten.

"He was forced to kneel on a stool with his hands pinned by handcuffs high above his head to a grating," the *News Bulletin* stated. "He was then beaten on the soles of his feet and heels. He was then treated with a dose of tear gas—straight into the eyes."

The result was a severe burning of his retina and partial blindness. Mnich also was fired from his job at the mine.[46]

Others, including several of the Solidarity activists who had visited the UAW in 1981, suffered in General Jaruzelski's prisons as well.

Fraser received a letter in September 1982 from Julian Dziura, who had visited Detroit with the Solidarity delegation. Dziura thanked Fraser and the UAW for the support for Solidarity.

"I apologize to you, Mr. President, and through you to all the members of the UAW for my silence," he wrote. "It was not my fault . . . but on December 13, 1981, at 1:40 a.m., I was jailed and was isolated from society until September 7, 1982. I am now working in my plant as a constructor. I end these few words. More can be written when this strange 'war' ends in my country."[47]

The guy sitting across from me in Billy Bob's in the Fort Worth, Texas, stockyards wore a large cowboy hat. With a capacity of 6,000, Billy Bob's claimed to be the "World's Largest Honky Tonk."

Perhaps not the best environment for a passionate discussion of events in Poland, but Solidarity exile Mirek Chojecki had joined me there on a break from the UAW's convention held in Dallas in 1983.

Chojecki the next day accepted the UAW's highest honor, the union's Social Justice Award, on behalf of Lech Wałęsa. Recipients of that award have included Eleanor Roosevelt, John

F. Kennedy, Carl Sandburg, Norman Thomas, Martin Luther King Jr., and Cesar Chavez.

"Today we assert the unbreakable bonds of brotherhood that unite Polish, American, and Canadian trade unionists," UAW President Fraser said as he handed the plaque to Chojecki. The inscription on the award saluted Wałęsa and the 10 million Solidarity members for their courage.

"Your struggle for free trade unions cannot be crushed no matter how oppressive the tactics of the Polish rulers," it read. "Besieged by the brutal force of martial law and the official banning of Solidarity, you have shown that the movement for workplace democracy and social progress lives on."

Although unable to travel to accept the award due to the harsh restrictions of martial law, Wałęsa sent the UAW a message delivered by Chojecki.

"I consider this honor a symbol of recognition for Solidarity, as well as a gesture of support for our union's struggle for

UAW President Doug Fraser (right) gave the union's Social Justice Award to Lech Wałęsa at the union's convention in 1983. Mirek Chojecki, an exiled leader of Poland's Solidarity union, held up a "Free Poland" bumpersticker as he accepted the award on behalf of Wałęsa.

the respect of human rights and democratic freedoms, the right to work, and the dignity of man," Wałęsa's message stated.

Chojecki was able to attend the UAW convention only because he had been in France when the imposition of martial law occurred in December 1981. He remained in exile and was one of those the UAW secretly worked with on smuggling equipment into Poland after General Jaruzelski's crackdown.

By 1986, the Polish regime declared an amnesty for Solidarity activists and allowed the union to re-emerge without full legal status. Wałęsa and other activists established a provisional executive committee and escalated the union's activism.

A wave of strikes began in May 1988, as Solidarity raised the pressure on the government.

Owen Bieber, who succeeded Fraser as UAW president, sent telexes to Polish strikers at the Gdańsk shipyard and the Krakow steel mill pledging UAW support yet again.

"The struggle of Polish workers focuses on the need for families to earn enough to live above the poverty line," Bieber stated. "But it is also a struggle for union freedoms, for an end to employer negligence and exploitation, and for inalienable, democratic rights denied by the Jaruzelski regime.

"The UAW stood with you in your struggles in 1980 and saluted the achievements of Solidarność. And we shared your pain, as much as was possible from afar, when the government repressed Solidarność so brutally in December 1981, and thereafter. . . . You will win, in the end, because your struggle is just and because your courage cannot be suppressed by any government."[48]

Faced with the new wave of strikes and activism, the regime seemed to realize that it had tried arrest, torture, delegalization, conscription, propaganda, and many other tactics aimed at destroying the opposition, and all had failed. There had been a stalemate of sorts reached by 1988 that could not continue.

Lech Wałęsa and the Solidarity union won a big political victory in the 1989 elections.

At the Communist Party congress that year, the government was authorized to begin roundtable negotiations, which started in February 1989.

Wałęsa was the leader of the "nongovernmental" organizations at the talks, which ended in the full legalization of Solidarity and a commitment to hold elections for the Polish parliament.

"The courage of Polish workers has brought about a remarkable victory," UAW President Bieber said after the agreement was reached. "Solidarność has won the restoration of its legal status and the Polish people have won commitments for the first free and open elections since World War II."[49]

The UAW president also noted that the roundtable accords provided commitments to reform the legal system, agriculture, healthcare, housing, and the structure of local government.

"Solidarność will have a half hour of air time weekly on TV and one hour weekly on radio, as well as its own legal daily national newspaper and regional weekly papers," Bieber said. "As a realist, I know that the key test is whether the commitments made by Poland's communist leadership are actually honored.

"Solidarność itself faces extremely difficult challenges in the weeks and months ahead, but I am confident they will continue their march toward freedom."[50]

Wałęsa set up a political group that was related to the union, but separate. Called the Solidarity Citizens' Committee, the new organization won all of the seats subject to open election in the parliament and all but one in the newly established senate.

On my way to Bielsko-Biała from Warsaw, I gazed out the train window in a pale, oyster light at small plots of farmland now idle after the fall harvest in 1989.

Alder trees had turned golden and contrasted with the green of the conifers that lined the occasional river next to paths where horses pulled farmers' carts.

Sometimes the train rumbled through a town where I could see aging factory yards full of rusted metal, broken windows, and small groups of workers out back smoking and talking in the grayness of a Poland run to ground by martial law.

I was heading to the FSM auto plant to meet Andrzej Kralczyński, the Solidarity activist who had visited Detroit in 1981, shortly after the new union had emerged from the Gdańsk shipyard strike.

Kralczyński had just been elected on the Solidarity slate to the new Polish senate. He had been a victim of Jaruzelski's laws and soon was to have the chance to draft new ones as a senator.

Eight years earlier, six men armed with pistols pounded on his door at 5:30 a.m. The secret police searched and found "illegal materials," which were merely papers from Kralczyński's job as leader of Solidarity at the huge auto plant in southern Poland.

Three days later, he ended up in prison.

"The worst period was while I was in solitary confinement," he told me. "I had no information about my family and no visitors for eight months. I didn't know what was going on outside the jail."

The autoworker's move from a Polish prison to the nation's senate was a journey few could have predicted in the eight years from arrest to elections.

But a few days in Poland that year showed me how daunting the task ahead promised to be.

Shortly after checking in to my $7-per-night hotel in Bielsko-Biała, I went to its small restaurant. An interpreter with me translated the menu, and I decided to have what sounded like a pork chop.

The waiter said that item was not available, but he would be pleased if I chose something else. I picked what seemed to be a beef patty.

Sorry, that's not possible either, the waiter replied.

Out of the eight entrees on the menu, only one was available due to the food shortages that still plagued Poland.

As I met with autoworkers at FSM and at FSO in Warsaw, they described huge challenges that went beyond the shortages of milk, bread, meat, and other food items that threatened to undermine the euphoria that followed Solidarity's political victories in mid-1989.

Among them:

- rampant inflation eroding workers' living standards to the lowest levels of the decade;
- housing shortages so severe that the average young worker faced a wait of 30 years or more for an apartment;

A huge crowd rallied in Hamtramck, Michigan, in April 1989 to support the Solidarity movement as hopes grew that there could be a shift to democracy and free elections in Poland.

- auto plants, farm machinery factories, and other facilities producing cars, tractors, and manufactured goods that frequently were only partially completed due to parts shortages and outdated, inefficient technologies; and
- an infrastructure of roads, bridges, sewers, and buildings that were falling apart.

Solidarity had inherited the task of trying to jumpstart an economic system scarred by many years of state-run inefficiencies.[51]

"Here in Poland, we survived war and we survived prison camps," Zbigniew Bujak told me. He was Solidarity's leader in the Warsaw region and a former electrician at the Ursus tractor factory that I visited. "We can't run from the problems that face us, and we have to have hope. We will have a year or two of a difficult life. If we survive that time, it will be good."

During my time at Ursus, I saw hundreds of tractors of various sizes throughout the grounds. They were uncompleted because of lack of parts.

UAW President Bob King joined Lech Wałęsa in 2010 at an exhibit on the Polish Solidarity movement at the Walter P. Reuther Library at Wayne State University in Detroit. ©Rick Bielaczyc/Walter P. Reuther Library

"It's possible for us to build 100,000 tractors a year here, but shortages make that impossible," the leader of the local union there, Janusz Sciskalski, told me. "We hope to complete 50,000."

After describing the recent visit of Joan Baez, the American folksinger who had performed at the tractor factory, Sciskalski went on to say the union there needed help on health and safety issues. Many of the problems that existed under communist rule had not gone away.

Indeed, the Communist Party continued to exist, and its members still held major positions in factory managements, government agencies, and elsewhere. Solidarity leaders at the FSM plant told me party officials still had their same offices and jobs.

A huge debate raged then about what type of economic reforms should be implemented. Unionists at the auto and farm machinery plants I visited in 1989 saw the need for radical reform, but also expressed a wariness about a rapid shift to a free-market economy.

Some in Solidarity favored "quick hit" proposals urged by Harvard Professor Jeffrey Sachs, who had been an adviser to the Bolivian government when it reformed its economy.

Sachs regularly related the story of a Bolivian official who had told him: "If you're going to chop off the tail of a cat, it's better to do it in one fell swoop, rather than a series of small cuts."

A Polish newspaper, reflecting doubts some had about radical reform, responded that "Professor Sachs is proposing to cut the tail of the Polish economy off at the neck."[52]

As Solidarity sought to deal with its new circumstances, the UAW once again provided important assistance.

The visits I made to various auto and farm implement unions in 1989 resulted in requests from union leaders in those sectors for more office equipment. The government-controlled official unions during martial law had commandeered the machines we had provided when Solidarity was legal.

For the third time, the UAW arranged for shipments of printing and fax machines for each of Solidarity's locals at Poland's auto plants and agricultural implement factories. This time we did it openly as a normal business transaction with no problems.

On December 9, 1990, Lech Wałęsa won election as president of Poland. He ran on the slogan, "I don't want to, but I've got no choice." He became the first democratically elected president of Poland.

In the years that followed, he navigated huge challenges as Poland adopted privatization and transitioned to a free-market economy with an inadequate safety net. He also helped Poland redefine its relationships with foreign nations and negotiated the withdrawal of Soviet troops.

His presidency had other ups-and-downs, some of them due to Wałęsa's personal style. That style, which had been so effective in the plain-spoken world of shipyards and auto plants, at times limited his ability to handle the government bureaucracy and master the new world of communicating to the public through television.

Wałęsa made several trips to Detroit and held discussions about Solidarity's history with the UAW after his term as president.

Whatever his failures as head of state and his inappropriate statements later in life,[53] Lech Wałęsa's earlier role as an electrician who led 10 million workers in Solidarity through a decade of repression to a new era of democracy and self-determination cannot be denied.

The UAW maintained close ties with Solidarity in the years that followed. And when we sought to organize a Johnson Controls plant in Dayton, New Jersey, Solidarity returned some of our support.

The plant employed a substantial number of Polish-speaking workers. Solidarity, at the UAW's request, sent a letter in Polish from the union leadership in Gdańsk urging the New Jersey workers to vote for the UAW.

They did, and that plant's workers became part of Region 9.

Solidarity, it seems, is a currency not to be hoarded, but to be spent.

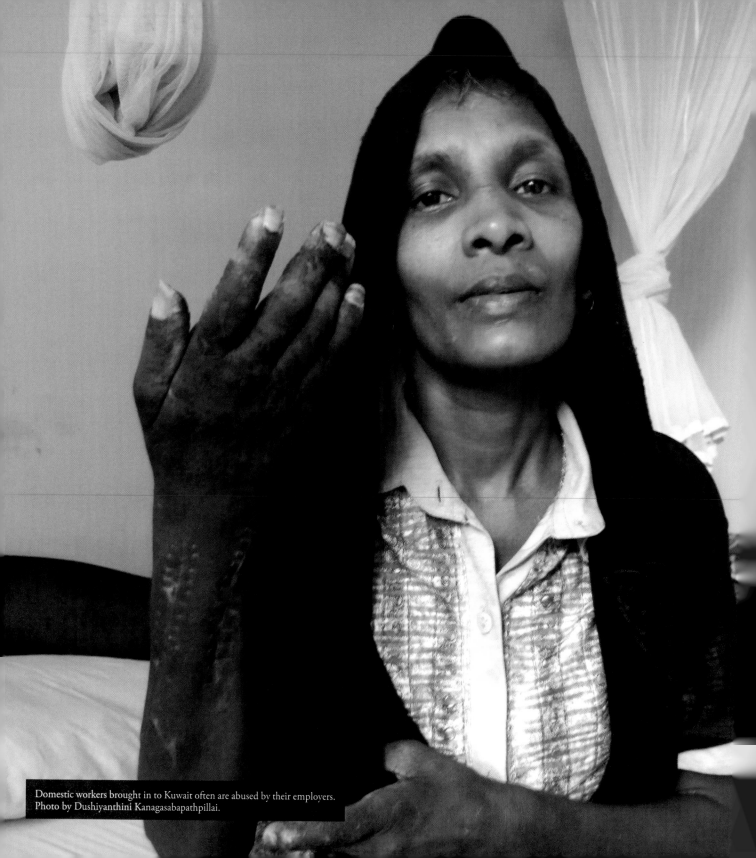

Domestic workers brought in to Kuwait often are abused by their employers.
Photo by Dushiyanthini Kanagasabapathpillai.

CHAPTER EIGHT

Kuwait: Recognize Labor, Human Rights

UAW Members Helped Liberate Country In 1991

Todd Dunn saw death for the first time during Operation Desert Storm.

"I was a 19-year-old kid when I went off to the Persian Gulf," Dunn recalls. "When we'd go into Kuwait, there'd be a lot of secondary gunfire, you know, from buildings along the way."

Today, Dunn is president of UAW Local 862 in Louisville, Kentucky. And like many UAW members, he's proud to have served his country as a member of the military.

"We kept supply routes open to run missions into Kuwait, and later I worked for General [Norman] Schwarzkopf as part of a quick reaction force and personal support to him," says Dunn, who was in the 89th Military Police Brigade. Some members of that unit were exposed to chemical weapons, such as nerve agents sarin and cyclosarin, in the aftermath of demolition operations at Khamisiyah in 1991.

The first Gulf War in 1990–91 occurred after Iraq, then led by Saddam Hussein, invaded Kuwait, an Arab country in the Persian Gulf that has the world's fifth-largest oil reserves[1] and is the 11th richest country in the world per capita.[2]

"First and foremost, American soldiers like me were there to liberate Kuwait," Dunn remembers. "We were dealing with atrocities and torture by Saddam's guys of the Kuwaiti people. I'll never forget the small children that would climb on our vehicles—they were hungry, and there we were. We gave those kids food and liberty.

"There was a lot of American sacrifice," Dunn says. "We lost American soldiers on foreign soil fighting for democracy."

Although young and not yet a UAW member, Dunn took note during his service in the Gulf of one group that stood out.

"Over there, foreign nationals did most of the grunt work," he recalls. "They were paid low wages and had horrible working conditions. We had conversations with some of them and with their bosses, who would say that it was just the way of the land to abuse those foreign [non-Kuwaiti] workers . . . it was just accepted."

David Herron, a crew chief on a C-130 with the 3rd Air Force, has a similar recollection of workers being mistreated. He spent 11 months as part of the Desert Storm effort and now is a UAW member at Local 412 at the Chrysler Tech Center in Auburn Hills, Michigan. He flew into Kuwait on supply missions with water, food, and material for coalition forces.

"Workers over there were treated like dirt," Herron remembers. "I'm going to give it to you like it was: workers in the Gulf were poor as all get-out. The sheiks brought them over from Pakistan and the Philippines, and they'd hold their passports so they couldn't leave.

"They'd work them like dogs. No respect at all. The Americans—the guys I flew with—went out of our way to be decent to those workers, but they were just cheap labor for those sheiks and worked long hours for peanuts."

Scott Harwick, who works at General Motors' Detroit/Hamtramck assembly plant, also noted the tough lives of the foreign nationals living and working in Kuwait. A rifleman in the 3rd Battalion, 9th Marines, Harwick was involved in clearing operations around the Kuwait airport—actions that won his fellow Marines two Silver Stars and 12 Purple Hearts.

"I felt I was helping to liberate Kuwait from an oppressor

who invaded," Harwick says. "Kuwait asked for our help. The least they could do is provide a better world for the people who live and work there. I really believed that workers in Kuwait need fair wages and better working conditions.

"And they should have had a clear right to form unions," the Marine veteran says. "It's better to have a collective voice, not a single voice that the employer or the government can squash.

"I support the right to have unions here and everywhere, including Kuwait. It's almost a God-given right. No one should be oppressed."

The UAW heard the sentiments represented by Todd Dunn, David Herron, and Scott Harwick and took up the battle for union and worker rights in Kuwait shortly after they and other American troops returned home from the Gulf in 1991.

The union chose a path that had paid off earlier when it had pressured an agency of the U.S. government called the Overseas Private Investment Corporation (OPIC). A UAW effort to cut off OPIC benefits for South Korea because of that country's labor rights violations had succeeded, and top union officials believed a similar case could be made against Kuwait.

OPIC provides a variety of benefits to American corporations that wish to operate in foreign countries, particularly emerging markets, including financing, guarantees, political risk insurance, and support for private equity investment funds.

In Kuwait, following the first Gulf War, OPIC's political risk insurance was seen as crucial by U.S. firms anxious to invest there and reap the postwar profits they believed they were entitled to by virtue of America's role in liberating Kuwait.

But, at the same time, investing in Kuwait posed significant risks. The United States and its allies had pushed the Iraqi troops out of Kuwait and back into Iraq, but President George H. W. Bush had chosen not to expand the war and left Saddam Hussein in power in Baghdad.

U.S. companies wanted to invest in Kuwait, and OPIC wanted to facilitate that investment through providing those companies with insurance against political risk. If Saddam chose to invade Kuwait again and American firms lost their new Kuwaiti plants in the oilfields, those companies could be reimbursed courtesy of OPIC.

But for OPIC to provide such benefits and others in Kuwait, the federal agency was allowed to do so only as long as Kuwait was taking steps to adopt and implement "internationally recognized worker rights," as defined under the Trade Act of 1974. This labor rights clause was one the UAW and other American labor groups had lobbied hard to see included in a number of U.S. programs, such as the Generalized System of Preferences (GSP) program and OPIC projects.

On November 12, 1991, just months after many UAW members who fought in Operations Desert Shield and Desert Storm returned home, the UAW filed a petition with the Overseas Private Investment Corporation demanding that it cut off benefits to Kuwait because of that country's failure to take steps to adopt and implement internationally recognized worker rights.

"The UAW recognizes the unique and difficult situation confronting Kuwait in the aftermath of the brutal and illegal occupation the country experienced following the invasion by Iraq on August 2, 1990," the union petition stated. "The American labor movement strongly condemned the invasion and occupation of Kuwait and supported sanctions and other efforts to force a withdrawal by Iraq.

"When the decision was made to go to war to liberate Kuwait, we again strongly supported the American and allied troops deployed to achieve that goal. Indeed, a significant number of UAW members and those belonging to UAW families served the United States in Operation Desert Shield and Operation Desert Storm. The UAW is proud of the contribution it made to the effort to free Kuwait from the vicious oppression of Saddam Hussein and the occupying Iraqi forces."

The union noted the situation facing Kuwait in the aftermath was extremely complex. It stated the recovery effort should "go forward in a positive and prompt manner, so that those living in Kuwait can return to some degree of normalcy as soon as possible—we recognize the role that U.S. corporations have to play in that process."

UAW Local Union 862 President Todd Dunn addresses the crowd at the dedication of the Hero Reward Ranch, a new veterans facility built by members of the union who work at Ford Motor Company. Dunn served in the first Gulf War.

While acknowledging the desire of U.S. companies to receive OPIC insurance and other support for activities in Kuwait, the petition warned that "UAW members and other Americans certainly have a strong position from which to raise questions about the performance of the Kuwaiti government in terms of worker rights.

"Having fought in a war that spilled the blood of American men and women to free Kuwait, it is far from unreasonable for us to desire that democratic rights, including the basic worker rights embodied in the statutes under which OPIC must abide, be respected," the UAW said.

What were the failures of worker rights that led the union to seek an end to OPIC activities in Kuwait?

They were many, but central to all was that about 80 percent of the workforce in Kuwait in the early 1990s was non-Kuwaiti. The large number of migrant workers—Palestinians, Egyptians, Lebanese, Indians, Bangladeshis, Sri Lankans, and others—provided the labor on which the wealthy Kuwaitis depended.

Kuwait's labor code was extremely restrictive. Law No. 38 of 1964 prevented non-Kuwaiti workers from joining unions until they had resided in Kuwait for five years. Because 80 percent of the workforce was made up of migrant workers from other countries, the law essentially meant that they could not unionize.

Of the 13 unions that had formed there, nine were civil service unions, three involved the oil sector, and one represented bank workers. About 90 percent of the Kuwaitis who worked did so in the public sector, and the remainder were to be found in banking, finance, or private firms. Of the roughly 27,000 organized workers, the overwhelming number were Kuwaitis.

Government restrictions meant very few of the migrants making up four of every five workers in Kuwait could join unions. For the few non-Kuwaitis who actually did make it into unions, they then were denied the right to vote within those unions.

The statutory limits on worker rights for non-Kuwaitis were severe, but those who did seek union freedoms faced harsh government repression.

The U.S. State Department Country Reports in 1991 analyzed worker rights in Kuwait and said this: "The [Kuwaiti] Government would deport any non-Kuwaiti [worker] deemed a troublemaker."

The UAW petition to OPIC also pointed out that a worker who wished to join a union had to present a certificate of good reputation and good conduct before he or she was allowed to become a union member.

There were other restrictions that limited worker rights:

- The Kuwaiti government had wide powers of supervision over the records and books of unions; the International Labor Organization (ILO) criticized the extent to which that government could intervene in the financial and internal affairs of unions.

- The government there had the power to dissolve any union that committed acts that violated laws "connected with the preservation of public order and morals."

- There were severe limits on the right to strike. In the five years preceding the UAW petition, there was only one threatened strike, and it was called off.

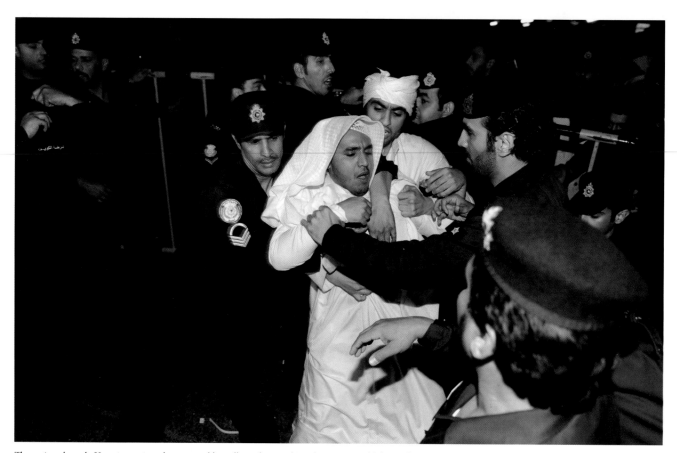

The emirs who rule Kuwait continued to respond brutally to those seeking democracy and labor rights.

- Unions in Kuwait were barred from engaging in any political activity.

In March 1989, Kuwait adopted a new law on expatriate workers. It provided that private sector workers could change jobs only if they had either served a full three years in their current jobs or had been in Kuwait legally for more than 10 years.

Non-Kuwaitis were banned from taking up employment with anyone other than their official sponsors. Government officials could reject any work permit application, renewal, or transfer without revealing the reason and could ask employers to cancel the work permit of a particular worker and deport the worker to his or her home country.

The UAW blasted that law, saying the "contract" system "smacks of indentured servitude." The system severely limited job mobility and freedom of workers to better their lot by hiring on with employers that offered improved economic and working conditions.

The union also stood up for domestic workers, who it said were badly exploited. Virtually all of them came from other countries, such as the Philippines, Sri Lanka, and Thailand. It cited abuses such as nonpayment of wages for maids and household servants and quoted an official of the International Metalworkers' Federation, Denis MacShane, who wrote in *The Nation* magazine:

"For the 35,000 Sri Lankan domestic servants in Kuwait, the provision of sexual services has been an unwritten part of their contract."

Finally, the UAW cited the crucial role that unions had played in the struggle for democracy in other countries, such as the efforts of Solidarność in Poland, which helped topple the country's communist dictatorship, and those of independent black trade unions then in the forefront of the battle to destroy apartheid in South Africa.

"It is not difficult to understand why the ruling emirs of Kuwait lack enthusiasm for democracy and choose to ban any political activity by labor," the UAW petition stated. "But as the pressure for greater political freedom (in Kuwait) grows, we strongly believe unions should have the right to engage in political activity."

The UAW case was a strong one on two fronts: first, Kuwait clearly repressed worker rights for 80 percent of its workforce of foreign nationals and even its own citizens; and second, American workers, including UAW members, paid in blood and treasure to liberate Kuwait and bring some opportunities for freedom to those who lived and worked there.

OPIC took its time investigating the union's arguments on Kuwait. In the majority of labor rights cases, the agency could rely on an elaborate process coordinated by the U.S. Trade Representative's Office, which administered the Generalized System of Preferences (GSP) program. OPIC would follow the USTR petition and review process on labor rights cases.

But because Kuwait did not receive GSP benefits, OPIC had to conduct its own investigation of that country's labor rights record. It involved the U.S. Labor Department and State Department, as well as relevant members of its own board of directors in that process.

The UAW heard little from OPIC on the Kuwait petition in 1992 and 1993, but in September 1994 the union received word from George Kourpias, then president of the International Association of Machinists and also an OPIC board member, that Kuwait had failed to take steps to adopt and implement internationally recognized worker rights.

OPIC was considering a proposal for a major petrochemical project in Kuwait in 1995 and agreed to use the proposed deal to seek actions from the Clinton administration that would pressure Kuwait to reform its labor laws and punish employers who abuse and repress workers there.

"In 1994, the Overseas Private Investment Corporation had decided to withhold its approval of insurance for investment in Kuwait until the State Department conducted a high-level dialogue with Kuwaiti officials on worker rights and made future commitments contingent on positive steps taken by the Kuwaiti government," said Human Rights Watch in describing the result of the UAW petition.[3]

With the pressure of the UAW petition still pending, the Clinton administration began to raise the issue of worker rights with Kuwait's leaders. President Clinton, Secretary of State Warren Christopher, and Secretary of Defense William Perry all visited Kuwait in 1994. Robert H. Pelletreau, assistant secretary of state for Near Eastern Affairs, began raising human and labor rights in discussions with Kuwaiti officials.

But Pelletreau also had been tasked with helping win contracts from Kuwait for U.S. companies.

"From President Clinton down, this administration has made crystal clear its view that supporting American business overseas would be at the heart of our foreign policy interests," Pelletreau told Congress in October 1994. "Our embassies have been active . . . in the Gulf helping American business to secure, for instance, over 500 construction contracts in Kuwait worth approximately $5 billion."[4]

That same month, Saddam Hussein ordered about 70,000 troops from his elite Republican Guard to an area within Iraq near the Kuwait border. The Pentagon responded by sending thousands of U.S. troops to the region and promising to engage Iraq if Saddam failed to withdraw his forces from the border area.

The combination of an increased focus by the Clinton administration on Iraq's continuing military threat to Kuwait and its emphasis on winning reconstruction contracts for U.S. firms no doubt diluted the pressures upon Kuwait to reform its labor laws and improve its worker rights performance.

But OPIC, facing the pressure of the UAW labor rights petition, used its own leverage. The agency withheld approval of insurance for the planned petrochemical plant, demanded tougher actions to deal with the exploitation of foreign workers including maids and household servants, and decided to condition additional insurance on achieving progress on worker rights.

Kuwait, faced with pressure sparked initially by the UAW effort, did amend its labor laws in 1995, including some expanded financial penalties for employers violating the law and, in certain circumstances, imposing criminal penalties of up to three years in prison for employer violations. Fines for employer violations of labor law could be doubled in the case of repeat offenders.

"The UAW effort to pressure Kuwait on labor rights won some gains, and OPIC began writing binding worker rights conditions into contracts for every project it supports," UAW President Owen Bieber noted. "But we wish the Clinton administration had pushed Kuwait harder and achieved the really major reforms our union, and the entire international labor movement, sought."

Today, Kuwait still restricts the right of freedom of association to only one union per occupation and continues to deny foreign workers, who make up more than 80 percent of the workforce, the right to join unions until they have spent five years in Kuwait working in the sector.

But a new private sector labor law enacted by Kuwait's parliament in 2010 did provide private sector workers with higher severance pay, longer vacations, and maternity leave. It also required that wages be paid to workers' bank accounts, rather than through cash transfers that often were abused. The new law included establishment of a state-owned recruitment company aimed at halting abuse of visa trading and illicit recruitment of foreign workers. However, domestic workers were excluded.

When the UAW began its effort on behalf of Kuwaiti workers—particularly the exploited foreign nationals denied worker rights—strikes seldom if ever occurred there.

In May 2013, more than 1,000 workers at the state-owned Oil Sector Services Company (OSSC) went on strike until the company management was forced to agree to workers' demands four days later. The striking workers belonged to the Oil & Petrochemical Industries Workers Confederation, which is an affiliate of IndustriALL, the global union federation to which the UAW belongs.[5]

The Kuwaiti oil workers' victory does represent progress, UAW Local 862 President Todd Dunn says. "I'm proud of the way my union fought for worker rights in Kuwait, and I'm proud of all the UAW members who risked their lives in Desert Storm to liberate Kuwait more than 20 years ago."

The former combat military policeman who helped keep supply routes open for coalition missions in Kuwait now spends some of his time assisting fellow veterans and first responders to get the help they need for post-traumatic stress disorder and other problems. With support from the UAW and Ford, Dunn and others on "ramp" teams recently built part of a facility that provides help for those suffering from PTSD and other illnesses in Indiana.

CHAPTER NINE

Immigrants Organized And Built The UAW
Union Now Demands Immigration Reform

Eduardo Rivera, a UAW member and a hi-lo operator at M&W Industries in Romulus, Michigan, showed up for work on March 27, 1996, ready for a good day.

But a few hours into his shift, federal immigration agents raided the auto parts plant. After blocking all the exits, they roughed up a number of workers, including Rivera—a U.S. citizen from Puerto Rico.

"One officer put me in a headlock before even asking for identification," the UAW member said. Even with ID, the agents claimed he wasn't a legal citizen, apparently because he looked Hispanic, according to an account of the raid in *UAW Solidarity*.[1]

But Rivera fared better than 21 workers from the UAW plant who actually were jailed for more than a week with no bond, as if they were dangerous criminals. Four minors were sent to Texas, where they, too, were put behind bars.

UAW President Steve Yokich strongly denounced the immigration raid five days later in his speech to delegates at the union's Special Collective Bargaining Convention in Detroit.

They took the workers and "just put them in the county jail and left them there," he said. "They sent children, immigrant children, to Texas and put them in detention."[2] Agents of what was then known as the Immigration and Naturalization Service (INS) failed to follow the agency's normal procedures, according to the workers' lawyer, Noel Saleh.

The workers should have had bond set so they could get out of jail. The children should have been processed in the facility nearest them, which was Detroit. They did not have access to their lawyers in Texas, nor could they see their families.

"All these actions seem to be intended to intimidate these workers into waiving their right to a trial, which would determine whether or not they truly were undocumented immigrants," the Rev. Joe Gembala told a rally of UAW members protesting the raid outside Federal Immigration Court in Detroit on April 3, 1996.

Cindy Estrada, then an organizer in Region 1A where the auto parts plant was located, urged UAW members to speak out against abuse of suspected undocumented immigrants.

"We have to remember that we are all workers, and we can't let politicians divide us," said Estrada, who years later won election as a UAW vice president. "NAFTA has created economic turmoil in Mexico that has forced people there to look elsewhere for work. They deserve to be treated fairly under existing immigration law."[3]

Saleh, in an interview in early 2014, recalled that the INS district director tried to block the demonstration at the courthouse but failed.

"Some UAW members at the plant like Rivera, who was a U.S. citizen, got swept up," the attorney said. "The agents locked down the plant—they sort of took hostages and asked their questions later, in contrast to INS policy, which was to ask for nationality and identification upfront.

"Those who were deportable were denied bond, despite numerous ties to the community. The good news was that the workers had a union, so in this case Cindy Estrada and others from the UAW moved quickly to provide help to them."[4]

Immigrants organized and built the UAW, just as they did our nation. Here's how the union put it in a 2013 administrative letter spelling out the UAW's policy on comprehensive immigration reform:

"Because the United States is a nation of immigrants, the UAW's mission to seek social and economic justice for all domestic and global workers is directly influenced by thousands of immigrants who arrived in Detroit and other cities after the turn of the 20th century to work in the auto industry.

"In our union's formative phase to gain a seat at the table to bargain fair wages and work conditions at Chrysler, General Motors, and Ford Motor Company, immigrant auto workers helped lead and participated in the sit-down strikes and other worker actions that have distinguished our union as a fearless fighter for workplace democracy.

"Those worker-driven actions still inspire and inform our organizing work today, as immigrant workers have helped lead recent UAW organizing in auto, gaming, and higher education."

In the late 1930s and early 1940s, many of those who sought UAW representation had names that were Polish, Italian, German, Czech, Slovak, British, Dutch, Romanian, Greek, and Hungarian. They reflected immigration patterns during that time when many new Americans came from Europe.

Today, much of the inflow of aspiring citizens comes from Latin America and Asia. The more recent immigrants, like those who came before them, continue to seek out the UAW and other unions because they want a better life.

As the UAW has broadened its reach beyond auto, aerospace, and agricultural implement plants, many of the union's newest members are immigrants.

Cindy Estrada (center), then an organizer and now a UAW vice president, and workers from M & W Industries discuss an immigration raid in which UAW members who were U.S. citizens were roughed up and arrested in 1996. Photo by Rebecca Cook.

In Washington state, for example, the UAW represents graduate researchers at the University of Washington. More than one-third of them are immigrants, many with doctoral degrees. They are driving the research pipeline that fuels innovation and economic growth.

Krishna Nadella, for example, took research he did as a member of UAW Local 4121 and turned it into MicroGREEN, which makes recyclable beverage cups out of discarded plastic bottles. Nadella's work created about 200 jobs for American workers in the Puget Sound area, but because of his immigration status, he needed a U.S. citizen to co-found the business.

David Parsons, president of Local 4121, has helped lead the union's fight for immigration reform. He has done so in part to keep members such as Nadella from suffering from the current two-tiered system based on employer sponsors. Many visa applicants must remain with a sponsoring employer to obtain and keep their visas. This makes it harder for all workers to maintain protections and living standards that have been established through decades of effort.[5]

New immigrants often face difficulties when employers use their undocumented status to pay them less, force them to work in unsafe or harsh conditions, and threaten deportation if they seek to join unions. They can be treated as scapegoats, particularly in difficult economic times, when some people feel their ability to sustain their living standards is under attack and their jobs are in jeopardy.

There is a long history of such scapegoating. "No Irish Need Apply" signs often were posted in shop windows in the 1850s. Austrian, Hungarian, Italian, and German coal miners were slaughtered by Pennsylvania police when, after being imported as strikebreakers, they decided to form a union in 1897.[6]

Congress established immigration quotas in 1921 that favored Anglo-Saxons and kept out most blacks, Asians, Latinos, Slavs, and Jews. In World War II, about 110,000 Japanese-Americans were moved from their homes in the United States to internment camps amidst war hysteria and racism.

In 1994, California's Republican Governor Pete Wilson fought for and helped win an anti-immigrant initiative called Proposition 187 that was strongly opposed by the UAW. It prohibited undocumented workers and their children from using the state's education and healthcare systems and other government services. The immigrant-bashing proposition later was found by the courts to be unconstitutional.

Another Republican governor, Jan Brewer of Arizona, pushed through legislation in 2010 that required police to detain people they suspected were in the country without authorization and to verify their status with federal officials. The law made it a state crime not to carry immigration papers, provoking a prominent church leader to compare it to "Nazism." The U.S. Supreme Court voided most of the provisions of the Arizona law.

Alabama adopted its own anti-immigrant legislation in June 2011. It prohibits undocumented workers from receiving any public benefits at the state or local level, bars them from attending public colleges/universities, prohibits landlords from renting to them, and prohibits them from applying for work.

Courts again have stayed some provisions of Alabama's anti-immigrant law. And the state, which has sought to attract foreign investment, suffered serious embarrassment when a German executive from Mercedes-Benz was arrested as an "illegal immigrant" because he had left his passport at the Alabama hotel where he was staying. Similarly, a Honda executive from Japan was stopped at a checkpoint and cited as an "illegal" despite having a valid passport, a U.S. work permit, and an international driving permit.[7]

The UAW strongly opposed the anti-immigrant laws passed in Arizona and Alabama during the devastating economic downturn that began under President George W. Bush in 2008.

Even more important, the union became a prominent

force in the broad coalition fighting for federal legislation that would provide far-reaching and comprehensive immigration reform.

In 2013, the UAW International Executive Board approved a resolution compelling the union's "direct engagement to help overhaul our nation's punitive and dysfunctional immigration system." The IEB:

1. Calls on the U.S. Congress to pass a fair, comprehensive immigration reform law that includes a genuine path to citizenship for the nation's 11 million undocumented immigrants, a data-driven employee-centered worker program that ensures equal workplace rights for all workers, an expanded pathway to citizenship for international academic workers in the United States and their families, a humane family reunification program, and rational border-control measures;

2. Instructs the UAW's Community Action Program to engage in activities on a national, regional, and local level to ensure that fair, comprehensive immigration reform passes;

3. Joins other labor and faith, student, veteran, immigrant, and community organizations to mobilize and act for fair, comprehensive immigration reform; and

4. Directs the UAW Education and Mobilization Department to make educational tools available for regions and locals to use to promote and advance understanding about immigration reform for UAW members and their families, friends, and neighbors, including the union's position on immigration reform.

"We are certain that this political, educational, and mobilization action plan will contribute immensely to the overall effort for fair immigration reform and result in a deeper democracy, with liberty and justice for all," the union stated.

Years earlier, the Stabilus Company, a supplier of gas springs to GM, Ford, Chrysler, BMW, and Toyota, fought the UAW at every turn.

A strike in 1986 resulted in a court ordering the company to pay $2 million in back pay to UAW members, but Stabilus flouted the ruling and took eight years to pay up. The Colmar, Pennsylvania, firm repeatedly stalled on negotiations, forced workers to put in seven-day work weeks, and only allowed OSHA inspections after the union won a court order.

In 1994, the company thought it had a secret weapon in its war against the union: the sizable contingent of immigrant workers it could pressure to vote out the UAW.

More than a quarter of the workforce were immigrants from Korea, India, the Philippines, Egypt, and elsewhere. Their status made it easy for management to threaten and coerce them as a decertification election pushed by the company neared.

Then Region 9 Director Tom Fricano and organizer Barbara Rahke coordinated with UAW Local 1612 activists to counter the effort to have the union voted out. They brought in an organizer who spoke Korean to talk to Korean workers in their own language. At a local diner, union activists brought in additional interpreters so immigrants of other nationalities could hear the case for the UAW.

In the end, the immigrant workers at Stabilus proved key to defeating the decertification effort by the company by a 2-to-1 margin.

"They refused to give up on the union," Fricano said after the vote. "It just doesn't get any tougher than what those folks have been through. For them to stick with the UAW was very commendable. It sets an example for how Americans should act."[8]

Workers with a union have a voice, whether or not they are immigrants. But nonunion employers who hire undocumented workers often exploit their vulnerabilities.

UAW Local 2300, which represented auxiliary staff at

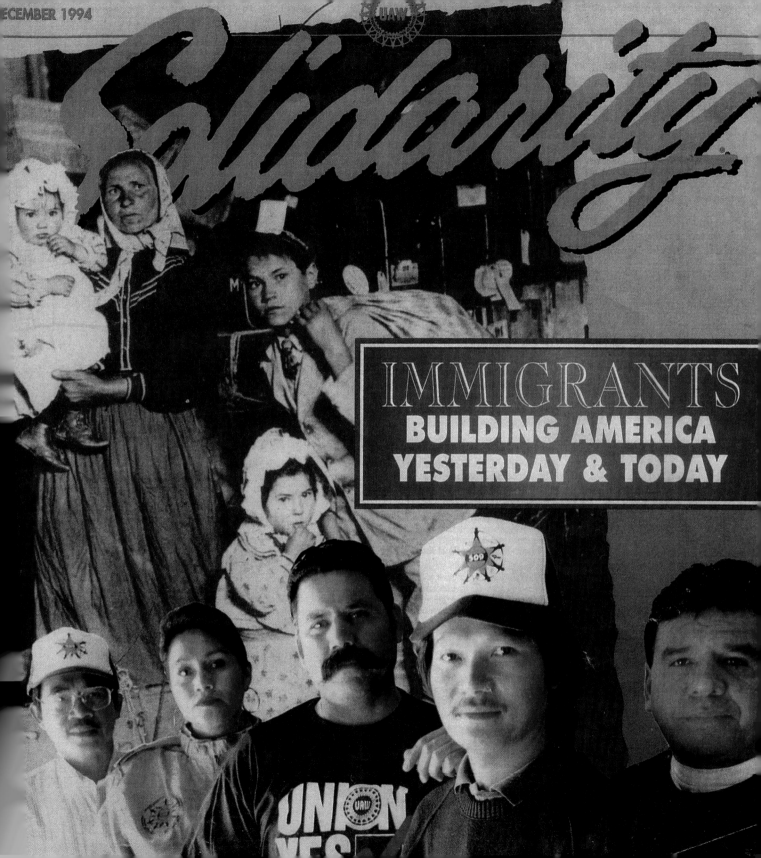

ECEMBER 1994

UAW

Solidarity

IMMIGRANTS
BUILDING AMERICA
YESTERDAY & TODAY

UAW President Bob King and Vice President Cindy Estrada joined advocates of immigration reform at the Fast for Families tent near the U.S. Capitol in December 2013. Eliseo Medina, longtime SEIU leader, had fasted for 22 days on water only in an attempt to pressure Republican House Speaker John Boehner to allow a vote on immigration reform legislation.

Cornell University and some Ithaca, New York, businesses, saw firsthand what an unscrupulous employer could do to the undocumented.

Salvadoran cooks and dishwashers at Cristiano's pizza parlor, one of Ithaca's most popular eateries in the early 1990s, got paid $2.50 an hour or less. A number of them worked 80 to 100 hours per week for $200 and then did not receive their paychecks.

They sought help from Local 2300 after the employer told them they had to work for free on Sundays, because that was "an American tradition."

Instead, with the UAW's help, the immigrant workers went on strike. The union and the local central labor council joined with Cornell students to launch a boycott. In addition, the UAW helped file a claim against Cristiano's with the U.S. Department of Labor and also organized a dance to raise money for the strikers' rent.

The owner, who had been prosecuted before for employing undocumented immigrants, eventually paid about one-quarter of what he owed in back pay. But he closed the pizzeria and moved it in the middle of the night to Massachusetts.[9]

The UAW also strongly supported one of the largest groups of immigrant workers who suffered exploitation: farm workers, particularly in California, Washington, Texas, and Florida. Abuses of workers brought in from Mexico and Central America by farm labor contractors in agricultural states have occurred for decades.

"Growers routinely violate child labor laws, use deadly pesticides, provide substandard living quarters, and steal from paychecks," according to a report on immigration in *UAW Solidarity* in December 1994.

Some of the worst treatment of immigrant farm workers was stopped by pressure from the United Farm Workers union, which the UAW supported financially and politically in its formative days. But given the seasonal nature of farm work and the itinerant nature of the workforce, much of the abuse continues today.

The UAW over the years has represented legal services lawyers who have fought on behalf of agricultural workers.

"We've been chased off property more than once," said Erik Kerzee, who was a member of the National Organization of Legal Services Workers, UAW Local 2320. He and other UAW members represented some of the 175,000 workers in Washington state who picked apples, pears, cherries, asparagus, berries, and other produce.

During the 1990s, 80 percent of Washington's farm workers were immigrants. Most came from Mexico, El Salvador, and Guatemala, but some were born in Russia, Ukraine, and other countries.

One employer warned UAW activists that "My rifle is my lawyer" as he attempted to keep union legal services attorneys out of his labor camp. Because those camps often are in remote rural areas, Local 2320 members from Evergreen Legal Services could provide immigrant workers with help only by going to the camps.

Wage disputes, health and safety problems in both the fields and worker housing, and illegal and retaliatory firings of the immigrant workers made up most of Local 2320's work, along with pesticide education and protection.

"It's important that we get to the labor camps," said Kerzee in 1994, "because many recent immigrants just aren't aware of the legal protections available to them."[10]

UAW President Bob King and Secretary-Treasurer Dennis Williams elevated immigration reform to be one of the top issues on the union's legislative agenda in 2013 in part because they saw it as a civil rights issue.

"There are 11 million people who are being abused and exploited," King said, and it "hurts everyone's middle-class standard of living."

Speaking at the union's Community Action Program conference in 2013, King said millions of undocumented workers "pay property taxes, they pay income taxes, they pay sales taxes, they contribute to Social Security, yet they're not eligible for the benefits the rest of us have."

The exploitation of those workers fosters racial division in the United States and drives down other workers' incomes, King said.

"This is a 100-year-old tactic of the bosses to pit one ethnic group against another," he said. The campaign for immigration reform, including a roadmap to citizenship for the 11 million undocumented workers, "is a struggle for human dignity."

After President Obama called for a constructive framework for immigration reform that included a pathway to citizenship for undocumented immigrants, the UAW urged Congress to pass legislation in early 2013.

"Our country's immigration system is broken," the UAW

said in a statement. "Without a pathway to citizenship, millions of workers are forced into a shadow economy and exploited by unscrupulous employers.

"That drives down wages and working conditions for all workers, and puts employers who want to do the right thing at a competitive disadvantage. It's past time to lift the fear of deportation for individuals who are contributing to our country."

UAW Vice President Cindy Estrada, who led the union's organizing efforts in the auto parts industry, blasted the status quo because it "divides families and forces workers to live in fear."

"No child should be separated from their parents," Estrada said. "Too many children go to school in the morning not knowing whether their parents will be home when they return. Our country can do better for our families."

Underscoring Estrada's point, nearly 23 percent of all deportations ordered between July 1, 2010, and September 31, 2012, involved parents with children who were U.S. citizens. More than 200,000 parents of U.S.-citizen children were ordered to be deported during that period.

In late June 2013, after intensive lobbying by immigration reform supporters including the UAW, the U.S. Senate voted 68–32 to adopt the Border Security, Economic Opportunity and Immigration Modernization Act (S. 744).

The legislation would have provided immediate legal

UAW members joined other unionists and immigration reform advocates in urging Congress to pass a bill that would provide immigrants with a path to citizenship. Photo by SEIU Local 99.

status and a 13-year path to citizenship for the 11 million unauthorized immigrants in the United States. But right-wing Republicans, such as Senator Bob Corker of Tennessee, insisted the bill provide about $40 billion over the following decade to build fences along the southern U.S. border and other measures with little likelihood of effectiveness, such as surveillance towers along the border.

"We are deeply disheartened that Republicans insist on wasting billions more to further militarize the border at a time when schools, military, and infrastructure are facing extreme budget cuts," the UAW said in a statement after the Senate adopted S. 744. "But today's 68–32 passage represents a positive step forward, and we call on House Speaker John Boehner to allow a vote on comprehensive immigration reform to preserve the pathway to citizenship for the 11 million aspiring Americans."

Despite the bipartisan support for the Senate legislation, the Republican leadership in the House remained strongly opposed to allowing a vote on the Senate bill or anything similar to it. Instead, the GOP-controlled House focused on legislation that would devote billions to border fences and other strategies that would exclude the path to citizenship at the core of immigration reform.

Under the spell of the far-right Tea Party and other extremists, the House refused to act in 2013 and 2014.

One of the issues adding to the pressure on Republicans, most of whom are opposed to immigration reform, is that it would be a boon to the American economy.

The nonpartisan Congressional Budget Office (CBO) studied the 2013 Senate bill and found that any additional costs that arise from immigration reform would be more than paid for by tax contributions of immigrants. In effect, the CBO said immigration reform pays for itself.

Federal tax revenues were projected to grow by nearly $460 billion by 2023 and by an additional $1.5 trillion by 2033 if the Senate immigration bill were to be implemented.

While state spending on education, healthcare, and other programs would increase as immigrants became eligible over time, the CBO estimated that state tax revenue would increase by about $748 billion by 2033—additional revenue that would more than cover the increased costs.

Other studies have indicated that a path to citizenship could raise wages for immigrant workers by about six percent. The wage gains and related productivity increases would ripple through the economy—immigrants are not only workers, but also consumers and taxpayers. As they spend their increased earnings on the purchase of food, clothing, housing, cars, computers, and other items, that spending would stimulate demand in the economy, according to the Economic Policy Institute.[11]

As the immigration debate continued in 2014, the UAW expanded its efforts to educate the public on the issue.

In her speeches, Cindy Estrada, who directs the union's General Motors Department, regularly explained who the people are who are included among the 11 million undocumented immigrants in the United States:

- They are kids who were brought into this country by their parents seeking economic and physical security.
- They are individuals who entered the United States legally on a visa, but overstayed, losing their documented status.
- They are guest workers who came into the United States on a work visa and lost their documented status when they left their employer after being victimized by wage theft or health and safety abuses—or both.

A sizable number of unauthorized immigrants can be traced to the impact of trade actions, such as the North American Free Trade Agreement (NAFTA), that the UAW strongly opposed. The union correctly predicted that NAFTA not only would cost hundreds of thousands of good-paying American jobs, but also would result in increased illegal immigration.

In the aftermath of NAFTA, more than one million Mexican farmers were driven out of business in Mexico, and undocumented Mexican immigration to the United States rose 60 percent.

The broader impact of the current form of globalization, in which corporations operate to maximize profits by seeking out low-wage production and the absence of governmental regulation, is the creation of huge economic dislocation. It has resulted in widespread emigration of workers from their home countries to others where they hope to find a better way of life.

"Corporate bosses and right-wing media use immigration as a wedge issue to divide us and keep the status quo: low wages and workers without rights," Estrada said.

"It's classic union-busting strategy: get the first shift fighting against the second shift . . . white workers fighting black workers . . . skilled trades fighting production. The boss gets everyone fighting against each other, so that people lose sight of what they have in common and stop organizing."

Here are some of the typical hang-ups that many Americans—and even some union members—have about immigration reform and Estrada's responses:

1. **Immigrants will get amnesty.** Opponents say the 2013 Senate bill gave the undocumented a free pass to U.S. citizenship right away. Not true. It allowed legal status only after payment of fines and penalties. They go to the back of the immigration line, and it takes a total of 13 years to get citizenship after paying more fees, learning English, and meeting other requirements. That isn't "amnesty."

2. **They'll take our jobs.** Current unemployment problems stem from the failure of a polarized Congress to pass jobs legislation, bad U.S. trade policies, globalization, technology, and corporate outsourcing. Immigration reform would help to level the playing field in the U.S. so employers can't pit worker against worker in a wage race to the bottom.

3. **Our country can't afford that many more people.** The 11 million are already here, so they are in the system. With legalization, our tax revenue will grow by almost $500 billion in the next 10 years. The undocumented do pay about $90 billion per year in taxes now, and they use about $5 billion in services.

4. **Immigrants broke the law and reform will reward them. They should have gotten in line and come here legally like my family did.** Many of our grandparents and parents came into the United States when the requirements were much looser. Today, there isn't really a line to get into. In 2005, the U.S. government gave only 5,000 permanent legal resident visas for nonprofessional workers. Even immigrants married to U.S. citizens have to wait for years to come to the United States to join their families.

Mario Rivera, a UAW Local 509 bargaining committee member at Johnson Controls, became a U.S. citizen in 1989. He was born in Guatemala but lived most of his life in America, where he married and raised three children in a suburban home near Disneyland.[12]

Despite living an all-American life, Rivera suddenly found himself with a pistol to his head in the early 1990s. The Anaheim, California, police surrounded his home, barged through the front door, and called him a "stupid Mexican." In front of his Mexican-born wife and his daughter, Rivera was handcuffed and hauled off to jail. He was charged with an unpaid $15 parking ticket.

The arrest came during the heated debate around California's Proposition 187. The UAW member's 16-year-old daughter helped organize a protest walkout at Loara High School, where she and 150 other students received two-day suspensions

for attending a speak-out on Proposition 187 at a college.

"I asked my dad how he'd feel if I walked out," Gabie Rivera told *UAW Solidarity* in 1994. "He told me I had his support. At 9:30 in the morning, we were sitting in biology class. We were scared, but when a couple of students stood up and quietly walked out, I followed.

"We walked five miles to the college, where we listened to speakers on both sides of 187. They were students from all over Anaheim. I was mad and I showed what I believed in. My dad really supported me."

The fight against Proposition 187 by Gabie Rivera, her father, and millions of Californians ultimately succeeded when a federal court found it unlawful. But the fight for the rights of aspiring Americans continued to face huge obstacles.

California Governor Gray Davis, a Democrat elected with UAW support, opposed Proposition 187. When he took office in 1999, Davis halted the legal appeals that had been filed by the previous Republican governor seeking to uphold the anti-immigrant initiative.

Four years later, the UAW sought to raise the need for comprehensive immigration reform as part of an Immigrant

Workers Freedom Ride. The effort took inspiration from the freedom rides of the civil rights movement in the early 1960s.

Advocates of immigrant rights crisscrossed the country seeking to raise public awareness. The UAW hosted the immigrant freedom riders in Dearborn, Michigan, on September 27, 2003, at a rally where workers carried signs such as "The People United Will Never Be Defeated" and "Civil Rights & Civil Liberties for Immigrant Workers."

Elvira Arellano, an airplane cleaner at Chicago's O'Hare Airport, addressed the crowd at the rally through an interpreter.[13] "I didn't come here to do harm to anyone," she said. "I came looking for a better future and for an opportunity for my son that he would never get in our country." Arellano was a single mother originally from Mexico. She had been ordered deported after a series of immigration raids at 13 U.S. airports. Her deportation was stayed after Congress passed a bill temporarily preventing it.

"When I was arrested, I felt like the worst criminal," Arellano said at UAW Local 600. "All I want is to be treated like a human being."

One of the final stops on the UAW-backed Immigrant

Workers Freedom Ride, also sponsored by the AFL-CIO, was in Doraville, Georgia.

Gary Casteel, then the UAW Region 8 director, told the crowd: "The UAW's support of workers is not confined to UAW members. The corporate greed that has shown itself to be prevalent in this nation today is driving the exploitation of the immigrant worker.

"It is not our intent to stand idly by and let this injustice continue."[14]

The union did not stand idly by over the next decade, but the far right and many Republican politicians broadened their attack on aspiring Americans and their children.

After Barack Obama received more than two-thirds of the Latino vote in 2008 and 2012, a small number of Republicans began to urge a more tolerant approach to immigration reform out of fear that a growing Hispanic vote could doom the GOP's election chances in the years ahead.

With the passage of immigration legislation in the U.S. Senate in 2013, hopes grew that a real pathway to citizenship might be possible. But then the House Republican leadership led by Speaker John Boehner refused even to allow a vote on the Senate bill.

UAW President Bob King and Vice President Cindy Estrada joined other union and faith-based advocates of immigration reform in December 2013 at a tent complex in front of the

U.S. Capitol where activists had conducted a water-only fast.

Some, such as Eliseo Medina of the Service Employees International Union (SEIU), had gone for more than 22 days without food as part of an effort to pressure Republican leaders in the U.S. House of Representatives to allow a vote on immigration reform.

King, Estrada, and then UAW Secretary-Treasurer Dennis Williams brought support to the Fast for Families in an effort to transform public consciousness over the immigration issue. Much in the way that Cesar Chavez, the late leader of the United Farm Workers, galvanized the nation with his long fasts seeking gains for Latinos laboring in the fields of California and Arizona, so, too, did the Fast for Families leaders hope to refocus the political debate on immigration reform.

President Obama and his wife, Michelle, also joined Medina and others in the tent and gave momentum to labor's call for House Republicans to allow a vote on immigration overhaul. They also urged Medina to end his fast for health reasons and let others carry it on, which he did after losing 24 pounds.

"While many CEOs get millions in bonuses for shipping jobs overseas, many working immigrants have no rights or protections to fight against employers who exploit their status," King said. He pledged a redoubling of the UAW's efforts in 2014 for fair and comprehensive immigration reform.

But House Republicans refused to allow an immigration bill to come to a vote in 2014, despite the likelihood that some version similar to the Senate bill would have passed.

President Obama took executive actions on immigration in November 2014 in an effort to make some progress on reform. UAW President Dennis Williams praised Obama, but noted the executive actions were "limited in scope and are not a substitute for comprehensive reform."

"The members of the UAW believe that Congress must pass immigration reform legislation that includes a pathway to citizenship for 11 million aspiring Americans, promotes family unification, and improves worker protections," Williams said. "Our current system destroys families, rewards unscrupulous employers, and hurts our economy."

The union president said that since the time of Walter Reuther, the UAW has led the struggle to secure economic and social justice.

"Comprehensive immigration reform supports the rights of all workers to have a voice on the job and a better opportunity to provide a decent standard of living for their families," Williams stated.

Some Republican state attorneys general and governors filed a lawsuit against Obama's executive actions and a conservative federal judge in Texas who had been appointed by George W. Bush blocked them from being implemented.

In early 2015, it appeared that months of legal appeals would be needed to resolve the issue. But the UAW and other labor and immigration rights supporters pledged to fight on until true reform is the law of the land.

CHAPTER TEN

UAW Stood With Central American Workers
Thousands Killed By Death Squads

Being a mother of three, including a 6-month-old infant, took much of her time. But skill, toughness, and an outgoing personality helped Febe Elizabeth Velasquez become a top leader of her union in El Salvador.

Velasquez spent the morning of October 31, 1989, carrying out her duties as an executive board member of the National Federation of Salvadoran Workers, known as FENASTRAS. With labor in El Salvador in the 1980s under extreme attack by right-wing forces and death squads, Febe treasured every day, knowing how risky union work had become.

Sometime after noon that day, she joined other FENASTRAS leaders and members for lunch in a small cafeteria at the union's headquarters, which was located just two blocks from the National Police headquarters in San Salvador. Despite constant monitoring by security forces, the FENASTRAS building had been bombed twice that year, but no one had been killed.

At about 12:30 p.m., a powerful explosion destroyed much of the union building. In the rubble, 10 people lay dead, many missing body parts. Febe Elizabeth Velasquez, age 35, mother and union leader, lost her life in that bombing.

About 30 other unionists had been injured in the blast.

By the time Febe and other FENASTRAS unionists were killed, El Salvador had experienced a decade of civil war. A small elite that controlled an economy based on coffee exports, backed by the military, battled an impoverished majority made up of peasants, trade unionists, and grassroots organizations

that opposed the government's massive repression.

U.S. President Ronald Reagan routed millions of dollars of American military aid to the Salvadoran government at a time when its systemic use of death squads, torture, kidnapping, and assassination regularly targeted union activists, religious leaders, and civilian opponents of the military regime there.

The UAW and other progressive unions in the United States became vigorous opponents of Reagan's military aid to El Salvador and regularly spoke out strongly to condemn the massive violence suffered by workers there.

Months after the FENASTRAS killings, a UAW delegation from Region 1A stood at Velasquez's gravesite in San Salvador. It was a solemn moment for the UAW to pay respect to her and others killed in the bombing as well as thousands of other unionists who lost their lives to right-wing death squads and Salvadoran military forces.

"The Salvadoran people and, in particular, the people of the Salvadoran labor movement are a people of great courage, great inner strength, great perseverance and stamina, but most importantly a people of great hope," Region 1A Director Bob King told FENASTRAS members and others. The UAW delegation had attended the annual convention of FENASTRAS, where they presented a check for $5,000 collected from local unions in Region 1A before the trip.

King expressed sympathy for those killed and injured in the bombing and pledged the UAW's strong support for the Salvadoran labor movement "on behalf of our 150,000 active and retired members of UAW Region 1A, and on behalf of our

Opposite page: Death squads in El Salvador marked the doors of union members and other victims they murdered with the "mano blanca," the white hand. Photo © by Susan Meiselas/Magnum Photos.

president, Owen Bieber, who has been one of the greatest leaders and most active fighters in the fight to end U.S. military aid to El Salvador."[1]

In addition to the graveside visit and attending the union convention, the UAW group went to a child care center organized by union women; visited Salvadorans who were forced to live in housing built on a garbage dump; and witnessed the construction of a new union hall.

"People live under conditions that most of us would not believe unless we witnessed it," then UAW Local 900 president Jeff Washington, a Ford worker from Wayne, Michigan, told *UAW Solidarity* after the trip. "Neighborhoods built on trash dumps . . . Children playing in raw sewage; homes built of tin, cardboard, and wood found along the roadside; as many as 17 people living in a two-room shack."[2]

The rampant poverty of so many Salvadorans actually made them targets of their own government. The wealthy coffee growers and exporters and others in the business elite deeply feared a popular revolt by workers and peasants. Thus, the military regime's violent repression kept escalating throughout the 1980s.

Three military coups occurred between 1979 and elections in 1982. Shortly after the first coup, many protesters had been killed, and opposition forces began to respond. The left demanded land reform, democratic elections, and more equitable distribution of El Salvador's gains from the coffee, sugar, and banking sectors.

As violence escalated in 1980, Roman Catholic Archbishop Oscar Romero strongly urged the United States to suspend military aid to the Salvadoran government.

"Political power is in the hands of the armed forces," the archbishop said in an open letter. "They know only how to repress the people and defend the interests of the Salvadoran oligarchy."

The Catholic Church played a huge role in El Salvador and had been a generally conservative force there since the 16th century. With about 5 million Catholics who made up the ma-

jority of the population, the archbishop's criticism of the military regime had an impact.

Archbishop Romero followed his open letter with an admonition to soldiers and security force members not to obey orders from their commanders to kill civilians. The next day, March 24, 1980, Romero was assassinated while celebrating a mass in San Salvador. As mourners left his funeral at the National Cathedral a week later, military snipers in the National Palace and on the periphery of the Gerardo Barrios Plaza fired on the crowd, leaving 42 mourners dead by gunshot and trampling in the ensuing panic.

Roberto D'Aubuisson, a former army major, was arrested with others in May 1980, and documents that were seized showed he had organized the archbishop's assassination. D'Aubuisson had been trained years earlier at the School of the Americas by U.S. Army instructors.

The Salvadoran government quickly released D'Aubuisson despite the evidence. In 1993, a United Nations truth commission on El Salvador conducted a detailed investigation of the case and confirmed that D'Aubuisson had planned and ordered Archbishop Romero's killing.

UAW President Douglas Fraser strongly condemned the assassination in 1980. But the union was even more shocked as the military regime soon engaged in widespread killings across the country. Nearly 12,000 trade unionists, peasants, teachers, priests, and others died violently in 1980.

The National Guard and a paramilitary force, for example, carried out a massacre at the Sumpul River in northwestern El Salvador. About 600 were killed, mainly women and children who had sought to cross the river into Honduras to escape the violence. The Honduran military turned them back, and Salvadoran troops then fired on them on May 14, 1980.

But it took events in December of that year to galvanize the growing dismay over repression in El Salvador into a broader international movement.

Two American churchwomen were among those who stood vigil all night beside the coffin of Archbishop Romero during his wake: Jean Donovan and Sister Dorothy Kazel.

Donovan had earned an MBA from Case Western Reserve University in Cleveland, Ohio, and worked as a management consultant for Arthur Andersen, a national accounting firm. But after volunteering with the Cleveland Diocese Youth Ministry, she became a lay missionary who went to El Salvador to work in poor, rural communities in 1977.

Sister Dorothy Kazel, an American Ursuline religious sister, also worked with the Cleveland Diocese program in El Salvador. Both she and Donovan knew how dangerous life had become in that country.

Here's what Donovan wrote to a friend in 1980:

"The Peace Corps left today and my heart sank low. The danger is extreme and they were right to leave. . . . Now I must assess my own position, because I am not up for suicide. Several times I have decided to leave El Salvador. I almost could, except for the children, the poor, bruised victims of this insanity. Who would care for them? Whose heart could be so staunch as to favor the reasonable thing in a sea of their tears and loneliness? Not mine, dear friend, not mine."[3]

On December 2, 1980, Donovan and Sister Kazel drove to the San Salvador airport to pick up two Maryknoll sisters, Ita Ford and Maura Clarke, whose flight arrived a little after 9 p.m. Five members of the Salvadoran National Guard had seen them on an earlier airport run, phoned their commander for orders, and changed out of their uniforms into plain clothes.

The four American churchwomen left the airport, but the five National Guardsmen quickly stopped their white van. The soldiers took them to an isolated area where they were beaten, raped, and murdered.

Some residents near the town of Santiago Nonualco about 15 miles east of the airport saw the white van drive by and,

Ten members of the FENASTRAS union federation in El Salvador died in a bombing October 31, 1989, committed by right-wing "death squads" under the direction of top officials of the Salvadoran military.

shortly afterward, heard machine-gun fire followed by single shots. In addition, they saw five men drive the van back with the radio blaring. The van was found burned out by the side of the airport road the next morning.[4]

Other local residents discovered the bodies of the American churchwomen that morning and were told by authorities to bury them in a common grave in a field close to where they were found. They did so, but one of the men told the parish priest, who informed the local bishop, and the word quickly reached U.S. Ambassador Robert White, who had hosted Donovan and Kazel for dinner at the American embassy two nights earlier.[5]

Ambassador White, along with several nuns and a group of reporters, went to the shallow graves on the morning of December 3. Donovan's body was the first to be recovered, followed by Sister Kazel's, Sister Clarke's, and finally Sister Ford's.

The two Maryknoll nuns were buried in Chalatenango, where they had served the poor. Sister Kazel's body was returned to Cleveland. Jean Donovan's body was flown to Sarasota, Florida, where her parents lived. The U.S. State Department charged the Donovans $3,500 for the return of their daughter's body.[6]

The brutal rapes and murders of the four American churchwomen set off an intense debate in the United States over who was responsible. With Ronald Reagan sworn in as president just a few weeks later, the U.S. policy of providing military aid to El Salvador became more hotly contested.

The new Reagan administration, strongly opposed to the Sandinista government in Nicaragua, saw the armed insurgency in El Salvador in Cold War terms. It began to send additional military aid to the Salvadoran government because it believed there was a real threat of a Marxist takeover there. By ignoring or discounting the legitimate grievances of the huge majority of peasants, unionists, and organizations of the poor, the United States chose instead to align with the very same forces that were killing labor activists and religious leaders such as Archbishop Romero and the American churchwomen.

Four American churchwomen working with the poor in El Salvador were taken by the U.S.-funded Salvadoran National Guard in December 1980. The churchwomen were beaten, raped, and murdered and then buried in crude graves near the airport. Photo © by Susan Meiselas/Magnum Photos.

Six weeks before the bombing that destroyed the FENASTRAS office in 1989, National Guard troops raided a factory in Santa Mercedes that workers had occupied in December 1988 when the employer shut it down. They also arrested additional workers in raids on four homes.

FENASTRAS conducted a protest the next day—a march during which union workers obstructed traffic. Two buses were burned. Members of the National Police chased the protesters, who took refuge in the Central American Mission Church. After forcing them out of the church with tear gas, the National Police arrested 64 protesters—kicking and striking them as they forced the demonstrators onto a bus that took them to police headquarters.

Julia Tatiana Mendoza Aguirre, a 22-year-old who did press work at FENASTRAS headquarters, suffered blows to the head and back. Upon arrival at National Police headquarters, she was blindfolded. Her interrogators accused her of belonging to the FMLN, an umbrella group of guerrilla forces.

FMLN, the Farabundo Marti National Liberation Front, was formed in 1980 to bring together guerrilla groups opposed to the military government of El Salvador. When the war ended, the FMLN demobilized and became a leftist political party. In March 2009, Mauricio Funes, the FMLN candidate, won election as El Salvador's president. Voters elected another FMLN candidate, Salvador Sanchez Ceren, as president in 2014.

On her third day in detention, Mendoza was taken to a room where a man with a soft voice told her to cooperate with the police, according to an Americas Watch report based on her testimony. He then raped her.[7]

That evening, the same man took her to a room for what she hoped would be an interrogation. Instead, he forced Julia, still blindfolded, to lean forward over a chair and sodomized her.

The young union activist appeared before the First Penal Judge in San Salvador on September 21. She denied being a member of the FMLN but proudly acknowledged belonging to FENASTRAS, her union.

After informing the judge that she had been sexually assaulted, he ordered an examination by a forensic physician. The doctor confirmed that the young union activist had been raped.

The judge then ordered Julia released.

In a few days, she returned to work at the FENASTRAS headquarters and, while there, provided testimony to Americas Watch investigators about the beatings and rapes while in custody.

Mendoza joined her union colleague Febe Elizabeth Velasquez and others in the FENASTRAS cafeteria at about 12:30 p.m. on October 31, 1989.

She also died in the blast.

A few days after the explosion, Major Roberto D'Aubuisson, who had been implicated in the assassination of Archbishop Romero nine years earlier, declared that "there are strong suspicions that the bombing was produced by the manipula-

tion of explosive artifacts that the unionists were making."[8] The government's police explosives unit also blamed the trade unionists and concluded that forces aligned with FENASTRAS committed the bombing as part of a conspiracy to discredit the Salvadoran government.

El Salvador's president, Alfredo Christiani, then announced the creation of a high-level commission to investigate the bombing. He chose representatives of the government and international organizations and also named Jesuit Father Ignacio Ellacuria to the commission.

Although FENASTRAS allowed visiting FBI agents to examine what was left of the building and collect evidence, along with the presiding judge in the case and a team of the Special Investigative Unit, the union said it would not participate in the commission investigation without strict conditions.

Father Ellacuria also had his doubts about the commission, and he said he would not serve on it because the government had a record of failing to prosecute military officers.[9] He and his fellow Jesuits at Central American University (UCA) had played a major role in trying to encourage dialogue between government/military forces and the FMLN guerrillas. But in advocating peace talks and urging a negotiated solution to the conflict, Father Ellacuria was viewed by the Salvadoran army as a subversive.

His refusal to serve on the commission to investigate the FENASTRAS bombing became moot a few days after President Christiani appointed him.

On the evening of November 15, 1989, an elite unit of the Salvadoran army called the Atlacatl Battalion, which had been created at the U.S. Army's School of the Americas in 1980, went to the UCA campus where the Jesuit residence was located.

The soldiers ordered Father Ellacuria and four other priests to lie facedown in the back garden, while others searched the residence. Then Lieutenant Jose Espinoza Guerra gave an order to fire. The five priests were shot and killed. A sixth Jesuit was killed inside the residence, as were the housekeeper and her 16-year-old daughter.

The Atlacatl Battalion soldiers then fired a machine gun at the façade of the residence and launched rockets and grenades. In an attempt to blame the opposition FMLN forces, they wrote on a piece of cardboard: "FMLN executed those who informed on it. Victory or Death, FMLN."

In both the FENASTRAS bombing and the Jesuit massacre cases, top officials of the U.S. government echoed claims of the Salvadoran military that the killings had resulted from actions by the FMLN guerrillas. U.S. Ambassador William Walker told congressional investigators six weeks after the Jesuit murders there was no evidence to implicate the Salvadoran military. He said leftist rebels might have committed the act while dressed in soldiers' garb.[10]

Walker and the entire Bush administration feared that the atrocities committed at FENASTRAS and the Jesuit university could damage U.S. political support for the Salvadoran government and embolden members of the U.S. Congress to end or limit the millions of taxpayer dollars being sent to the very forces that committed those horrible crimes.

More than three years later, in 1993, the United Nations Commission on the Truth for El Salvador found no involvement of union members or the FMLN in the FENASTRAS bombings or the Jesuit murders. Instead, the commission, after examining the evidence, concluded the Salvadoran military, including top generals and colonels, had ordered both atrocities and later sought to conceal the military's role.

UAW Region 9A Director Ted Barrett traveled to El Salvador in early June 1983 with a group of U.S. labor leaders. The trip was organized by the National Labor Committee in Support of Democracy and Human Rights in El Salvador (NLC), which was co-chaired by UAW President Douglas Fraser.

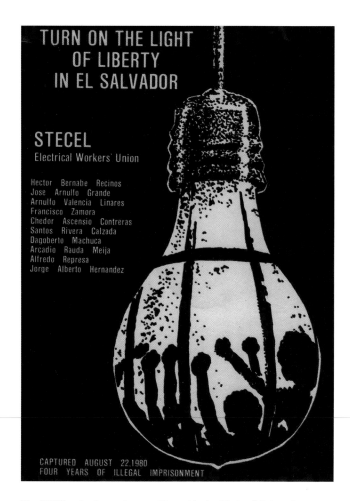

The UAW and other unions working with the National Labor Committee launched a postcard campaign aimed at pressuring the U.S.-backed government of El Salvador to release jailed members of the electrical workers' union called STECEL.

I also made several trips to El Salvador at Fraser's direction to examine firsthand the reports the union had received of Salvadoran death squads and military forces killing workers and labor activists there as the civil war intensified in the early 1980s.

What the Region 9A director found squared with my own experiences. Here's how Barrett and his colleagues described the labor situation upon returning to the United States:

"Trade unions exist in El Salvador. The workplace landscape of El Salvador abounds with the acronyms of labor organizations. . . . But there is no trade union freedom in El Salvador, no semblance of the trade union rights we as North American trade unionists consider fundamental to democracy.

"In El Salvador, we spoke to trade unionists whose wages had been frozen, whose meetings had been disrupted, whose offices had been bombed, whose bodies had been tortured, whose co-workers had disappeared—and been murdered."

As I had, Barrett visited Mariona Prison near San Salvador where he and his NLC delegation met with 10 imprisoned members of the hydroelectrical union called STECEL, led by Hector Recinos, the secretary-general since 1976. They had been arrested during a nationwide strike in 1980 to protest attacks by the government against STECEL and other unions. Death squads had killed 18 members of STECEL during 1979–80, and the local at the Lempa River had been dynamited.

About 15 STECEL leaders first were taken to the Treasury Police headquarters, where they were beaten repeatedly. Interrogators told them their families would be killed. During the 70 days they were held there, authorities provided so little food some feared they would die of starvation.

Then authorities transferred the trade union leaders to Santa Tecla Prison. Five other unionists arrested with them were released (including Miguel Angel Centeno, who was murdered by government security forces eight months later).

The STECEL union was dissolved by government decree in 1980 after the strike cut off electrical power throughout much of El Salvador. Americas Watch, in a report on labor rights in El Salvador, found that the summary action "violated the dissolution procedure established in the country's labor code."[11]

While STECEL leaders were imprisoned, Salvadoran authorities forced them to sign extrajudicial statements that they were not allowed to read. Later, the union leaders learned these papers were "confessions" implicating them in the transport of arms and other "terrorist" activities. In fact, they had only participated in a 24-hour strike.

Still, the government did not put them on trial, or even formally charge them.

But the union activists were punished in other ways. Jose Valencia, one of the STECEL leaders, received word that his 17-year-old daughter had been abducted from their home on June 11, 1981. Her bullet-riddled body was discovered in a public garbage dump in Santa Ana some days later.

Recinos, the top STECEL leader, learned on August 20, 1982, that his wife, Maria Adela Cornejo de Recinos, and 13-year-old daughter, Ana, had been arrested by uniformed and civilian men. Maria had been active in the Mothers of Prisoners and the Disappeared. His remaining children had to take on assumed names in order to go to school. Ultimately, they fled El Salvador to the United States out of fear that they, too, would be "disappeared."

After Region 9A Director Barrett and the National Labor Committee delegation met with the STECEL prisoners in 1983, the committee launched an international campaign seeking their release. Like other campaigns to follow, the NLC worked with the 22 North American unions that made up the committee to get letters and telegrams sent to the government of El Salvador demanding the STECEL leaders be freed.

In addition, we filed a human rights petition with the Organization of American States (OAS). AFSCME and ACTWU produced 20,000 brochures on the STECEL case that included sample letters. A number of UAW regions participated in the campaign, including 1A, 4, and 9A.

Dan Cantor, who had been hired by the NLC to help organize grassroots activities, located Hector Recinos Jr., the son of the jailed STECEL leader, in California and, with

Following page: A wife carries her murdered husband's body home on a cart to bury him. Photo ©by Susan Meiselas/Magnum Photos.

UAW help, had taken him on a publicity tour of northeastern cities.

In 1983 as we waged this campaign, Owen Bieber succeeded Doug Fraser as UAW president. Bieber also became co-chair of the NLC while Fraser remained involved as co-chair emeritus. Like Fraser, Bieber found the torture and killings of Salvadoran unionists to be outrageous. He was particularly disturbed by the fact the Reagan administration funded the military regime there and regularly defended its actions.

UAW members seemed to support that view. Region 3 (Indiana and Kentucky) conducted a secret ballot vote at its summer school in 1983 on the question of whether "the U.S. should stop all forms of military aid and assistance to El Salvador." The results: 92 voted for stopping military aid; 23 voted for continuing it; and 21 were not sure.

The time was 4 a.m. on October 15, 1984. I was in San Salvador, but hadn't been to bed and decided lying down would be a big mistake at that point. Instead, I went to the lobby of the Camino Real Hotel, a 235-room island in the middle of a civil war that featured incessant decapitations, murders, rapes, kidnappings, and an air of fear blended with unreality.

One could also find a bit of bravado, gallows humor, and lots of booze at the Camino Real, which played host to hundreds of journalists from all over the world who came to report on the conflict between the U.S.-backed military regime and the FMLN insurgents.

On my previous trips, I chose the Camino Real because I found the journalists to be good company and knowledgeable about events on the ground. I never stayed at the Sheraton, where Michael Hammer, an official of an AFL-CIO institute and the brother of a UAW member, had been gunned down with two others in the coffee shop in 1981.

My friend Janet Shenk had introduced me to Susan Meiselas, a superb documentary photographer who had covered the war for many months. I learned valuable lessons from Meiselas, as on the day we were going to Usulutan in a van with a big "PRENSA" sign on the side announcing that reporters were inside.

Meiselas suddenly demanded that the driver pull off to the roadside and stop. Nothing seemed to be going on, so I asked her why we had stopped.

"No vehicles have passed us coming from the opposite direction," she said. "That usually means there's a firefight or some sort of battle up ahead. We'll just wait here for a while, until the traffic resumes, and hopefully things will be safe for us."

Meiselas herself had been seriously injured in 1981 when a car she was in heading north out of San Salvador hit a land mine; a South African journalist with her was killed.

I also learned to carry a few tampons in my bag while out in the field in El Salvador. Journalists who were veterans of war zones found them excellent for gunshot wounds to help stanch bleeding in a relatively sterile manner.

The lobby of the Camino Real, even at an early hour, had 20 or 30 journalists, photographers, and members of TV crews coming and going as they prepared for the biggest event in many months: the opening of peace talks between the government and the rebels in a town called La Palma in northern El Salvador. For the first time since the hostilities began in 1979, the warring forces would actually talk to each other.

But I was there on behalf of the UAW for another reason. I had been on my way to Honduras as part of a delegation of the Commission on U.S.-Central American Relations when news came that the National Labor Committee's campaign to free the STECEL trade union leaders had succeeded.

After their four years in prison without charge or trial, the government had yielded to the pressure and agreed to release them on the same day as the La Palma peace talks opened.

Some of those the UAW had worked with on the STECEL

UAW Region 9A Director Ted Barrett (far right) met with members of the STECEL union who had been jailed for years in Mariona prison in El Salvador. The UAW sent a number of delegations to Central America in the 1980s to offer solidarity support to unions there. Photo by David Dyson.

campaign were excited to have a victory, but I had a vague sense of unease. The timing seemed quite strange. The imprisoned unionists would be freed on the very day that virtually every single journalist in El Salvador would be en route to the La Palma talks several hours away.

Given that the wholesale slaughter of trade unionists had proceeded unabated, it did not seem to be a stretch to think the STECEL leaders would be gunned down at the airport as they prepared to fly to the Netherlands, which had offered them asylum.

Why would government security forces and death squads be willing to have these articulate labor leaders free to travel globally and describe to the broader international community the nature of Salvadoran repression?

I called Dave Dyson, the executive director of the National Labor Committee, and told him of my fears. I urged him to join me in San Salvador and see if we could find a way to protect the STECEL leaders as they went to the airport and departed the country.

Dyson, a superb organizer, also had great courage. On his earlier trips to El Salvador, he had gone to garbage dumps and morgues with Salvadoran unionists and human rights workers to recover bodies. He knew firsthand what the dangers were.

With Dyson on board, I called Janet Shenk in Washington, D.C. She had been with me on my previous trips and delegations. Her book, *El Salvador: The Face of Revolution*, described what was going on there better than anything I had read. Shenk was fluent in Spanish, knew everyone from peasant leaders to cabinet ministers, and was both fearless and smart. She, too, understood what was at stake for the STECEL leaders and agreed to join us.

A few days earlier, one of the worst of the death squads, the Secret Anti-Communist Army (ESA), had issued a press release announcing that trade unionists would be the target of a new killing campaign. ESA had close ties to the National Police and other internal security forces, so it operated with impunity.

That alone was cause for worry.

When Dyson and Shenk arrived, they met me at the Camino Real, where I filled them in. That afternoon, I had a briefing from U.S. Ambassador Thomas Pickering along with other members of the Commission on U.S.–Central American Relations.

During the meeting, I asked the ambassador if he would arrange for me, Dyson, and Shenk to visit the STECEL unionists in the prison. His response: "Perhaps if President Reagan calls (Salvadoran) President Duarte, it might be possible, but nothing short of that will get you in."

The U.S. embassy there repeatedly had sided with the Salvadoran government and found its forces blameless in so many atrocities. So Pickering's comments added to our worry.

From a journalist, I learned that a "Commandante Lara" would be in charge of Mariona prison that evening. Shenk put in a call to the prison, and the second-in-command agreed to let us see the STECEL prisoners if we came right over.

The prison was brightly lit, and armed guards approached

Hector Recinos (left), leader of the STECEL union, meets family members and unionists at the San Salvador airport about an hour after his release from prison. Photo by David Dyson.

us as we pulled up. Shenk talked to the guards, and they allowed her to enter, which worried me. But she was back out in five minutes with bad news. The officer she spoke to checked with the higher-ups, and word came down that under no circumstances were we to be allowed to see Hector Recinos, Jose Valencia, or any of the STECEL unionists.

Hugely disappointed, we departed for the Presidente Hotel in search of Jan Willen Boertens, a diplomat from the Netherlands with whom I had spoken on a number of occasions about the STECEL prisoners. When the Netherlands had agreed to provide the STECEL leaders asylum, Boertens had been at the center of the negotiations with the Salvadoran government.

The first person I saw in the Presidente lobby was Senator Paul Tsongas, a Massachusetts Democrat who had played a role in pushing for the La Palma peace talks. He was with some Salvadoran army leaders, so we said a brief hello and moved on.

The Dutch diplomat was by the pool in a larger group. He joined us off to the side and said the union prisoners were set to be released very early in the morning.

The International Red Cross had agreed to pick them up

and transport them to the airport, where they were to board a commercial flight to Guatemala and then a KLM flight to Amsterdam.

I told Boertens that Dyson, Shenk, and I wanted to join the International Red Cross at the prison and travel together with them to the airport. He responded that the Salvadoran government would not even allow him to do that.

Shenk asked about the unionists' families. Boertens told us that he and an assistant would meet the family members, who also were going into exile, at a home in San Salvador and would transport them by bus to the airport.

Once the prisoners were there, they and their families—a total of 44 people—would be in a locked VIP room along with us and the Dutch diplomats.

Boertens said that when he met with the prisoners in Mariona, they asked what the Netherlands was like. "Well," he told them, "we are a coastal country in western Europe and half of our land is below sea level."

The men huddled and came back to ask: "How can this be? Do people live on barges?"

"No, we have dikes which hold back the water," Boertens replied. On his next visit, he brought some glossy KLM Airlines brochures with photos of blonde women in pigtails with starched white hats, neatly stacked Gouda cheese, and Heineken beer bottles.

The STECEL leaders, in their fourth year in prison, looked at the brochures, talked among themselves briefly, and then told Boertens: "Holland it is!"

Dyson, Shenk, and I returned to the Camino Real fairly hopeful that the arrangements for the release, particularly the involvement of the International Red Cross, would work.

But back at the hotel, the Dutch diplomat had left a message for me. The Salvadoran government, inexplicably, had denied the use of the locked VIP room to the STECEL leaders and their families for the next morning. Instead, they would be forced to wait in the open, accessible to everyone.

That's why I couldn't sleep.

With all the journalists heading north to La Palma, Shenk, Dyson, and I departed for Comalapa Airport at 5 a.m. Our goal was to get there before the STECEL leaders and their families so we could mingle with them and provide some minimal disincentive to a death squad attack.

With an 8-month-old daughter, a 3-year-old son, and a wife back in D.C., this role wasn't particularly appealing to me. But, given the courage shown by so many Salvadorans in their daily lives during the civil war, it seemed like the right thing to do.

Near the airport, we saw two small passenger buses traveling together. Shenk believed it was the families, so we drove along with them for a while.

Once at the airport, Shenk ran up the stairs to a second-level terrace and yelled back at us, "They're here. They're upstairs."

One of the STECEL union leaders, Jose Valencia, made this truck during his years in prison for the grandson he had never seen. The UAW helped win the release of the jailed Salvadoran unionists and their safe transit to exile in the Netherlands. Photo by David Dyson.

There was absolutely no security, no Red Cross, no Dutch. But the STECEL leaders were safe. We all embraced. It was an emotional moment, but I kept scanning the terminal fearing that the worst could happen.

Dyson told Hector Recinos that his son had been on a speaking tour seeking his release and knew now that he would be freed. Jose Valencia showed us a wooden truck he made in prison for a grandson who lived in San Francisco after his wife and two children fled the country.

Then Valencia's smile went away as he told us about another daughter, the 17-year-old who was "disappeared" and later was found in the Santa Ana garbage dump. "She had bullet holes everywhere," he said.

Shenk asked Recinos about his family members who were kidnapped two years before. He responded that the day before, his last day in prison, someone from the army got word to him that his wife and 13-year-old daughter were killed 16 days after he and the other STECEL leaders had been arrested and taken to the Treasury Police headquarters.

The men also informed us that another STECEL member, Ismail Antonio Alvarado Andino, had been in Mariona prison with them. He had been jailed after the original group and had been released April 23, 1984. His body was found May 29.

Recinos said death squads took credit for the killing. Andino had left him a makeshift will "in case anything happened." In the will, he asked STECEL to care for his family.

Then a large group of FENASTRAS members rushed up the stairs, followed by two busloads of family members. The Dutch diplomats were with them.

Children hugged fathers they had not seen in four years, husbands and wives embraced, and the tears flowed.

Andino's widow and two children arrived with the big group of family members. The union looked after its own.

Dyson, Shenk, and I thanked Boertens for all the Netherlands had done to help secure the releases and to provide the

Salvadoran unionists and their families with asylum.

We stood with the large group until they boarded the TACA plane without incident.

Soon, it was wheels up.

The death squads, it seemed, had other business that day.[12]

The National Labor Committee grew to involve about 25 U.S. unions by 1985. UAW President Owen Bieber then co-chaired the group with the Amalgamated Clothing and Textile's Jack Sheinkman, who was the most active union leader in opposing the repression of Salvadoran unions.

The total membership represented by the NLC amounted to more than 7 million workers in the United States, which constituted a majority of the unionized workforce.[13] The size of the NLC and the fact that its membership was made up of some of the most effective unions in the AFL-CIO gave it huge impact but also set the stage for conflict within the labor movement.

Fraser and then Bieber helped set an agenda for the National Labor Committee that often was at odds with the AFL-CIO under its president, Lane Kirkland, a staunch Cold Warrior, who devoted much of his time to fighting what he saw as the evils of worldwide communism.

The UAW often had disagreements with Kirkland's predecessor, George Meany, particularly on foreign policy issues. Those differences and other issues helped spur then UAW President Walter Reuther to orchestrate the union's departure from the labor federation in 1968.

The UAW had reaffiliated in 1981 in hopes that a united labor movement could counter the harsh anti-labor policies of the new Reagan administration, such as the firing of the striking air traffic controllers. But the union remained miles apart from the AFL-CIO on international issues.

The NLC's initial goals were to oppose the repression of workers in El Salvador and press to halt the killings, torture, and imprisonment of trade unionists there. It sought to change the Reagan policy of expanded military aid to the repressive government of El Salvador and feared the former Hollywood actor would send substantial American troops to fight in Central America.

Under Sheinkman, Fraser, and Bieber, the committee saw workers and unions as the victims of political repression there and believed American unions should support their right to organize, bargain, strike, and fight for labor and human rights in the face of right-wing repression.

"An underlying political goal of the committee was to challenge the Cold War framework of U.S. foreign policy, and it argued repeatedly that the conflicts in Central America were caused not by communist subversion or Soviet intervention, but by long-standing poverty and injustice," wrote Professor Andrew Battista in *The Revival of Labor Liberalism* (2008).

"The committee's institutional objective was to promote within the labor movement a new international outlook and role, different from that of the AFL-CIO. . . . For three decades, the AFL-CIO had monopolized control of foreign affairs and remained uncompromisingly anti-communist."[14]

The UAW's policy prioritized worker rights and international labor solidarity and opposed the repression by the right-wing military governments that held power in El Salvador during much of this period. The AFL-CIO, for its part, prioritized staunch anti-communism there that was not inconsistent with the Reagan policy. Throughout much of this period, the National Labor Committee and the UAW opposed military aid to El Salvador, while the AFL-CIO favored it.

"The AFL-CIO saw U.S. military aid and Salvadoran political negotiations (between the government and the FMLN) as complementary, whereas the NLC viewed them as contradictory," Battista wrote.

"The federation accepted the Reagan administration's claim that military aid was necessary to prevent outright victory by the guerrillas and to force them to the negotiating table.

NLC believed military aid undermined negotiations by inducing the Salvadoran military to continue the war and pursue military victory."[15]

Given the size of the labor coalition Fraser, Bieber, and Sheinkman had built, the NLC succeeded at both the 1983 and 1985 AFL-CIO conventions by inserting language into the international affairs resolutions stating that a negotiated settlement in El Salvador was far better than a military solution and calling for negotiations between the government and the opposition.

At both conventions, Jack Howard of AFSCME and I were asked to negotiate with the AFL-CIO international staff and that of the government-funded American Institute for Free Labor Development (AIFLD). They vigorously opposed our approach, but had to yield partially to it because they feared defeat on the convention floor.

The UAW repeatedly had adopted its own convention and International Executive Board resolutions opposing military aid to El Salvador. The union under both Fraser and Bieber lobbied hard in Washington against that military aid and for a negotiated settlement, but that view was opposed by Kirkland's AFL-CIO.

"[The AFL-CIO] remained committed to a particularly hawkish version of anti-communism and Cold War, exemplified by its unstinting support for the war in Vietnam, its fierce opposition to détente, its own international operations in Latin America . . . and its broad sympathy for U.S. policy in Central America in the 1980s," Battista wrote.

"The elaborate bureaucratic apparatus in charge of the federation's international affairs, including the Department of International Affairs and its four overseas institutes . . . helped to sustain a hard Cold War outlook in the AFL-CIO. This apparatus received extensive funds from the U.S. government, amounting to nearly $40 million in 1985, and was led and staffed by hawkish anti-communists drawn from Social Demo-

crats USA. The financial benefits, ideological orientation, and institutional influence of this foreign-affairs bureaucracy all contributed to maintaining a Cold War posture in the AFL-CIO."[16]

Essentially, there were two different world views here. The UAW and the majority of American labor had moved to oppose reflexive U.S. support for authoritarian regimes abroad.

We sought arms control and détente with the Soviet bloc and prioritized economic and social development over militarized Cold War policies favored by Kirkland and the cadre of hard-liners around him who relied on Reagan administration funding for most of their international programs.

The UAW saw the AFL-CIO's support of policies that sustained authoritarian regimes as not only morally wrong, but also harmful because those repressive governments regularly crushed unions and sought to maintain very low wages that harmed both workers in those countries and workers in the United States who had to compete with them.

Much of the internal debate on Central America within American labor, and specifically between the UAW and the AFL-CIO, took place at a time when President Reagan and many American corporations had launched an extremely harsh attack on unions. This placed the Cold War hard-liners in the AFL-CIO's international operations in a difficult place: they were defending much of the Reagan administration's policy in Central America, including military aid, at a time when that same administration sought to crush AFL-CIO unions at home.

Despite the contradictions, the AFL-CIO continued to allow AIFLD and hard-line staffers to call the shots on much of its Central American policy. That policy was moderated to some degree by the fact that two AIFLD organizers and a peasant leader had been murdered in the Sheraton Hotel coffee shop in 1981 by death squad forces tied to the Salvadoran military.

But despite that horrific event, the AFL-CIO continued to support U.S. military aid to the Salvadoran government in various forms throughout the decade of the 1980s. It also supported military aid to the Nicaraguan Contras, military forces that sought to overthrow the Sandinista government in Nicaragua with help from the Reagan administration.

The UAW strongly opposed Reagan's funding of the Contra rebels. The union's legislative department regularly lobbied members of Congress to reject Contra aid. UAW Community Action Program (CAP) delegates every year made the rounds on Capitol Hill urging representatives and senators to reject Reagan's military funding for El Salvador and Contra aid as well.

In a letter signed by UAW President Bieber and other union presidents, the Reagan program in Central America was strongly criticized in 1986.

"The Reagan policy is wrong: it is wasting money . . . it is costing the lives of thousands of innocent people, it is ignoring numerous opportunities for negotiations, and it threatens to draw us into a deeper escalation of the conflict," Bieber and others wrote.

More than 1,000 local union delegates to the UAW CAP Conference in 1986 affirmed a task force report that stated:

"Legislatively, it's important for us to continue opposing military and other aid to the Contras. Aid to El Salvador should not be provided until that country reforms its judicial system, ends the killing of its citizens by death squads and security forces, and implements true land reform and full trade union rights among other conditions."

The UAW delegates did not hesitate to criticize the Sandinistas, noting that "in Nicaragua, abuses of democracy by the Sandinistas continue." But they concluded that, "We must insist on human rights and social justice in both El Salvador and Nicaragua; a diplomatic solution—not a military one—must be our constant objective for peace in that area."[17]

UAW Region 1 Director Perry Johnson went to Nicaragua and El Salvador in 1985. He reported back that some criticisms of the Sandinista government made sense, particularly limits it imposed on the right of unions to strike from 1982 to 1984. But he warned that the Reagan administration policy of providing military aid to the Contras posed the risk of pushing Nicaragua toward the Soviet Union.

Johnson said he and others on a National Labor Committee delegation found widespread opposition to the U.S.-backed Contras. The top Nicaraguan labor leader, who opposed the Sandinista government, told the group that "we do not support U.S. aid to the Contras."[18]

The UAW lobbied hard to defeat a Reagan proposal in the U.S. House of Representatives to provide $100 million in direct military and other aid to the Contras in 1986. The union had also joined in earlier successful efforts to limit Contra aid proposed by U.S. Rep. Edward Boland.

Secretly, the Reagan administration then funded the Contras through an "arms for hostages" deal. It involved facilitating the sale of missiles and other military weaponry to Iran, despite a pledge Reagan had made not to fund terrorists. This violated an arms embargo against Iran.

Lt. Col. Oliver North, a top official in Reagan's National Security Council, and others took proceeds from arms sales to Iran and diverted the money to fund the Contras seeking to overthrow the Nicaraguan government. What became known as the "Iran-Contra affair" ended in 11 convictions of those involved, including high-ranking Reagan administration officials. Some convictions were vacated on appeal, and later President George H.W. Bush pardoned the others.

UAW member John Linder was one of many labor activists who joined in large protest demonstrations in Washington on April 25, 1987, urging a negotiated settlement to the Central American conflict. Linder, a member of UAW Local

1921, was a laid-off aerospace worker who had worked at Martin Marietta.

His brother, Ben Linder, was an American engineer doing volunteer work with Nicaraguan peasants, helping to build a dam that would provide water and electrical power to people there.

Contra forces shot and killed Ben Linder on April 28, 1987, in an ambush near the dam construction site. An autopsy showed he had been wounded by a grenade, then shot at point-blank range in the head.

Later, Linder's mother, Elisabeth, said: "My son was brutally murdered for bringing electricity to a few poor people in northern Nicaragua. He was murdered because he had a dream and because he had the courage to make that dream come true."[19]

But Elliott Abrams, then Reagan's assistant secretary of state and a strong backer of the Contra war, blasted Ben Linder, saying he should have known better than to have been in a combat zone. Republican U.S. Rep. Connie Mack echoed Abrams in a congressional hearing. He told Linder's grieving mother that he was going to be tough on her because "I really feel you have asked for it."[20]

Ben Linder's death came as the Iran-Contra affair had become a huge national scandal for the Reagan administration.

UAW member John Linder spoke to tens of thousands in Nicaragua on May 1, 1987, and told the crowd about his brother, who used his talents as a clown, juggler, and unicyclist to entertain local children in El Cua, where he lived.

"It is a crime that the U.S. government, speaking in the name of democracy, is waging a war against the interests of the big majority of the U.S. people," he said.

The Iran-Contra scandal got most of the political attention in the late 1980s, but the situation in El Salvador worsened during this time. Public television carried a documentary in 1988 called "El Salvador: Our Forgotten War." Yet both Rea-

gan and George H.W. Bush who followed him in early 1989 continued to send $1 million of taxpayer funding each day into El Salvador while death squads still ran rampant.

In February 1989, after much pressure from the UAW and other unions in the National Labor Committee, the AFL-CIO Executive Council called for an end to all military aid to El Salvador until the "violators" of human rights were brought to justice. The council also supported "negotiations leading to an end to the conflict in El Salvador."

The month before, I had joined Jack Sheinkman, who by then had become president of the Amalgamated Clothing and Textile Workers Union, and William Winpisinger, president of the Machinists union, on another trip to El Salvador.

We visited trade unionists at workplaces and in union halls throughout the country. One union we met with had lost seven activists in 11 months. Six had been assassinated in broad daylight, while one was "disappeared."

In a report on that trip, "El Salvador: Critical Choices," our delegation stated:

"Most Salvadorans still live in abject poverty; the economy continues to crumble; the 'death squads' are on the rise; trade unions are prime targets; the civil war rages; and innocent people still die.

"Runaway shops from the U.S. are lured to the region by the prospect of cheap labor and 'free trade zones.' When Salvadorans try to organize, union halls are bombed and organizers are shot. Despite a dismal and well-documented record of labor rights abuses, El Salvador continues to receive special trade preferences from the United States."

One of the union leaders we met was a hospital worker, Freddy Torres. He was a world-class judo champion who competed in the Olympic Games in both Los Angeles and Seoul, South Korea. The day before Torres was to leave for the 1988 games, he was attacked by armed men who screamed they were going to kill him. Because of his strength and judo skills, he fought his attackers and escaped.

Torres grew up in the slums of San Salvador and started work at age 9 in a mattress factory. By 17, he was married and a father. He took a job at the Social Security Hospital in 1982 and joined the union there.

In 1984, Torres and other union members went on strike and won wage increases. They struck again the next year, but their pay couldn't keep pace with the rampant inflation in El Salvador. Three years later, he became one of the hospital union's top staff members and soon was targeted by management.

"They always accuse us of being with the guerrillas," he told us. "They say that so that they can justify whatever they do."

As Torres was leaving judo class in April 1988, he was kidnapped by 10 armed men, who said they had taken his family as well. Everyone would be released, the paramilitary troops said, if he would admit he was a guerrilla.

After taking him to a cell block in the notorious Treasury Police headquarters, soldiers stripped Torres and made him stand for hours without sleep. When he defended the union, they forced him to do exercises for hours. After he did 3,000 deep knee bends, his kidnappers laughed and said he had just broken the Salvadoran record.

"Had I not been in top shape, I would have died," Torres told us. After being moved to Mariona Prison, he eventually was released.

"They told me if I continued to work with the union, they would come back, and this time they would finish the job," he said.

One of Torres' union colleagues, Eliseo Cordova, also was targeted by paramilitary forces. Immediately prior to the opening of contract negotiations, Cordova was abducted along with his nephew and a lawyer. All were blindfolded and driven around until dark. They were taken to an abandoned field, where the troops took off their blindfolds, but shined lights in their faces.

"Then they told us to run," Cordova's nephew recalled. He and the lawyer escaped. "Then I heard shots. I never saw my uncle again."

By 1989, real wages in El Salvador were half what they were in 1980. Only 30 percent of Salvadoran workers had jobs. The minimum wage was 40 cents an hour in the city, 20 cents in the countryside. Most two-income families earned only 50 percent of the minimum amount needed to maintain basic nutrition.

The Reagan and Bush administrations had poured in more than $3.3 billion in economic aid during that decade, yet the country had become poorer than before U.S. intervention. America provided 55 percent of El Salvador's national budget in 1989, yet much of that taxpayer money funded a government and a military that targeted trade unions and opponents for kidnapping, torture, and death.

By then, more than 70,000 Salvadorans had been killed—many of them trade unionists.

The far-right ARENA party took control of the government in 1988. In our NLC delegation report, we noted: "In the year since the ARENA party gained control of the National Assembly, the levels of torture, disappearances, assassinations, and political imprisonment have increased."

ARENA, the party founded by death squad leader Roberto D'Aubuisson, also controlled the judiciary. The National Labor Committee noted "not one officer or public official implicated in the murders of tens of thousands of innocent civilians has been brought to trial."

But perhaps the most important conclusion of our delegation was that, after eight years of massive U.S. aid and tens of thousands of deaths, the United States continued to stand by a "failed policy."

"More military aid, and the destruction it brings, will not address the underlying poverty, injustice, and despair which are

After nearly 13 years of civil war, a United Nations peace process that had begun in 1990 actually began to make progress. In early 1992, the FMLN and the Salvadoran government initialed a peace agreement that was followed by a nine-month cease-fire.[21]

The peace deal required that the Salvadoran government reduce the armed forces by 70 percent. It also caused the hated National Guard, Treasury Police, and National Police to be disbanded and the intelligence services to be removed from military control and transferred into the office of the presidency. The armed FMLN forces also disbanded.

By 2009, the FMLN, which had reorganized as a political party, won the Salvadoran presidential election. It won again in 2014. A number of Salvadoran activists who the UAW worked with in the 1980s ended up holding top positions in the new, progressive governments, including Francisco Altschul, a close ally of the UAW during the conflict, who became Salvadoran ambassador to the United States in 2010.

The progressive governments went on to adopt many social reforms aimed at combating poverty. Among them:

- pensions for the elderly;
- monthly stipends for workers receiving job training;
- land reform that more fairly distributed land;
- free meals and uniforms for schoolchildren;
- abolition of healthcare fees and introduction of community health programs;
- higher teacher salaries; and
- programs to reduce illiteracy.

Much of the progress made in El Salvador in recent years amounted to the adoption of the agenda pushed by worker activists and trade unions.

Sadly, thousands of unionists killed by right-wing security forces and death squads are not there to see that progress.

at the root of the civil war," the report said.

Despite a number of peace proposals put forward by the Catholic Church, other Central American leaders, and the international community, the calls for a negotiated settlement to the conflict got little attention from the right-wing government of El Salvador, nor from the Republican administrations in Washington, D.C.

"In El Salvador, the Army is the real power," our delegation found. "As long as their bills are paid by U.S. tax dollars, resistance to any 'peace plan' is understandable."

CHAPTER ELEVEN

UAW: Close School Of The Americas
U.S. Trained Human Rights Abusers

Yes, they killed nuns, often raping them first. Yes, they killed children, too. Not only the 15- and 16-year-olds, but toddlers and babies as well.

And, of course, they killed unionists and worker activists, who were prime targets.

The list is so long: teachers and peasants, priests and archbishops, students and the elderly—thousands killed in the most horrific ways over the years by graduates of the School of the Americas (SOA).

SOA, now renamed the Western Hemisphere Institute for Security Cooperation, is a combat training school for Latin American soldiers and police paid for by the American taxpayers.

Since 1946, more than 64,000 of those forces have been trained by the U.S. military and then returned to their countries, where some have committed horrible atrocities.

"Unfortunately, it's been a real bad history of graduates of the School of the Americas being involved in some of the worst human rights abuses in Central America," UAW President Bob King told WMNF radio in 2010.[1] Each year since 2001, UAW members from across the country have joined in protest vigils near Fort Benning in Georgia, where SOA has been based since 1984.

"We're there demanding the School of the Americas be shut down, because an attack on a trade unionist in Central or South America is an attack on the UAW," King said. "Over the years, the soldiers from SOA have led death squads, killed striking workers and union organizers, raped nuns and children, and suppressed popular movements."

The now retired UAW president, an Army veteran, made clear that he and other labor protesters have great respect for the U.S. troops who work at Fort Benning, which is the army's major training facility that enables highly skilled American troops to be deployed wherever needed to protect the nation. The problem is with the far smaller separate operation that trains about 700 to 1,000 Latin American soldiers each month.

The UAW has supported SOA Watch, which began the effort to close the school in 1989 after 26 soldiers in El Salvador entered the Pastoral Center at the Central American University in San Salvador. The troops forced five Jesuit priests to lie facedown on the ground in the courtyard and then shot and killed them. A sixth priest, the housekeeper, and her 16-year-old daughter were murdered inside the residence (see previous chapter).

"The Jesuits had been labeled 'subversives' by the Salvadoran government for speaking out against the socio-economic structure of Salvadoran society," according to Amnesty International.

The human rights group found that 19 of the 26 soldiers involved in the horrendous killings had received training at the School of the Americas at Fort Benning.

SOA Watch repeatedly has documented the role of the School of the Americas in sending soldiers back to their home countries, where they have joined death squads, secret police units, and shadowy paramilitary groups. Among the atrocities SOA soldiers have been found guilty of or linked to are:

- the El Mozote massacre of about 800 civilians, including children and babies, in El Salvador in 1981;
- the assassination of Salvadoran Archbishop Oscar

Romero in 1980;

- the killings of eight members of the San Jose de Apartado peace community in 2005 in Colombia;
- the overthrow of the democratically elected president of Honduras in 2009; and
- the rapes and murders of four American churchwomen in El Salvador in 1980.

In addition, a number of U.S.-trained SOA graduates went on to become dictators of their home countries.

Take Efrain Rios Montt of Guatemala, who took power there in a military coup in 1982. Earlier in his military career in 1951, he received training from U.S. forces at the School of the Americas, which then was based in Panama.[2] After seizing power, Rios Montt launched a scorched earth campaign that killed more than 3,000 people each month. He declared a state of siege that severely restricted trade unions. Labor activists were targeted by his death squads. Amnesty International estimated that about 10,000 indigenous Guatemalans and peasants were murdered during a six-month period in 1982.

U.S. President Ronald Reagan, a strong supporter of Rios Montt, provided his regime with more than $10 million in military supplies while the slaughter went on. Reagan repeatedly praised the Guatemalan dictator, who had by then left the Roman Catholic Church and become close to right-wing American evangelicals including Jerry Falwell and Pat Robertson.

Years after the slaughter of many thousands of Guatemalans, the School of the Americas graduate finally faced trial. Rios Montt was convicted of genocide and crimes against humanity on May 10, 2013, bringing further shame to the SOA and its American supporters.

Judge Yasmin Barrios found that Rios Montt "is responsible for masterminding the crime of genocide." The former dictator received a sentence of 80 years in prison and became the first former head of state to be convicted of genocide by a court in his own country.[3] Some 200,000 people were killed

in Guatemala's civil war, which went on from roughly 1960 to 1996. Prosecutors detailed how Rios Montt ruled during the bloodiest phase. They argued that the School of the Americas graduate turned a blind eye as soldiers used torture, rape, and killing against those suspected of supporting leftist rebels in Guatemala.[4]

Predictably, despite the overwhelming evidence, Guatemala's Constitutional Court ordered the trial be "reset" to its status as of April 19, 2013, on what most objective legal observers found to be questionable grounds. In January 2015 the trial resumed, but was suspended until an appeals court selected a new judge.

The UAW's strong push to organize pressure to close the School of the Americas clearly would have been justified for the SOA's role in training dictators such as Rios Montt. But the broader record is even more appalling. Here are some examples.

Argentina

Leopoldo Galtieri received SOA training paid for by U.S. taxpayers and went on to lead the military junta in Argentina during which at least 30,000 people were killed or disappeared.

Many of the victims were worker activists and union leaders. An investigation by the National Commission on Disappeared Persons, a government body that in the 1980s examined what occurred during the military dictatorship, found that abductions of union activists occurred at Ford and Mercedes-Benz auto factories in Argentina. UAW President Douglas A. Fraser protested the repression by the Argentine military regime at the time.

Some Ford autoworkers survived Galtieri's human rights crimes. Pedro Troiani, for example, worked on the line at Ford's Buenos Aires plant, when he was paraded through the factory at gunpoint, bound with wire for eight hours, and then taken in a company truck to a soccer field where the army had opened a detention center.

He later described being repeatedly beaten, tortured, and deprived of sleep and food, according to a *New York Times* account.[5]

"Jail was pure terror because people were disappearing all the time and you didn't know if you were going to be the next to be killed," Troiani said.[6] Although he survived, Ford had fired him for absenteeism. Troiani, who was held in three different prisons, eventually lost his claim for back pay from Ford for the time he was imprisoned on the grounds that the statute of limitations had expired.

Chile

The majority of the Chilean military leaders who overthrew the democratically elected government of Salvador Allende in 1973 attended the School of the Americas.[7]

Many of the leaders of DINA, the Chilean intelligence agency, also were SOA graduates who have faced "innumerable accusations of summary executions, assassinations, torture, murder, kidnapping, and disappearances."[8] A Spanish judge sought indictments against 30 Chilean officers for crimes of terror, torture, and kidnapping, and 10 of those had been trained at the School of the Americas.

Bolivia

General Hugo Banzer Suarez, a graduate of the SOA, led a bloody coup against Bolivia's President Juan Jose Torres in 1971. The seizure of power by the military occurred after Torres had allowed a labor leader, Juan Lechin, to return to his position as leader of the Bolivian Workers' Union. The coup appeared to have the support of the Nixon administration. General Banzer moved immediately to suspend the Bolivian Workers' Union and took thousands to "the horror chambers" in the basement of the Ministry of the Interior, where they were tortured and some were killed.

Captain Tito Montano Belzu, whom American taxpayers funded to study small unit warfare at the SOA, went on to be convicted of murder and genocide in connection with a bloody 1980 coup.[9] In 2002, Bolivian Captain Filiman Rodriguez studied at SOA (by then renamed WHINSEC) despite the fact that the Bolivian Chamber of Deputies found him responsible for the earlier kidnap and torture of Waldo Albarracin, then director of the Popular Assembly for Human Rights.[10]

Haiti

Colonel Franck Romain, an SOA graduate, opened fire on a church where he shot and killed 12 parishioners and wounded at least 77 others. Then, he set the church on fire and later claimed the massacre was justified.[11]

Another SOA graduate, Colonel Gambetta Hyppolite, ordered his soldiers to fire on an election office in 1987.

Honduras

Juan Lopez Grijalba, a School of the Americas graduate, has been accused of leading a special military unit responsible for the disappearances of more than 150 people. He was located in the United States in 2002, deported in 2004, and found responsible by a Miami federal court for torture and disappearances.[12] Other Honduran SOA graduates, including Generals Luis Alonso Discua, Gustavo Alvarez Martinez, and Bali Castillo, operated the notorious army death squad known as Battalion 3-16. Here's how author Lesley Gill described their work: "Small groups followed victims for days or even weeks before agents driving vehicles with stolen license plates kidnapped them and took them to clandestine jails, where the disappeared were tortured, interrogated, and usually executed."[13]

Panama

More than 3,600 soldiers from Panama attended the SOA. Manuel Noriega, an SOA graduate whom American taxpayers paid to train, became the country's dictator. He was forcibly extradited by U.S. forces and continues to serve time for drug trafficking, now in Panama.

Paraguay

A School of the Americas graduate, General Roberto Knopfelmacher, was charged with the assassination of peasant leaders and the forcible removal of families from their homes and land.

Peru

General Ismael Araujo, an SOA graduate, has been accused of involvement in a prison massacre in which 120 people were killed, most of whom had already surrendered.[14] Another SOA alum, General Juan Velasco Alvarado, overthrew an elected government. Fellow graduates were accused of drug trafficking, summary executions, leading death squads, and torture. Three high-ranking Peruvian military officers who attended the School of the Americas were convicted in 1994 of murdering nine university students and a professor. General Nicolas Hermoza Rios was imprisoned after he pleaded guilty to taking more than $14 million in illegal arms deals.[15]

Venezuela

In April 2002, Army Commander-in-Chief Efrain Vasquez and General Ramfrez Poveda, both School of the Americas graduates, helped lead a failed coup. In 1996 General Ramon Davila Guillen, an SOA graduate, was indicted for shipping one ton of cocaine into Miami. He claimed the shipment was authorized by the CIA, which dismissed the CIA agent involved and called the shipment "a regrettable incident."[16]

John Davis, who worked 28 years for General Motors, had never heard of the School of the Americas. But in the fall of 2005, Davis drove five hours to Columbus, Georgia, to join with other UAW members, including two busloads from Atlanta organized by Region 8. They were there for the annual vigil to commemorate victims of the SOA and to demand the school be closed.

Davis, the Region 8 webmaster, turned to the Internet to learn about the SOA. He didn't like what he found after just an hour of online research.

"Basically, it was clear that the School of the Americas was using our tax dollars to train mercenaries for Central and South America," Davis recalled in a phone interview. "Those mercenaries returned to their countries and murdered priests and nuns and union people—anyone who pushed for social justice.

"It seemed we were training terrorists, and they then would kill people in Latin America and hold down those in poverty," he said. "The goal seemed to be to protect corporate America's operations there and keep people in poverty so they could be controlled."

Davis found many UAW members at the SOA vigil along with a diverse group of protesters. "The crowd was definitely a mixture, with everything from college students to elderly people in wheelchairs in attendance," he said. Attendees included members of Veterans for Peace dressed in their military uniforms, nuns and priests in formal habit, Buddhist monks in robes, and workers from other unions, such as SEIU and the Steelworkers.

"Labor was founded on the idea that an injury to one is an injury to all," Davis later wrote. "If we truly believe in democracy, then we can't tolerate the killing of innocents and the shedding of blood for corporate profits. Taking lives in South America is just as much of a tragedy as taking lives in North America."[17]

Davis took note of the poor state of the housing near Fort Benning where families of troops serving in Iraq, Afghanistan, and elsewhere lived while awaiting their soldiers' return. To him, it seemed wrong that millions of dollars of defense funding were going to the School of the Americas while the troops' families were stuck, in some cases, in substandard housing.

After hearing speeches by leaders of SOA Watch, religious organizations, human rights groups, and the UAW, Davis said his mind "was racing with mixed emotions."

"It is unnerving to know that our government is training potential terrorists with our tax dollars," Davis said. "But the showing of young people at the vigil left me with hope."

Despite a very clear record of human rights atrocities by its graduates, the SOA always has had defenders. The most common argument they use is that it is only a few "bad apples" who have given the school a bad name.

This is hardly a compelling defense, given the huge number of fully documented cases of assassinations, killings, rapes, torture, disappearances, military coups, and other crimes committed by SOA graduates.

But it is particularly difficult for SOA supporters to defend the repeated targeting of trade unionists, worker activists, and their families by those who have graduated from the school.

In 1996, Dana Priest of *The Washington Post* reported that U.S. Army manuals used to train Latin American military officers and soldiers at the SOA advocated executions, torture, and blackmail against a range of citizens, including those who:

- support "union organizing or recruiting";
- distribute materials "in favor of the interests of workers";
- "sympathize with demonstrators or strikes"; and

Graduates of the U.S.-funded School of the Americas assassinated San Salvador's archbishop, Oscar Romero, in 1980. Demonstrators above marched on the fifth anniversary of Romero's killing. In February 2015, Pope Francis declared Romero a martyr, a step toward sainthood.

Another atrocity committed by military forces trained by U.S. taxpayers occurred in 1989. Salvadoran soldiers murdered six Jesuit priests who were scholars at Central American University. They also killed the Jesuits' housekeeper and her daughter.

- make "accusations that the government has failed to meet the basic needs of the people."[18]

The SOA training manuals specifically identified as targets "religious workers, labor organizers, student groups, and others in sympathy with the cause of the poor."

The manuals, paid for with U.S. taxpayer funds, encouraged the use of fear, payment of bounties for enemy dead, beat-

ings, false imprisonment, executions, and the use of truth serum, according to a secret Defense Department summary put together during an investigation of the instructional materials being used at Fort Benning by the SOA.

One of the manuals said SOA graduates returning to their home countries might cause the "arrest of the employee's parents, imprison the employee, or give him a beating" to coerce cooperation.

More than 1,000 of the torture manuals were distributed in countries such as El Salvador, Guatemala, Ecuador, and Peru in addition to their use at SOA in Fort Benning.

An internal investigation of the materials occurred after the U.S. Southern Command evaluated the manuals in 1991 for use in expanding military support programs in Colombia.[19] Dick Cheney, then secretary of defense, received the report that five of the manuals "contained language and statements in violation of legal, regulatory, or policy prohibitions."

Cheney, later to become a strong advocate of torture during his time as vice president in the post-9/11 era, reviewed the investigation of the illegal manuals and had little choice but to order they no longer be used.

Details of the SOA manuals and the targeting of trade unionists for torture and execution became public in 1996. In the aftermath, *The Los Angeles Times, The New York Times, The Chicago Tribune, The Boston Globe, The Washington Post, The Atlanta Constitution, The Cleveland Plain Dealer*, and many other papers either ran articles critical of the SOA or called on the United States to close it altogether.[20]

Around the time the torture manuals surfaced, Sister Dianna Ortiz, a U.S. citizen and Ursuline nun, received new attention for her horrifying story. She was kidnapped by Guatemalan troops in 1989 while teaching Mayan children to read. Here is what she said:

"I was tortured and raped repeatedly. My back and chest were burned more than 111 times with cigarettes. I was lowered into an open pit packed with human bodies of children, women, and men, some decapitated, some lying face up and caked with blood, some dead, some alive and all swarming with rats. . . .

"The memories of what I experienced that November day haunt me even now. I can smell the decomposing bodies. . . ."[21]

The arrest and torture of Sister Ortiz became public, in part because she was an American citizen. But the U.S. Embassy in Guatemala (during the presidency of George H.W. Bush) initiated a smear campaign against her.[22] Later, a U.S. court found General Hector Gramajo, an SOA graduate, responsible for Ortiz's abduction and torture. In his court statement, the general blamed her hundred-plus burn marks on a failed lesbian affair. Two years after the torture of Ortiz, General Gramajo delivered the commencement address at the School of Americas.

Jerry King works in the trim department at a Chrysler plant in Warren, Michigan, where the Dodge Ram is assembled. He helped organize a large delegation from Local 140 that attended the November 2013 protest vigil at Fort Benning.

"I read about the School of the Americas in *UAW Solidarity* magazine and I had my curiosity sparked," Jerry King said.

King went to the SOA vigil in 2012 with two other UAW members after he learned more about it through his involvement in the union's Community Action Program (CAP) and his attendance at the UAW Black Lake education program.

"This year [2013] I'm more armored. I know more about the SOA and how it all ties in to the fact that greed drives the machine," the Local 140 member said. "In the UAW, we have to stand up for other people so they can't pit us against workers in other countries. We need to get everybody's standards to come up."

In the fall of 2013, King used his Facebook page to invite 600 "friends" and had 32 commit to attending the vigil several weeks before it occurred.

Brian Schneck, president of UAW Local 259 in New York, regularly shows members a DVD detailing the atrocities committed by SOA graduates.

"Most people don't know anything about the School of the Americas and the fact that American taxpayers have paid to train terrorists who have gone back to the militaries in Central and South America to keep the people down," he said.

Schneck credits Father Roy Bourgeois, who founded the SOA Watch, with inspiring him and many other UAW members who have joined in the vigils at Fort Benning. Father Roy was invited to a UAW conference in Pittsburgh attended by then Local 259 President Bill Pickering.

"Bill came back and said you've got to check this out—it's unbelievable how this could be happening in our country," Schneck told me. "I had a strike going on, but I went down to the vigil in 2003 on the weekend. Father Roy and people from all different walks of life really inspired me to get involved in the union's effort to close the School of the Americas."

Another UAW member paid a tough price for her opposition to the School of the Americas. Rebecca Kanner "crossed the line" at the protest vigil at Fort Benning in November 2000. She and 25 others were convicted of criminal trespass in the U.S. District Court for the Middle District of Georgia in May 2001.

Kanner had engaged in nonviolent civil disobedience in previous years and crossed the line in 1997, 1999, and 2000. She received a six-month sentence, which she spent at the Women's Work Camp in Pekin, Illinois.

"This trial is not about whether I crossed that line at Fort Benning or not," Kanner said in her court statement. "Rather, this trial is about bringing truth to the lie that SOA/WHINSEC helps Latin American governments to promote stable democracies. This is an obscene lie. The opposite is true.

"The victims of SOA graduates are those working for a

better life: working for land reform, for better wages, for adequate housing and healthcare for the poor," she told the court. "Over the years, we've learned that SOA graduates have been responsible for countless atrocities . . . the atrocities continue."

Kanner had helped organize workers at the Ecology Center of Ann Arbor (Michigan) who now are members of UAW Local 174.

Bob King, then a UAW vice president, read about Kanner's civil disobedience in a local newspaper. "When we talked, Bob asked what he could do to support me," Kanner said later. "I asked if he would take my place in the November 2001 vigil, since I'd be in prison, and so Bob joined the SOA protest that year and has not missed one since."

Kanner noted that then UAW President King also lobbied Congress to shut down the School of the Americas.

"He has joined religious leaders, torture survivors from Central and South America, human rights activists, and other labor people in going to Capitol Hill to urge members of Congress to close SOA," Kanner told me.

She said elected officials and aides they met would often ask: "What's the UAW doing here lobbying on this issue? We don't see how it relates to unions."

Kanner said labor activists had to educate representatives and senators and their staffs about targeting of union activists in Central and South America by School of the Americas graduates.

"The biggest victims of SOA violence are those who are organizing in these countries to make their lives better," she noted. "Often, it's union organizers and worker activists who bear the brunt of the repression."

In an eight-page spread in *UAW Solidarity* magazine in 2010, the UAW president pointed out that "in our early organizing days, the UAW would never have been successful without the support of other unions and people of conscience—we have a moral responsibility to support unionists, community

activists, and others in Central America working for democracy and justice."[23]

U.S. Representative James McGovern, a Democrat from Massachusetts, has led the congressional effort to deal with the abuses of the School of the Americas, or WHINSEC. His bipartisan bill, the Latin America Military Training Review Act, was cosponsored by U.S. Rep. John Lewis and had strong support from the UAW, AFL-CIO, Steelworkers, NAACP, Veterans for Peace, Amnesty International USA, and many religious groups.

In a letter to members of Congress in 2011, McGovern urged them to join in cosponsoring H.R. 3368 in the 112th Congress and made a number of arguments:

- SOA/WHINSEC now refuses to allow public access to the names of students for the last six years, which reversed the 40-year policy that allowed taxpayers to monitor the abuses SOA graduates committed upon returning to their home countries. How do we advance military-to-military relationships when the Pentagon insists it will not and cannot monitor, track, or remain in contact with SOA graduates once they return to their home countries?

- None of the fundamental issues raised around the need to close the SOA have been addressed by the renamed WHINSEC: not its training methods, nor its lack of oversight, nor the school's record of graduating human rights abusers.

- The U.S. Army and the Office of the Secretary of Defense have failed to deal seriously with the record of the SOA. A comprehensive review of U.S. military training of Latin American soldiers and police needs to be undertaken, as well as an *independent* inquiry into past training abuses.

- Human rights abuses and problems with civil-military relations are not, unfortunately, a thing of the past in Latin America. We need to look no further than recent events in Mexico, Honduras, Colombia, Haiti, Guatemala, and Bolivia to understand that Latin America is still grappling with the question of how to train, respect, and institutionalize, within its military establishments, proper civil-military relations. The Pentagon and Justice Department have reputable long-standing programs aimed at promoting human rights within Latin American military institutions. SOA/WHINSEC training programs add little to those respected efforts and bring instead a history that is greatly tainted.

- In no other region of the world has the Pentagon determined that a separate military training institute is necessary in order to build military-to-military relationships. Why are Latin American military officers alone singled out for such privileges, especially when so many past graduates have failed the test of leadership when challenged to protect and promote human rights and the rule of law upon returning to their own countries?

"For most Latin Americans, the U.S. has focused too much attention on courting its militaries, and not enough on strengthening civil society, democratic institutions, or effectively addressing long-standing problems of inequality and poverty," McGovern said in his letter. It urged that SOA/WHINSEC operations be suspended and a bipartisan review be conducted to examine foreign military training needs in Latin America and the Caribbean.

The UAW supported the McGovern legislation and, indeed, has had a long record of urging Congress to act on the School of the Americas.

In May 2004, UAW Legislative Director Alan Reuther wrote to House of Representative members that "the UAW believes that WHINSEC is a relic of the Cold War that serves no meaningful purpose today."

Reuther pointed out the U.S. Army officially closed the "infamous" School of the Americas in January 2001 and "sub-

sequently reopened a virtually identical Department of Defense facility at the same location named the Western Hemisphere Institute for Security Cooperation.

"It is now apparent that the Army has simply changed the name of the school, and has not taken steps to address the many serious concerns which have been raised by Congress," the UAW legislative director said.

He said the renamed SOA merely continued virtually the same courses, had not changed staff, and kept the same training approach.

"Thus, it is evident that the Army has failed to deal seriously with the problems that led to the closure of the SOA," Reuther said. "Instead, it has simply tried to paper over the problems with a change of names without any underlying reforms to the operation of the school."

The UAW argument was underscored by the late Republican U.S. Senator Paul Coverdell, a strong supporter of the School of the Americas, who called the name change to WHINSEC "cosmetic" and agreed the shift was merely to allow SOA to "continue its purpose." A strong opponent of the SOA, the late U.S. Rep. Joseph Moakley, said at the time of the name change that it was "like pouring perfume on a toxic dump."[24]

School of the Americas Watch leaders held a meeting with Denis McDonough, then deputy national security adviser to President Obama, in November 2012. They gave him a letter from the UAW urging the closure of the School of the Americas/WHINSEC.

McDonough, who became President Obama's chief of staff, has a deep Roman Catholic justice background, graduated from St. John's University and Georgetown, and comes from a family that includes two priests. He acknowledged past support for SOA/WHINSEC but expressed openness to hearing more from those opposed to it.

One of those who met with McDonough, Adrianna Portillo-Bartow, told him how troops in Guatemala directed by

UAW members from Region 1A marched with union members in El Salvador to commemorate the one-year anniversary of the murders of the Jesuit priests, their housekeeper, and her daughter. The killings were committed by graduates of the U.S.-funded School of the Americas.

SOA graduates trained in the United States executed six members of her family, including her 9- and 10-year-old daughters. In Latin America, she said, the SOA is a symbol of horror, pain, and suffering, and there is deep resentment that it remains open and unaccountable.[25]

The issue of what benefit American taxpayers get from the millions of dollars that go to the renamed School of the Americas gets less attention than it should from Congress and the Obama administration. But more and more countries in Latin America have doubts about the value of sending their soldiers to Fort Benning for training.

The disillusionment began in the 1980s when Panama demanded that the United States remove the SOA from its country. Jorge Illueca, then Panama's president, said the School of the Americas was the "biggest base for destabilization in Latin America." Later, his anger was underscored by the repression and drug trafficking of SOA graduate Manuel Noriega that did great harm to Panama.

More recently, SOA has hemorrhaged support. Argentina, Bolivia, Ecuador, Venezuela, and Uruguay all have withdrawn from participation in the program. Other countries, such as Colombia, where very serious human rights abuses occur regularly, including the killings of trade unionists, still send soldiers and police to SOA/WHINSEC for training at U.S. expense.

Some of the erosion of support came as the result of democratic elections in some Latin American countries, as military regimes have given way to new leaders with popular support.

To Rich Feldman, a UAW member who coordinated the 2013 union delegation to the SOA Watch vigil and protest in Georgia, the action is a deep expression of "the very soul of the union."

"The UAW loses its center of being if it becomes focused around only the struggle to make a living," Feldman told me. "Our union has a broad vision of the global fight we are in and how much deeper that fight is beyond just the closure of the School of the Americas.

"Our activism on SOA is linked to the UAW's effort to work in our communities to stop the race to the bottom," Feldman argued. "This fight is about values and how we can work to battle the way U.S. capitalism has allowed people in Latin America to be made into the 'other.'"

For Rebecca Kanner, the former UAW organizer who spent six months in prison for her civil disobedience at the School of the Americas in 2000, the fight still energizes her.

"One year, Bob (King) brought one of his daughters to the vigil in Georgia," Kanner recalled. "In a restaurant in Columbus, she summed it all up by saying that labor folks in Latin America were being killed for exactly the same sorts of activities her dad was doing here in the U.S."

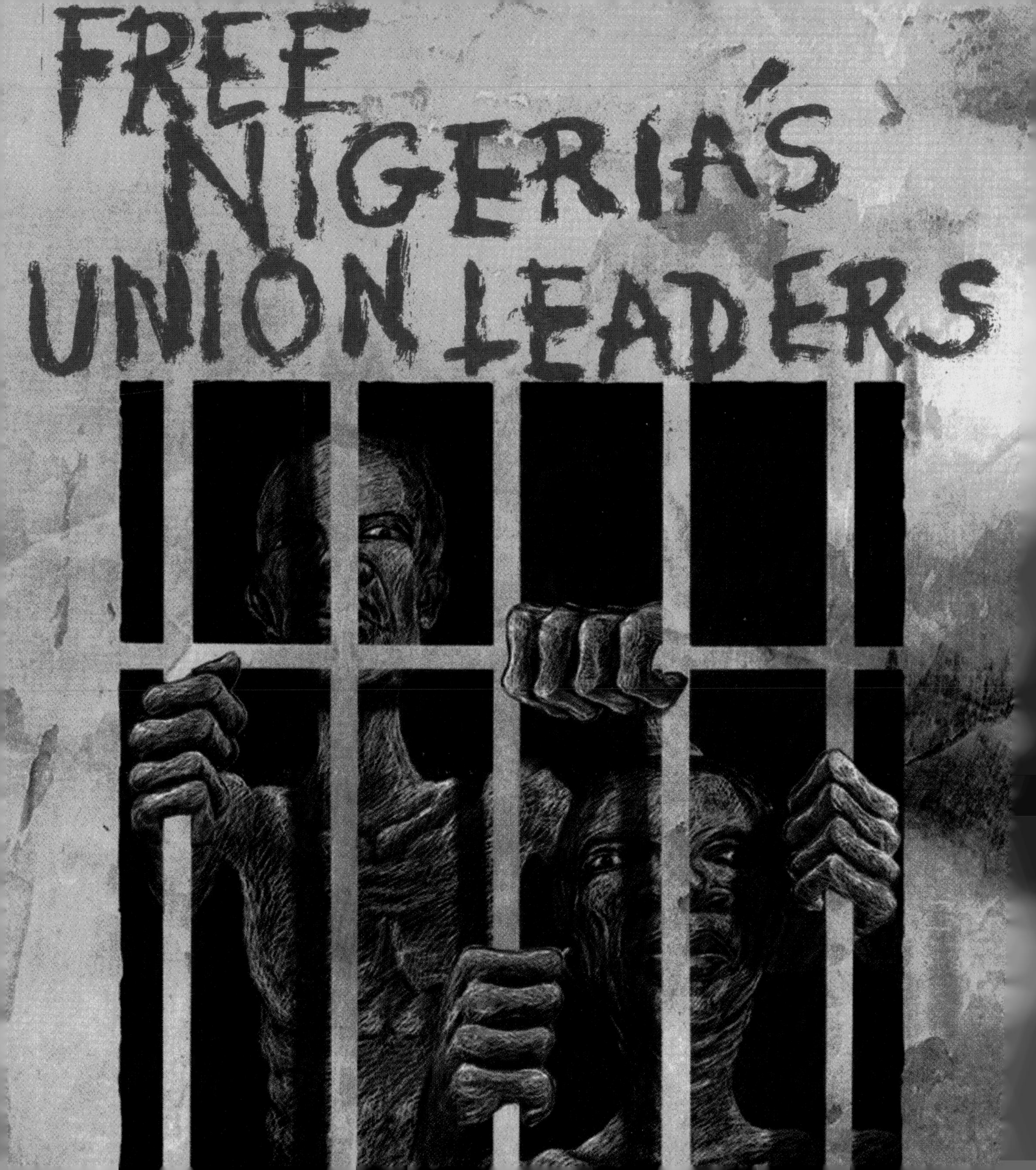
FREE
NIGERIA'S
UNION LEADERS

Nigeria: The Struggle Against Labor Repression
How The UAW Worked To Free Leaders Of Oil, Gas Unions

When the UAW's 32nd Constitutional Convention convened in Las Vegas in June 1998, President Stephen P. Yokich and the union's leadership faced a number of tough issues, including a dispute with General Motors in Flint, Michigan. It involved strikes by 9,200 members that had shut down 24 of GM's 32 North American assembly plants.

Yokich promised delegates the union would "last one day longer than GM." But on this day, the UAW president wanted several thousand union activists to focus on a different struggle—this one far away in Africa.

"I want you to join me in celebrating the UAW's success in winning freedom in Nigeria for the two leaders of the oil and gas unions, Frank Kokori and Milton Dabibi, who were released a week ago after years in prison for leading strikes there," Yokich said. "This huge victory comes after years of work by our union and our allies, but the fight for labor rights and democracy in Nigeria is far from over."

It was a special moment for Yokich, who had taken up the fight for trade unions in Africa that former UAW President Owen Bieber had waged so vigorously before him, particularly on behalf of South African workers repressed by apartheid. The African American leadership of the UAW had played an important role in the union's anti-apartheid effort and also pushed for support for workers' struggles elsewhere in Africa and globally.

Some of the interest in Nigeria grew from contacts the UAW had through the International Metalworkers' Federation, the Geneva-based global union federation in which the union was a major player. Bieber, Yokich, and I had met with Nigerian autoworkers at international meetings, particularly those from

the General Motors plant outside of Lagos, Nigeria.

As labor militancy in South Africa played out on the international stage, unions in other African countries emerged as potent forces pressing for worker gains and greater democracy. Workers had been crucial to the independence struggles in Africa in the 1960s. It was the trade union movement that helped put an end to one-party regimes in Malawi and Zambia, and in the 1990s workers fought for democratic freedoms in the streets of Nigeria, Kenya, Mali, and Zimbabwe.

The surge in union activity alarmed the rulers of a number of African countries, including Nigeria, one of the most populous and resource-rich nations on that continent. In 1993, the military annulled the results of Nigeria's presidential elections after the labor-backed candidate, M.K.O. Abiola, won the vote and declared himself the duly elected president.

Abiola, a wealthy businessman with some ties to the military, had developed alliances with the democratic opposition, including the Nigerian Labour Congress (NLC), one of the few organizations with both national scope and mobilization capacity. The military, which had some erosion of its own political base in the predominantly Hausa-speaking and Muslim north, moved to void the election and then jailed Abiola, the newly elected president.

In July 1994, the oil and gas unions called a general strike against the anti-labor policies of General Sani Abacha, who had seized power and crushed the pro-democracy movement.

Nigeria at that time relied on oil exports for 95 percent of its foreign exchange earnings and 80 percent of its government revenue. The strike by the National Union of Petroleum and

Natural Gas Workers (NUPENG) and the Petroleum and Natural Gas Senior Staff Association of Nigeria (PENGASSAN) threatened General Abacha and the military, which needed the oil and gas revenue to finance their regime.

Initially, the strike grew out of grievances including what the unions regarded as unjustified layoffs and the use of armed guards to break up labor disputes in the oilfields. But there were broader issues of democracy that fueled the stoppage.

"Our struggle for economic emancipation cannot be separated from the political struggle for democracy and accountability in government," said Milton Dabibi, PENGASSAN's general secretary, as the strike spread across Nigeria in 1994. Dabibi labeled the strike a "patriotic struggle" to save the industry and the nation from collapse.[1]

Frank Kokori, general secretary of the 60,000-member oil and gas union, was arrested August 19, 1994, as the strike in the oil and gas fields became a general strike embraced by the Nigerian Labour Congress. The military refused to negotiate and instead sent troops to crush the protests. In addition to Kokori, security forces sought to jail Dabibi of the gas union, but he went underground and evaded them for two years.

The dictatorship also issued a series of extraordinary decrees aimed at destroying the union power base. The decrees did the following:

- dismissed many of the striking workers;
- dissolved the oil and gas unions' executive councils and installed government-appointed officials to run the unions' affairs;
- dissolved the national executive committee of the Nigerian Labour Congress and put the federation under the regime's control;
- forcibly merged existing unions from 41 down to 29 unions and restricted who could be elected to run those unions;

- froze union bank accounts and banned checkoff of union dues;
- fired leaders of the three university unions, which had been active in the general strike, and banned those organizations from trade union activity; and
- occupied union offices with troops and/or police.

Later, as the UAW and other international labor allies came to the support of Nigerian workers, General Abacha voided the unions' international affiliations.

Although the repressive decrees and arrests did not end worker actions against the regime, the restrictions put labor on the defensive, and additional strikes by civil servants, teachers, and oil workers eventually came to an end.

Despite the continuing imprisonment of Kokori, efforts by the UAW and other allies seemed to yield a breakthrough in January 1996 when four leaders of the oil workers' union were released. Wariebi K. Agamene, A. Aidelomon, M. Eleregha, and F. Addo, important leaders of NUPENG, had been detained without trial in the summer of 1994.[2] But our optimism soon was crushed.

On January 25, 1996, Milton Dabibi, leader of the PENGASSAN, finally was discovered in hiding and jailed shortly after he returned from an appearance at the AFL-CIO convention in New York City, where the UAW and other unions forced out old guard leaders of the U.S. labor federation in the hopes of reenergizing it. The Nigerian dictatorship did not charge either Kokori or Dabibi with any crime. Both were denied medical attention and prevented from having access to lawyers. They were barred from contact with their unions, and family visits were severely restricted. General Abacha's harsh treatment of Kokori and Dabibi made it clear just how dangerous the collective power of the oil and gas unions was to the military regime.

This internal repression spurred new initiatives by labor in

Nigeria to seek allies outside the country, including the UAW, which had developed a strong profile for its solidarity work on behalf of the independent black trade union movement in South Africa. Some Nigerian unionists at the GM plant outside of Lagos, which by this time was barely producing because the economy had collapsed into disarray under Abacha, also reached out to the UAW through the International Metalworkers' Federation.

Another global union federation with which the UAW was affiliated, the International Federation of Chemical, Energy, Mine and General Workers (ICEM), put its resources behind the developing campaign to support Kokori and Dabibi and the Nigerian struggle. (ICEM and the IMF merged with the textile sector federation to form IndustriALL in 2012.)

During this period, UAW President Yokich had been spending more time in Washington, D.C., following his crucial role in electing SEIU President John Sweeney to head the AFL-CIO.

I had long discussions with Yokich about the need to reform the labor federation's international affairs operation. Un-

The UAW's African American leadership energized the union's postcard campaign seeking the release of the jailed leaders of Nigeria's oil and gas unions in 1996.

der George Meany and Lane Kirkland, the AFL-CIO international staff had been dominated by hardline anti-communist ideologues with minimal interest in the affiliates' priorities of global solidarity for organizing and bargaining, particularly at U.S. operations of foreign companies.

I suggested to Yokich that he urge Sweeney to take up the plight of Kokori and Dabibi and put the federation behind a campaign for their release and for labor rights and democracy in Nigeria. Given that Dabibi had been arrested just after attending the AFL-CIO convention, such a campaign seemed compelling.

Sweeney quickly agreed, but asked Yokich if the UAW would spearhead the effort. Barbara Shailor, international affairs director of the Machinists union, had just been appointed to that role at the AFL-CIO, and we worked with her on this project.

The template for the campaign grew out of the UAW's success in winning freedom for Moses Mayekiso, the leader of the metalworkers' union in South Africa, in the late 1980s. The UAW developed a "Free Kokori, Free Dabibi" campaign that was used to involve local union activists. We also produced a poster for local union halls and a brochure with more details on the case with tear-out postcards that could be sent to both the Nigerian embassy in Washington, D.C., and General Abacha, the country's ruler.

The text of the postcard read:

"I demand the immediate and unconditional release of union leaders Frank Kokori and Milton Dabibi and an end to suppression of human and labor rights in Nigeria. I support multi-party democracy and political freedom there."

UAW members and other labor and progressive allies who filled out the postcards provided their names and addresses. While the cards were addressed to the Nigerian leaders, the address where they were sent was the UAW Washington office.

This solved the confusion over postage to Nigeria for the

Abacha card, which earlier experience had taught us tended to cause some people to not carry through with sending the card off in the mail. But perhaps more importantly, we would receive the cards and tally the names and addresses of campaign supporters before forwarding them on. This enabled us to follow up with communications to those activists who already had invested in the campaign.

We would pass out the brochures, postcards, and posters at UAW meetings, just as we had with the Mayekiso materials. When possible, the postcards would be signed and collected on the spot. The supply of filled-out cards would then be sent in batches of 10–15 each day to Dr. Wakili Hassan Adamu, the Nigerian ambassador to the United States.

One of the most successful moments of the campaign came at a large-scale "Free Tibet" rock concert, where thousands of cards were distributed and gathered.

The UAW began meeting with a "roundtable" of groups in support of the campaign. The SEIU under new leader Andy Stern played a big role in the effort and assigned a staff member who was an immigrant from Nigeria to work fulltime on the issue. Amnesty International also supported the effort, as did other human rights and religious organizations. The Sierra Club also became active in the campaign, given the prominence of the oil issue.

In addition to the UAW and the AFL-CIO, other U.S. unions worked with us, particularly the Oil, Chemical, and Atomic Workers (OCAW), the Communications Workers of America (CWA), the United Mine Workers of America (UMWA), and the American Federation of State, County and Municipal Employees (AFSCME). Ken Zinn, with whom the UAW worked closely on the Shell Boycott campaign to support South African workers, played a big role as North America coordinator of ICEM.

Working with Shailor and the AFL-CIO, both the Inter-

After harsh years in Nigerian prisons, Frank Kokori and Milton Dabibi came to the United States to thank the UAW for its crucial role in winning their freedom. They met with the author in the union's Washington, D.C., office in 1998. Photo by Kristyne Peter.

national Labor Organization and the International Confederation of Free Trade Unions adopted resolutions calling for the release of Kokori, Dabibi, and all Nigerian political prisoners. The international groups also pushed for broader initiatives for labor rights and democracy in Nigeria, and some urged an embargo on Nigerian oil.

Dutch and Belgian unions also were important actors in the broader campaign. The Dutch, for example, staged a powerful symbolic protest at a soccer match between the Netherlands and Nigeria in the run-up to soccer's World Cup.

The union and human rights protesters, including the president of the Dutch labor federation FNV, wore T-shirts proclaiming an "alternative Nigerian" team that included Kokori and Dabibi. TV coverage of the soccer match beamed back to Nigeria showed Amnesty International advertising signs near the goals that demanded "Fair Play for All."

The campaign got a powerful and unexpected boost when Pope John Paul II, on his first visit to Nigeria in 16 years, called on the Abacha regime to release all political prisoners.

Back in the United States, we found a terrific ally in Cordelia Kokori, the daughter of the jailed oil union leader. Several years earlier she had relocated to America. Labor Rights Now arranged numerous speaking engagements for her to talk about her father's imprisonment and the need for labor rights and democracy in Nigeria.

Just as Moses Mayekiso's wife Khola had proven a natural on the campaign trail in union halls, churches, and press conferences, so, too, did Cordelia Kokori. Kristyne Peter of the UAW International Affairs Department arranged for her to speak at a convention of the Coalition of Labor Union Women (CLUW), which adopted a resolution calling for the release of Nigerian union leaders.

In addition, the UAW's top African American leaders enlisted a wide variety of organizations, such as the Coalition of Black Trade Unionists and the A. Philip Randolph Midwest Conference, which adopted statements demanding the release of Kokori and Dabibi.

AFL-CIO President Sweeney further raised the profile of the campaign with a letter to Hassan Sumonu, general secretary of the Organization of African Unity, urging that other African leaders pressure General Abacha to release Kokori and Dabibi and restore labor rights in Nigeria.

Another front in the effort was opened when we helped arrange for Cordelia Kokori to appear at the Mobil Oil shareholders' meeting. We viewed Mobil as a business partner of the Nigerian military regime and, with our allies, wanted to pressure it and other big oil companies to end their silence on Abacha's repression of their workers.

The shareholder resolution at that 1998 Mobil meeting in Reston, Virginia, was introduced by the SEIU Master Trust pension fund.

"Reports from Nigeria indicate that these union leaders are very sick and may die in jail," said the SEIU fund in a statement. "Mobil must use its influence with the Nigerian government to seek the release of the duly elected leaders of its Nigerian employees."

In the run-up to Mobil's annual general meeting, progressive shareholder groups had asked simply for Mobil officials to request a meeting with Kokori. The company refused.[3]

At the shareholders' meeting, Mobil CEO Lucio Noto disavowed all knowledge of Kokori.

When Cordelia Kokori eventually gained the floor, she confronted Noto: "You say you don't know my father. Let me tell you about my father." She then described how Frank Kokori had been imprisoned and abused for four years without any contact with his family.

Her calm but chilling story shamed Noto, who quickly dropped his bravado and told her: "I can't imagine what you and your family are going through. I will be in Nigeria this fall and will bring up the case of your father and other political prisoners."

Noto nevertheless opposed the SEIU shareholder resolution, but it received enough votes to be reintroduced the following year.

Another company, Sun Oil, faced a major demonstration at its shareholders' meeting in Philadelphia in May 1998. The Oil, Chemical, and Atomic Workers (OCAW) union organized that protest, which added to the negative media coverage of multinational oil companies operating in Nigeria.

Faced with mounting international pressure, much of it driven by the UAW and its allies in the international labor movement and progressive community, General Abacha began to promise to restore democracy in Nigeria. Yokich called me to ask how realistic Abacha's commitments were.

My response was simple: the Nigerian dictator felt the heat and feared economic sanctions, but clearly was promising democracy under tightly controlled conditions that negated his promise. None of the repressive laws had been repealed, nor were political prisoners released or organizations unbanned. The military government sought the trappings of democracy with none of its content as a means to transform Abacha from dictator to a "civilianized" president.[4]

He had called for a presidential vote on August 1, 1998, but had strong-armed the country's five political parties to endorse him, and became the only presidential candidate.

Then, in a bizarre twist, the 54-year-old Abacha suffered a massive heart attack on June 8, 1998. The Nigerian military maintained foul play was not involved, although before his death Abacha was reportedly in the company of two Indian prostitutes imported from Dubai, who allegedly had laced his drink with a poisonous substance.[5] With the military in disarray, the UAW and AFL-CIO called for a major demonstration on June 17 at the Nigerian embassy in Washington. Our sense was that this was the time to maximize our pressure on the regime.

General Abdulsalami Abubakar became the new military ruler of Nigeria after Abacha's death. He initially promised to follow Abacha's agenda, but soon felt the heat and embarked on a cautious but unmistakably clear democratization process.

Within a week of taking power, General Abubakar ordered that Frank Kokori and Milton Dabibi be released.

It was a huge victory for the UAW and for many other allies who had fought so hard in the campaign to win freedom for Kokori and Dabibi.

Later, we learned that the release of the oil and gas union leaders came so quickly after Abacha's death because General Abubakar believed the military would get "credit" with the broader international community that had threatened sanctions and economic reprisal for Nigeria's violations of human and trade union rights.

Two months after Kokori and Dabibi left prison, the Nigerian government repealed a number of anti-labor decrees. The oil and gas unions regained control of their organizations, as did the Nigerian Labour Congress and the three university staff unions. A number of the other objectionable decrees remained on the books until 1999, but then were lifted.

Auditors eventually discovered the military regime had looted about $5 million from the Nigerian union federation. When officers returned to their headquarters, they found their offices had been ransacked, stripped of computers, telephones, and furniture. General Abacha and his family later were shown to have stolen or embezzled about $4 billion in government and other funds.

Political life slowly normalized in Nigeria with local and state elections held on schedule and in a manner that observers concluded was free and fair. In February 1999, General Olusegun Obasanjo of the People's Democratic Party was elected Nigeria's president. Soon after his inauguration, Obasanjo ordered the retirement of 93 senior military officers, including the powerful heads of the army, navy, and air force and every officer who held a government position in previous military regimes, including those of Abacha and Abubakar.

The UAW, in an analysis commissioned after the campaign to free Kokori and Dabibi and to roll back the attack on labor rights had succeeded, nevertheless saw that "while much has been accomplished, much remains to be done."

Though there are many areas in which to advance solidarity, according to the 2000 study, four main themes stood out:

1. **Rebuilding trade union capacity:** Material and technical aid is needed to restore the Nigerian unions' physical infrastructure and administrative systems to overcome the destruction suffered during the Abacha years. Such assistance is essential to help develop the unions' capacity to engage government and business.

2. **Interventions to strengthen democratic institutions in Nigeria:** Labor will gain immensely from the deepening and consolidation of democracy in Nigeria. American trade unions can assist this process by building links to other organizations dedicated to ensuring a free Nigeria.

3. **Using pressure and supporting campaigns to resist World Bank and IMF** efforts to impose strict structural adjustment policies on Nigeria.

4. **Providing solidarity during campaigns** against multinational corporations, including oil companies, that violate Nigerians' labor, social, and environmental rights.

The UAW's analysis noted that such measures by themselves could not produce a democratic Nigeria, but in contributing to the development of labor rights they could help ensure that Nigerian workers were in a position to promote the political, social, and economic development of their country.

In October 1998, freed labor leaders Frank Kokori and Milton Dabibi came to Washington, D.C., to visit the UAW and the AFL-CIO to offer thanks for the global solidarity support during their imprisonment.

Kristyne Peter and I met with them in the conference room of the UAW's Washington office and asked for their ideas on what American unions could do to support the Nigerian labor struggle going forward.

Then we walked to the Tabard Inn, a restaurant a few doors down from our office. While there, Kokori related details of the abuse he suffered while in prison.

"They can keep you in an inhuman environment," he said. "The weather could be very, very hot. They will tell you to feed on substandard, subhuman meals in a very poor environment . . . very bad putrid smell.

"And they keep you in such a place without medical attention and in complete solitude," he said. "I was kept in a place where I was out of touch with my own tradition. I was in a place where the language I couldn't understand.

"If you are in prison and you are kept in a place where you can chat with fellow prisoners, it makes life go on," Kokori told us. "But if you are kept in isolation, in complete solitude, you will see that one hour is like the whole day. The day does not move. The time stays still, so the problem is boredom, extreme boredom for four years."

After we finished dinner and walked outside, Kokori embraced Peter and then me and said simply: "Thank you to the UAW for getting us out."

AÑA ALT

Photo by David Bacon.

CHAPTER THIRTEEN

Solidarity Helps Mexico's Workers Fight Back
NAFTA Hurts Those On Both Sides Of Border

Agapito Gonzalez Cavazos, a union leader in Matamoros, Mexico, left negotiations with factory managers to attend a party for his daughter on a dark night in January 1992 when about 30 plainclothes cops surrounded his car.

The "special team" from the Mexican federal judicial police grabbed the 77-year-old Gonzalez, who soon found himself on a government helicopter taking him to a jail cell in Mexico City.

The government, led by President Carlos Salinas, charged the union leader with cheating on his taxes in 1988. However, a judge quickly dismissed the charges on grounds that Gonzalez in fact had paid the taxes he owed.

Angry officials of the Salinas government soon found a friendly judge who ordered the union official held on another tax charge. Gonzalez, who had undergone several heart-bypass operations, collapsed and ended up in a hospital with police guards at his bedside.

Because the UAW had supported the workers in Matamoros, I soon received calls from reporters asking about the Gonzalez affair.

"He basically was arrested two days before a strike deadline for 33 more maquila factories," I told Tim Shorrock of the *Journal of Commerce*. "One would have to find the timing curious."[1]

Just before the federal police grabbed Gonzalez, selective strikes at 17 plants had been settled, with workers winning 25.4 percent wage increases. Nearly 15,000 workers had walked out at three plants owned by General Motors and six other workplaces.

With thousands more workers set to strike, the timing of the arrest of Gonzalez clearly appeared aimed at removing the union leader and weakening the workers' bargaining position at a crucial moment.

UAW President Owen Bieber compared it to "conduct we have come to expect in countries such as South Africa or Korea—countries known for their repression of workers and unions."

In a letter to Mexico's ambassador to the United States, Gustavo Petricioli, Bieber said: "At a time when our two countries are engaged in talks over greater economic integration, this incident raises serious questions about the degree of commitment to internationally recognized labor rights in Mexico."[2]

Before the arrest, the UAW had sent $15,000 for strike support to the union known as the Union of Day Laborers and Industrial Workers.

It represented about 34,000 workers in the Matamoros area who were employed at some 77 foreign-owned maquiladora plants. The factories operated in Mexico under special tax breaks that allowed them to assemble products from imported parts for export back to the United States duty free.

Because nearly all of the maquiladora workers in Matamoros belonged to the union, unlike those in other border towns, they earned slightly higher wages that averaged about $13 per day.

Gonzalez had angered the big American companies that had located there because workers did not hesitate to strike to win the gains they sought. Union leaders elsewhere in Mexico generally had been less than militant, due in part to their close ties to the ruling PRI party, which had controlled Mexico for decades.

The strike deadline for the 33 plants without contracts was postponed to February 10 after Gonzalez's arrest.

The UAW set out to determine how we could help get

Gonzalez released and back to the bargaining table. We knew there was little the UAW could do on the details of the tax charges against him.

But our Mexican allies told us that authorities there actually seemed to tolerate some level of tax avoidance. They questioned the timing of reviving allegations from 1988 on the eve of crucial strikes in Matamoros.

We quickly found some facts that confirmed our suspicions. Four days after the selective strikes that Gonzalez had called, Mexican President Salinas had met with a group of top executives, including some from General Motors, Zenith, and other maquiladora employers in Matamoros. Those businessmen had told Salinas that Agapito was being unreasonable.[3]

The Matamoros Association of Maquiladoras had taken ads in newspapers in Mexico City and Matamoros asking President Salinas to intervene in the negotiations.

"Agapito needed to be cut down to size," according to one member of the employers' group.[4]

Paul Blanco, a former president of the association, made the employers' position very clear: "We want someone [in the union] with a different attitude."[5]

This was not the first time the employers had appealed to President Salinas when Gonzalez and his union negotiated with greater militancy than those in other maquiladora zones. In 1990 the Associated Press reported, "There are indications the Mexican government wants to throttle Gonzalez."

It quoted Jim Ebersole of the Economic Development Council in Brownsville, Texas, across the border from Matamoros: "The [Mexican] government is really fed up with this guy because of the harassment he's given our companies."[6]

The earlier whining of the corporations that resented the union in Matamoros resulted in Salinas moving the negotiations in 1990 to Mexico City, with Gonzalez not allowed to participate. The companies won concessions "to discipline workers without union permission" and wage increases 10 per-

cent below what had been expected.[7]

In addition, two weeks after the settlement, government auditors from the Treasury Department in Mexico City went to the union headquarters in Matamoros and seized a truckload of documents from Gonzalez, which they took back to the Mexican capital.

"The move raised speculation the government might use the threat of investigation to keep Gonzalez in line," the Associated Press reported.[8]

Given this background, the UAW contacted political allies in the U.S. Congress, including U.S. Representative Don Pease and House Majority Leader Richard Gephardt, after Gonzalez was arrested in 1992. Both began to put pressure on the Mexican government to release Gonzalez.

UAW President Bieber received a response to his letter to Mexican Ambassador Petricioli, who wrote that "no one is above the law in Mexico; and anyone who commits a crime must stand before justice, regardless of his or her occupation."

Leonardo Ffrench, a spokesperson for President Salinas, defended the jailing of Gonzalez in the midst of the Matamoros bargaining and denied it had anything to do with the pressure from the maquiladora association in their discussions with Salinas just days before the arrest.

"This is a brouhaha over nothing," Ffrench said.

As for the employers' association, their spokesperson told the media the arrest of Gonzalez during the negotiations was nothing but "a bizarre coincidence."[9]

Gonzalez languished for months under "house arrest" in the Mexico City hospital. The union "had already begun to lose ground in the contracts negotiated after his departure."[10]

The labor leader's son, Agapito Gonzalez Benavides, who also was the union's attorney, acknowledged the setbacks caused by the combined strength of Mexico's government and the powerful American corporations operating the maquiladoras.

"You might say Agapito has got the message," he told reporters.

Twenty years after implementation of the NAFTA trade deal opposed by the UAW, about 42.2 percent of the Mexican people continued to live in poverty. Photo by David Bacon.

The UAW continued to fight for the release of Agapito Gonzalez, primarily through pressuring political leaders in Washington, D.C.

Congress had voted to place the free-trade agreement that eventually became known as NAFTA on a so-called "fast track." That meant that a Mexico free-trade deal had to be voted on in Congress promptly and without amendments.

To win enough Democratic votes to pass fast track, President George H.W. Bush promised that Mexico would uphold internationally recognized labor rights. With one of the few Mexican union leaders willing to challenge employers now being held under "house arrest" by the Salinas government, that promise seemed hollow.

"The Matamoros incident reflects what is wrong with President Bush's approach to trade," said Andrew Reding at the time. Reding directed the Mexico project of the World Policy Institute. "The administration has argued that free trade will expand employment and markets in both countries. The maquiladoras have indeed created hundreds of thousands of jobs. But they pay absurdly depressed wages, which do little to develop Mexico's market or stem the northward flow of migrants.

"Mexican workers are denied basic human rights," Reding noted. "U.S. workers are forced into surrendering wage gains or losing their jobs outright."[11]

Finally, in October 1992, President Salinas allowed Gonzalez to be released. He returned to Matamoros to lead the Union of Day Laborers and Industrial Workers.

UAW President Bieber continued to criticize the Mexican government's blatant interference in the bargaining but expressed relief that Gonzalez had been freed. Privately, he worried that the Mexican union leader's health had been harmed by the ordeal.

Steve Beckman, a trade expert on my staff, followed Mexican labor issues closely. Both he and I believed it had been important for the UAW to support the Matamoros workers in the bargaining and to fight for Gonzalez's release after the arrest.

But we knew full well that Gonzalez was no choirboy. His union lacked the democratic principles supported by the UAW, and he ruled by fiat. Gonzalez was a sort of old-school boss who tolerated no dissent.

Many of his negative qualities could be found in other labor leaders who made up the Confederation of Mexican Workers (CTM), but very few of them had Agapito's willingness to allow workers to challenge employers at the bargaining table and to strike to achieve real gains. After some 30 years of compliance with the companies, Gonzalez gave workers there some room to fight. It was this "weakness" in dealing with the workers that the government and the CTM resented.

Fidel Velazquez Sanchez, a reactionary in his late 80s who was doggedly loyal to the PRI, at that time ran the CTM.

Under Velazquez, CTM unions throughout the country entered into "protection contracts"—effectively sweetheart

contracts benefiting employers instead of workers, who often had no idea that a union actually represented them. Employers sought out the CTM regularly to prevent workers from being organized by independent unions that also faced government hostilities.

The UAW had little contact with the CTM and opposed its reactionary politics and its regular sellout of Mexican workers.

In the late 1980s, AFL-CIO President Lane Kirkland had pressed Bieber and other leaders of federation affiliates to participate in meetings with the CTM. After general discussion, smaller meetings of Mexican and American union leaders occurred on a sectoral basis.

The AFL-CIO and CTM paired Bieber with Hector Uriarte, who had been appointed by Velazquez to represent the CTM autoworkers. The UAW president came away unimpressed and, after two meetings, stopped participating.

A year or so later, Bieber was shocked to learn that the CTM's Uriarte had led a group of thugs into the Ford plant in Cuautitlan. About 2,500 Ford workers had stopped work after a small number of co-workers had been arrested as the result of disputes over Ford's cuts in the Christmas bonus. The workers also demanded the CTM allow them to elect their own leaders, rather than have them appointed by the CTM.

After the thugs entered the Ford plant, workers fought back with whatever they could find: scrap metal, tools, and other implements on the shop floor. They outnumbered the attackers and began to drive them back. At that point, the armed men fired on the Ford workers, wounding 12 of them. Cleto Nigno, who had been shot in the back, died several days later.

After firing on the Ford workers, the attackers refused to allow the Red Cross into the plant to treat the wounded. Some of them hid out in the plant but were apprehended by groups of workers who had searched for them. Three of the attackers were turned over to the police.

Ultimately, the three told authorities that Hector Uriarte had hired them. The Ford workers at Cuautitlan remained on strike, demanding union elections and the arrest of Uriarte. Velazquez, under pressure, decided to remove Uriarte as leader of the Ford union.

Mexico's attorney general, Humberto Benitez, announced in late January 1990 that a warrant had been issued for Uriarte's arrest. Uriarte ultimately was charged with homicide, criminal association, and injuries against workers.[12]

The CTM autoworkers' leader avoided arrest for four years but finally was detained by Commander Fernando Sandoval Acosta of the State of Mexico Judicial Police in late October 1994.

Sylvia Hernandez, who worked at a Zenith factory in Reynosa, Mexico, came to Kansas City, Missouri, at the invitation of UAW Region 5 to talk about the conditions she and other workers faced each day.

UAW members who gathered in Swope Park with the Maquiladora Task Force listened intently as Hernandez told them she earned about $35 for her 50-hour work week and described her living conditions: "There is no electricity, no drinkable water, and no sewers—intestinal illnesses are very common."[13] Maria Teresa Frias of the Border Committee of Women Workers said massive pollution in the maquiladora area harmed workers' health. Plants along the U.S. border routinely dumped fungicides, pesticides, and solvents into streams and canals, she told the crowd of about 350 workers.

After their speeches, Hernandez and Frias were presented bouquets of red roses by Dianna Forster, who had worked at Jerrold Electronics in Kansas City. Forster lost her job, along with 190 other workers, when the company moved the plant to Mexico to take advantage of the extremely low wages there and the nonexistent health and safety standards.

UAW President Owen Bieber closed the meeting by telling the workers that "ours is not a fight that pits American workers against Mexican workers. Ours is a fight together for basic fairness for workers in both countries."

That philosophy guided the union's solidarity work with Mexico. A number of UAW regions, including Region 5 and Region 1A, have sent delegations south of the border during the last 25 years. Often the focus of these trips was for UAW activists to meet with their counterparts at companies that had closed plants in the United States and moved them to Mexico.

A particular area of UAW solidarity work was health and safety. The union had highly skilled experts, some with doctoral degrees in the field. They often traveled to Mexico, particularly as the UAW developed close ties to independent unions such as the Authentic Labor Front (Frente Auténtico del Trabajo or FAT), and to groups such as the Coalition for Justice in the Maquiladoras.

One example was UAW support for workers at Autotrim and Customtrim, two factories in Tamaulipas, Mexico, owned by an American company, Breed Technologies. The Mexican workers produced vinyl covers and leather for gearshifts and steering wheels installed in vehicles bound for the U.S. market.

UAW occupational safety and health department staff had conducted workshops at the two firms and learned about the risks in their workplaces.

"My wife and I had a baby," one of the Mexican workers said in testimony before the National Administrative Office (NAO) of the U.S. Labor Department. "It lived only two days. If I had known about the chemicals I worked with, I would have done something."

Another said he had been exposed to toxic substances for seven years when the daughter born to his wife died two hours after birth from anencephaly. Eighteen days later, another worker's daughter died due to hydrocephaly.

Both Customtrim and Autotrim exposed their Mexican workers to glues, adhesives, and solvents used in mounting leather covers over plastic parts. In addition to miscarriages

and birth defects, the chemicals caused extremely high rates of respiratory difficulties, sleep disorders, memory loss, fainting spells, and other health problems.

"One day, I started to have trouble remembering names," another Mexican worker testified at the hearing. "I had trouble concentrating, too. I saw other workers with the same problems I had, and I could hear them breathing hard when they worked with the yellow glue."[14]

Dr. Lida Orta-Anes, a UAW ergonomics specialist, testified as an expert witness on behalf of the Autotrim and Customtrim workers. She described the irreversible damage to hands caused by severe production standards the companies required of the workers.

They had to perform repetitive motions while placing their limbs and bodies into distorted, awkward positions. Workers as young as age 31 had developed permanent disabilities in their hands, wrists, elbows, shoulders, and backs, the UAW expert told the NAO.

On April 6, 2001, the NAO issued a report confirming worker allegations of unsafe chemical exposure and injuries from poor ergonomic conditions.[15] It also highlighted the Mexican government's failure to ensure employers protected the health and safety of the country's workers.

Unfortunately, President George W. Bush and Secretary of Labor Elaine Chao showed little interest in taking the steps available under procedures established by the North American Free Trade Agreement (NAFTA) to see that Mexico's lack of health and safety enforcement was remedied.

The UAW's strategy evolved into a vigorous program of "training the trainers." A joint project with the Coalition for Justice in the Maquiladoras sought to educate Mexican workers who could be trained and then go back into factories where the knowledge they gained could be spread widely. The hope, sometimes realized and other times not, was to empower workers to demand safer workplaces.

The union worked with the Canadian Auto Workers and others to offer workshops in Spanish on ergonomics, toxicology, and other issues. The training was identical to that provided to UAW locals, using translated versions of the same health and safety materials.

UAW President Steve Yokich strongly supported the project and noted in the union magazine, "It is important to establish international solidarity with our Mexican brothers and sisters. We need to remember that it is the corporations undermining American jobs, not Mexican workers."

J obs were at the very center of the debate in the early 1990s over a proposed free trade deal with Mexico.

The UAW strongly opposed what developed into the North American Free Trade Agreement. President George H.W. Bush had begun negotiations with the strong backing of U.S. corporations, and soon Canada was included in the talks.

When President Bill Clinton took office, he made NAFTA his top priority and put healthcare and labor law reform on the back burner in a move that strongly alienated unions and many of the grassroots progressive forces that had helped elect him. Clinton won NAFTA's passage in 1993 in an orgy of crass backroom deals, mainly to win reluctant Democratic votes.

Clinton had claimed that NAFTA would create an "export boom to Mexico" that would create 200,000 U.S. jobs in two years and a million jobs in five years.[16] The president said NAFTA would produce "many more jobs than will be lost" due to rising imports.

"Fast forward 20 years and it's clear that things didn't work out as Clinton promised," reported the UAW-supported Economic Policy Institute (EPI). "NAFTA led to a flood of outsourcing and foreign direct investment in Mexico."

"By 2010, trade deficits with Mexico had eliminated 682,900 good U.S. jobs, most (60.8 percent) in manufacturing," the EPI found. "Worse yet, production workers' wages

The NAFTA trade agreement cost hundreds of thousands of jobs on both sides of the border. In Mexico, a farmer in Oaxaca rallied to protest the deal, which also severely hurt agricultural workers there.
Photo by David Bacon.

have suffered in the United States. Likewise, workers in Mexico have not seen wage growth. Job losses and wage stagnation are NAFTA's real legacy."[17]

Free trade supporters in 2013 continued to claim NAFTA had succeeded, and the corporate news media and dogmatic economists often echoed the claim. The U.S. Chamber of Commerce, for example, argued that NAFTA "trade" created millions of jobs. The EPI noted those claims were based on dishonest accounting, which counts only jobs gained by exports but ignores jobs lost due to growing imports.[18]

The UAW did not wait until 2015 to determine that NAFTA was a disaster. In his 1995 President's Report given to delegates to the union's convention, Owen Bieber noted, "UAW opposition to NAFTA clearly has been vindicated by the unfortunate developments in Mexico."

Bieber said NAFTA had been sold to Congress and the American people as a way to increase U.S. jobs through expanding exports to Mexico.

"In fact, the opposite has occurred," the UAW president said. "Thousands of Americans have lost jobs instead, as U.S. companies moved work to Mexico to exploit low wages and weak regulation there.

"I took on the Big 3 auto executives who touted NAFTA as the route to greatly expanded U.S. car exports to Mexico. What they failed to point out, of course, was that imports from Mexico would skyrocket as well."

The United States went from a pre-NAFTA surplus to an immediate trade deficit with Mexico. And in the auto sector, America suffered a disastrous $6.1 billion deficit with Mexico, including more than $2 billon in auto parts.

By 2012, the U.S. trade deficit with its NAFTA partners, Mexico and Canada, had grown by 580 percent from January 1, 1994, when the trade deal took effect. The NAFTA deficit amounted to $181 billion in 2012.[19]

Bieber also noted in 1995 that multinational companies that pushed so hard for NAFTA had argued the deal would reduce illegal immigration by Mexicans seeking a better life in the United States.

"It did not," he said. "Huge job losses have been devastating to Mexican workers who already faced declining living standards."

The UAW leader also called out the failures of other claims made by pro-NAFTA politicians and companies.

"NAFTA advocates said drug trafficking would be reduced," he said. "Instead cocaine and other illegal drugs move across our borders with greater ease due to reduced custom procedures."

Free trade supporters also had argued the deal would promote democracy in Mexico, but Bieber ripped that claim, noting that "instead, the elections there were marred by the assassination of the ruling party candidate and later by the killing of another party leader." He also pointed out the harsh measures taken against the revolt in Chiapas.

Bob Braner didn't need anyone to give him the statistics on NAFTA's failure. Three years after the deal took effect, he sat in the plant where he worked in Warren, Michigan, and watched as equipment was dismantled for loading onto trucks that would haul it to Mexico.

Braner had worked for 31 years at Sandvik Hard Metals, a small producer of parts for dental tools and ballpoint pens. At age 53, he had lost his job.

In 1995, company executives had pressed UAW Local 771 for concessions to make the firm more "competitive" with low-wage suppliers overseas. Workers had not received a raise in five years but agreed to an economic freeze for two more years to save their jobs.

Instead, in October 1996, the company announced it would move to Mexico and leave behind a workforce where the average worker had about 25 years' seniority.

"How can you compete against the 70 cents an hour that the Mexican workers are paid?" Braner asked during an interview with *UAW Solidarity*.[20]

Braner's experience at Sandvik was not unique:

- Some 117 members of UAW Local 2217 in North Baltimore, Ohio, lost their jobs when Abbott Corporation moved production of wire harnesses for Whirlpool appliances to Mexico. The workers had been commended for the high quality of their output just before they were fired. In the aftermath, Sharon Allgire, president of the local, reported that she went from earning $8 per hour in a 40-hour week at Abbott to $5 per hour working 20 hours a week at a child care center.

- Borg Warner in Muncie, Indiana, sold its manual transmission business to a Mexican firm with the loss of 650 UAW jobs paying an average of $17.50 per hour. The local Chamber of Commerce said the move south of the border would cost Indiana 4,000 jobs.
- About 200 jobs at Atlas Crankshaft in Fostoria, Ohio, moved to San Luis Potosi, Mexico. "The company loaded up two entire lines and hauled them away," said UAW Local President Ken Lortz. "Imagine my surprise when I turned on a TV news show one night and saw the same machines we'd been using running in a Mexican factory."[21]

At the time of these and many similar job losses for UAW workers, their counterparts in Mexico were not doing well either. Their wages had declined to $1.51 per hour in 1995 from $1.58 per hour in 1990 despite increased productivity.[22]

The UAW intensified its outreach to Mexican workers even as job losses mounted.

"These (Mexican) auto workers do the same work that we do," said Maria Winters, a member of UAW Local 845 who worked at Ford's Sheldon Road plant in Canton, Michigan. "But they make only $1 an hour or a bit more, and so, unlike us, they can't afford to buy the cars they build."

Winters was one of nine members of UAW Region 1A who visited Mexican auto plants in Toluca, Mexico, in early 1997.

"I think that by sharing information about what's going on in each other's countries, we can back each other up," she said.

Region 1A Director Bob King and other leaders encouraged additional groups to visit Mexico, such as the one that went to a General Motors plant in Matamoros that made most of GM's North American steering wheels.

"A GM manager told us that raising wages too much would damage Mexico's economy," said Brad Markell of Local 1776 in 1997. "Until Mexican wages rise considerably, this incentive to move jobs will remain."[23]

Back in Matamoros, Agapito Gonzalez kept a low profile after his arrest and long detention by Mexican President Carlos Salinas in 1992. But six years later, his Union of Day Laborers and Industrial Workers once again took on the big maquiladora employers.

In February 1998, five maquiladora plants went on strike after being unable to win an agreement with the employers' association. Workers there did not return until the union had won a 27 percent wage increase.

But that agreement covered only 7,000 workers, and contracts covering 40,000-plus workers still had to be achieved at 55 additional plants.

Corporate officials blasted the union for its militancy. "We went back to the years when Agapito's union and the maquiladora [owners] fought like cats and dogs," one said.[24]

The companies complained the strikes and big wage settlements had tarnished the image of Matamoros in the eyes of investors who sought a low-wage environment in which to locate production.

"That's baloney," responded Gonzalez. "We are just fighting for the rights of our people . . . rights embedded in our constitution."[25]

With pressure on Gonzalez from Tamaulipas Governor Manuel Cavazos Lerma, Gonzalez's union attorney son told the *Brownsville Herald* the maquiladora workers were not alone in their struggle.

"He said an American labor union, the United Auto Workers, is supporting the Mexican workers' cause," *Herald* reporter Tony Vindell wrote. "He showed this reporter a letter the union received from United Auto Workers President

Stephen P. Yokich."

The UAW letter, sent on January 23, 1998, stated: "In recent years, wages for Mexican workers have failed to keep up with the rapid pace of price increases, while the profits of the American companies with production facilities in Matamoros have been booming.

"Once before, in 1991–92, the UAW was able to provide support for your struggle with the maquiladora employers to achieve economic justice for your members," UAW President Yokich wrote to Gonzalez. "And just as you survived in that difficult time to return to the leadership of your union, we are pleased to see that the spirit of the workers of Matamoros has also survived to inspire their fight for better contracts."

Once again, the UAW provided financial assistance to the struggling maquiladora workers to help them get through the strikes.

In contrast to those with weaker CTM unions in other border areas, the Matamoros workers, with UAW help, achieved their victory.

More such struggles remained ahead.

Photo by David Bacon.

CHAPTER FOURTEEN

'Meat For The Crocodiles'
UAW Helps Save Top African Unionist

Chakufwa Chihana had the gift. While in his teens, he had become an activist in the Commercial and General Workers' Union in Malawi, a landlocked country in southeast Africa, and had fought for his country's independence from the British. By age 21, workers in the 4,000-member union had chosen him as their leader. He soon launched tough bargaining campaigns at the Imperial Tobacco Group and Malawi Railways.

By 1985, Chihana had become secretary-general of the Southern Africa Trade Union Coordination Council (which then represented 10 million workers in national trade union federations in 10 African countries).

I had been in contact with Chihana about UAW support for unions in South Africa but did not meet him until he attended an AFL-CIO convention in Detroit in 1991.

So when Kerry Kennedy, a human rights activist, called in the summer of 1992 and asked if I would meet with Chihana's son, Enoch, I immediately agreed even before she told me the African labor leader's life was in danger.

I had worked with Kerry seeking to halt the killings of unionists in El Salvador in the 1980s and also felt a special bond because I had traveled as a reporter with her father, Robert F. Kennedy, in the weeks before his 1968 presidential campaign ended with his assassination in Los Angeles.

Enoch Chihana, then a student at Wichita State University in Kansas, soon came with Kerry Kennedy to the UAW Washington office on N Street with news that his father had been arrested on orders from Hastings Banda, the dictator who then ruled Malawi as "president for life."

Banda had threatened pro-democracy critics such as Chakufwa Chihana, saying, "They will be meat for the crocodiles."[1] Chihana had spoken at a conference in Lusaka, Zambia, in March 1992, where he blasted President Banda's repression of workers and his stifling of free speech, press, and association. The union leader also denounced the Malawi government as "one of the worst dictatorships in Africa." He called on Banda to step aside and allow a multiparty democracy to build a "new, vibrant, democratic Malawi."[2] When Chihana stepped onto the tarmac upon his return to Malawi, he said:

"There comes a time in the history of every nation when all must recognize that change is not only desirable, but inevitable. For Malawi, the time is now."

Plainclothes police were waiting at the airport and quickly manhandled him into an unmarked police car. They went to the headquarters of the Southern Africa Trade Union Coordination Council, which they ransacked, and then to Chihana's home, which they searched. The police seized his money and evicted his wife before hauling him off to prison.

Chihana was no stranger to state repression. He had argued after independence in 1964 that labor unions in Malawi should be independent of the government and the ruling party. Banda ordered him sent into internal exile in northern Malawi, where he repeatedly was attacked by assailants and twice was left for dead. Roman Catholic priests smuggled Chihana into Kenya, where he served in various union leadership roles until he led a general strike in 1971 that resulted in Kenya's deporting him back to Malawi.

The regime there jailed him immediately. Chihana served seven years without a trial, five of those years in solitary confinement. For much of that time, he was kept naked and in hand and leg irons. His jailers beat him frequently, hung him upside down, and threw water on him, according to *Africa Report*.[3] Media accounts stated his imprisonment was due to his leadership of the Commercial and General Workers' Union, which had been banned, and his demands for an end to the dictatorship.[4] Moved out of solitary, Chihana then shared a cell with 86 other prisoners with only two buckets for use as latrines. "I saw people beaten with batons until they were maimed," he recalled. "Some lost eyes or ears. Some died. You saw people carried away in wheelbarrows and you never saw them again."[5]

Chihana won release in 1978 after Amnesty International declared him a "prisoner of conscience." Still defiant, President Banda reiterated that "if to maintain political stability and administration, I have to detain 10,000, 100,000, I will do it. . . . I will keep them there and they will rot."[6]

An important condition of the release was that Chihana go into exile, so he moved to England, where he studied at Ruskin College, Oxford, and then at Bradford University. By 1984, he had returned to Africa and settled in Botswana, where he became general secretary of the Southern Africa Trade Union Coordination Council.

Malawi experienced widespread protests in 1992, during Banda's 28th year as "president for life." The country's seven Catholic bishops issued the first major public criticism of the government since independence. The bishops' letter expressed concern about a "growing gap between the rich and the poor." It called for greater popular participation in politics and expanded freedom of expression and association. And the letter noted that the bishops could not "ignore or turn a blind eye to our people's experience of unfairness and injustice—for example, those who . . . are imprisoned without knowing when their cases will be heard."

Banda was not pleased. The chair of his Malawi Congress Party in the city of Blantyre reportedly said that if the government had known what the bishops planned to say, they would have been killed. Tape recordings later revealed that government officials actually discussed how to kill the bishops.[7] After weeks of student protests, Chihana gave a speech at a conference in Zambia calling for multiparty democracy and then was grabbed by police after arriving at Lilongwe International Airport in Malawi. As he was being held incommunicado, workers demanded the trade union leader's release.

On May 6, 1992, in Blantyre, 30,000 striking textile workers launched protests that immediately won broad public backing. The next day, thousands gathered at the High Court, where Chihana was to be produced for a bail hearing, but the government refused to allow him to appear. The crowd reportedly marched to Banda's party headquarters, which it burned to the ground. Some then looted stores in Lilongwe owned by Banda's company, Press Holdings.

Government security forces killed at least 38 protesters in response. Life-President Banda, shaken by developments, went on national radio to call for Malawian citizens "to behave like ladies and gentlemen." Soon, however, protests over Chihana's detention and the broader issues of the economy and one-party rule spread. Workers at tea and tobacco plantations demanded the union leader's release, higher wages, and a change in government.

During this time, Chihana's son, Enoch, sought help from the church he attended while a student at Wichita State University, the 1,800-member Wichita First Presbyterian Church. Enoch believed a letter-writing campaign by clergy and church members would spur Kansas Senators Bob Dole and Nancy Kassebaum, both Republicans, to work in Washington to keep the heat on Banda. Without such pressure from the United States, Enoch feared Malawi would execute his father, just as it had done with many other political prisoners.

Enoch came to Washington and spoke at a "Free Chihana" protest at the embassy of Malawi. UAW members joined with those of other AFL-CIO unions at the demonstration. Just days later, the younger Chihana learned the Banda government was livid over his role at the embassy protest. He was told the FBI "was taking precautions to monitor anyone from Malawi who might schedule travel to Wichita." The administration at Wichita State University moved Enoch to a new residence, gave him an alias, and deployed campus police to provide additional security for him.

For many years, the U.S. government turned a blind eye to repression in Malawi. Both President Reagan and President George H.W. Bush viewed Malawi as a valued bastion of anti-communism and a counterweight to the socialist governments of Mozambique and Tanzania in the region. They also saw Malawi as a conduit for trade with the apartheid government of South Africa.[8] But the broader international community reacted critically to the Banda regime's continual repression of Malawi's workers and other citizens. On May 14, 1992, a week after massive protests by striking textile workers over Chihana's jailing, labor and human rights groups' pressure finally helped push the World Bank to suspend Malawi's request for $74 million in new nonhumanitarian aid. It cited Banda's human rights abuses and refusal to allow multiparty democracy.

Senator Paul Simon, a close ally of the UAW from Illinois, chaired the Senate's African Affairs Subcommittee. He and Republican Senator Kassebaum wrote to the U.S. Agency for International Development and the State Department asking the Bush administration to "link future aid to the government of Malawi to respect for human rights and sustained progress toward multiparty democracy." In addition, they urged the United States to ask European donor agencies and the inter-

national financial community to adopt a similar approach. The Simon/Kassebaum letter specifically cited the imprisonment of Chihana.[9] Shortly thereafter, Malawi finally agreed to bring Chihana to trial and to allow an international delegation to see him in prison. As foreign pressure grew, the High Court of Malawi granted Chihana bail on June 11. Malawi under Banda had never granted bail for a political prisoner previously.[10] Uncowed by his time in detention, Chihana gave interviews to the BBC and Voice of America calling for reforms in Malawi. Two days after his release on bail, he was thrown into jail once again after the interviews.

Enoch Chihana had enlisted the help of another activist from Malawi whom he had met while studying at Wichita State. Enwood Longwe had become a guest minister at Spearville Federated Church, and he arranged an interview on the Christian Broadcasting Network, which had many listeners in western Kansas. Longwe detailed the repression of the churches in Malawi and also described Chihana's imprisonment. He closed by asking listeners to contact their senators to pressure Malawi to reform.

Republican Senator Bob Dole heard from constituents shortly after the interview. On August 28, 1992, Dole wrote to Jim Friedenwald of the First Presbyterian Church to report that he was concerned about Chihana's treatment and planned to examine the case along with Senator Kassebaum as they considered the 1993 foreign aid appropriation for Malawi.[11]

In the weeks that followed, Dole and Kassebaum also signed a letter to Banda with Senator Simon and others that stated:

"We strongly urge you to release Mr. Chihana and other democratic activists immediately. We will oppose . . . any assistance to Malawi as long as no significant progress is made."

Malawi then formally charged Chihana with three counts of sedition. He again was released on bail to await trial.

I came away from my meeting with Enoch Chihana at the UAW Washington office feeling we needed to expand our efforts on his father's behalf. After several discussions with UAW President Owen Bieber, we decided to use some of the same tactics employed in the union's successful campaign to free Moses Mayekiso in South Africa.

Underpinning all UAW global solidarity campaigns is the maximum involvement of the rank-and-file membership and a strategy to amplify and expand the impact of that involvement. The first step was to inform and educate on Chihana's plight.

UAW publications, such as *Washington Report*, carried articles on his imprisonment and the Banda regime's repression of unions and workers in Malawi. Bieber also began to mention Chihana as he spoke to UAW locals, at Black Lake education sessions, at Community Action Program (CAP) meetings, and in Washington, D.C.

We drew on the Mayekiso playbook by printing thousands of postcards with Chihana's photo, which we addressed to the Malawi embassy in Washington. Once again, UAW members responded by signing their names and addresses on the cards and mailing them.

In addition, we regularly passed out the cards at UAW meetings and collected them after they had been signed. As with other campaigns, this allowed us to put the postage on in the Washington office and then mail 15 or 20 cards each day to the embassy.

Here is how Professor Melvin Kahn described the union's "Free Chihana" effort in a 2006 academic paper:

"The UAW originally distributed 25,000 (postcards) and, when they were exhausted, passed out 15,000 additional ones. The Malawi Embassy was so inundated that the Ambassador pleaded with the UAW not to send any more."[12]

On September 25, 1992, Chihana won the Robert F. Kennedy Human Rights Award, which carried with it not only money and prestige, but also the commitment of a strategic partnership with the RFK Memorial Center for Human Rights (now called the Robert F. Kennedy Center for Justice and Human Rights). Ethel Kennedy hosted more than 1,000 people at her Hickory Hill estate in Virginia, and the awards ceremony generated extensive news coverage detailing Chihana's imprisonment and Banda's labor and human rights abuses.

The political skill and reach of the Kennedy family, particularly that of Senator Edward Kennedy, had considerable impact. Kerry Kennedy spent weeks making the rounds on Capitol Hill with Enoch Chihana. A skilled organizer, she once worked for Amnesty International in El Salvador. In short order, she had arranged meetings with Vice President Al Gore, members of Congress, human rights groups, and religious organizations.

We set up additional meetings with other trade unions and, working with the AFL-CIO, with some central labor bodies. The UAW's relationship with the AFL-CIO's international affairs operation had been strained for many years, but we attempted to work with the federation, then led by Lane Kirkland, on the Chihana case.

Tom Kahn, the hard-line ideologue who ran the AFL-CIO's international affairs department and frequently criticized the UAW, died several months before Chihana's arrest. Some at the federation seemed to welcome the UAW's activism on the Chihana case, while others remained hostile. Our strategy during this era was generally to work independently of the AFL-CIO on global issues the UAW members and leadership identified as important and to avoid internecine warfare.

Chihana had been charged with an additional two counts of sedition in September 1992. When he was brought to the High Court in Lilongwe in October, more than 30,000 union members and other advocates gathered there to show their support. They continued to appear each day until Banda's security forces began to harass and beat some protesters. Five

Chihana supporters were killed during the protests.

In an effort to defuse the angry public and deal with mounting international pressure, Banda announced on October 18 that Malawi would hold a referendum "on the question of whether people want our present one-party system or want to switch to a multiparty system of government." The dictator said he was confident "his people" would "reject the chaos and disunity of multiparty politics."[13]

Public excitement over the referendum was tempered by news two days later that Orton Chirwa, a widely respected political prisoner, had died in detention. He and his wife, Vera, had been kidnapped from Zambia in 1981 and sentenced to death in 1983 after a "trial" during which they were not allowed a defense attorney and were denied the right to call witnesses in their defense.

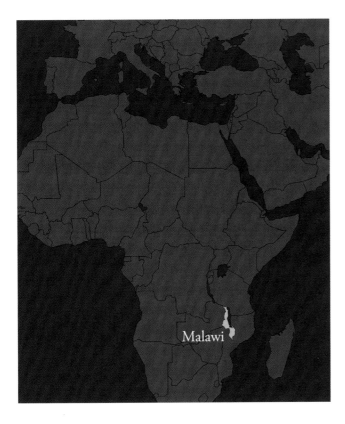

Chirwa was 73 years old when he died in prison shortly after a group of British lawyers who visited him reported he had been forced to squat on the floor for days with arm and leg irons chained to a metal rod behind his knees. The Banda government denied Vera Chirwa permission to attend her husband's funeral.

News of Chirwa's death gave a further sense of urgency to the UAW campaign to win freedom for Chihana.

As the union leader's trial moved forward, a delegation of the Law Society of England and Wales, the General Council of the Bar, and the Scottish Faculty of Advocates went to Malawi to examine the evidence against Chihana. After detailed scrutiny of that evidence, the prominent group of jurists concluded:

"It was plain from our examination of the evidence that Mr. Chihana had not committed any act which could reasonably be regarded as a criminal offence in accordance with basic human rights standards applicable to freedom of expression."[14]

The British jurists also pointed out that Banda had ordered his minister of justice, who was constitutionally responsible for the prosecution, to stand aside. Instead, Banda brought in two British lawyers—John Beveridge, a Queen's Counsel who handled commercial clients, and Andrew Nitch-Smith, a partner in a commercial firm.

This baffling news later was explained by the fact that both Beveridge and Nitch-Smith did legal work for Lonhro, a British conglomerate with mining and other investments in Malawi and elsewhere in Africa. Some labor rights advocates believed Lonhro wanted Chihana jailed for years to weaken unions not only in Malawi, but throughout Africa.

Despite the weak evidence and arguments of the prosecution, on December 14, 1992, Chihana predictably was found guilty of sedition for possession of papers he delivered to the conference in Zambia on the prospects for multiparty democracy in Malawi.

The court sentenced Chihana to two years of hard labor, which was reduced to nine months in March 1993.

UAW President Bieber blasted the Malawi Supreme Court when it validated the lower court's verdict.

"By upholding his conviction, the Supreme Court established in effect that advocacy of multiparty democracy is 'seditious' and an imprisonable offense," Bieber wrote in a letter to Banda.

The UAW leader called for the immediate and unconditional release of Chihana, who he said had been jailed "solely for his peaceful activity on behalf of political democracy."

Bieber also expressed worry about Chihana's poor health, which he told Banda was "a matter of deep concern." He said the African labor leader had lost weight, suffered from severe headaches and chest pains, and was coughing up blood.

"The UAW believes Malawi's treatment of Mr. Chihana violates the United Nations convention against torture and other cruel, inhuman, and degrading treatment," Bieber said. "Because of his role as a leading trade unionist in Africa, the entire international labor community is watching what happens to Mr. Chihana very closely.

"Given the notoriously harsh conditions in Malawi prisons, we frankly fear for his life," the UAW president wrote.

Bieber's tough criticisms were echoed in a joint resolution of Congress supported by the UAW and other labor groups, human rights activists, and congressional leaders, including Kennedy, Dole, Kassebaum, and Simon. The resolution set standards Malawi would have to meet for further U.S. aid, including protections for freedom of association, expression, and the press as well as reforms to guarantee multiparty democracy.

In the United States, voters in November 1992 had rejected a second term for George H.W. Bush and elected Bill Clinton as president. After just three months in office, Vice President Al Gore had become interested in the Chihana case after hearing from the UAW and the AFL-CIO as well as Kerry

Kennedy and Enoch Chihana. On April 14, 1993, Gore summoned Robert Mbaya, Malawi's ambassador to the United States, and demanded Chihana's immediate release.

"I am deeply concerned by the continued imprisonment of Chakufwa Chihana," Gore said in a statement after the meeting. "I believe the charges against him were politically inspired and the authorities should release him immediately so that he may join in the dialogue for change underway in Malawi."[15]

As the June referendum on multiparty democracy approached, Enoch Chihana told us and others, including Kerry Kennedy, that many citizens in Malawi had little access to information about the referendum, in part because Banda controlled the press. Kerry then approached Joe Duffey, a UAW ally from Connecticut, who had just become director of the U.S. Information Agency in the new Clinton administration.

Duffey agreed to shift funding so that Voice of America broadcasts heard in Malawi would not be just in English. Instead, those broadcasts provided objective information on the referendum in Chichewa, a vernacular understood by most of those in Malawi.

When the votes were counted after the June 14 referendum, nearly two-thirds of the voters rejected Banda's one-party system and supported a multiparty state. The outcome effectively ended the Malawi Congress Party's 37-year monopoly on power.

Banda soon was stripped of his "president for life" title and most of his dictatorial powers.

On July 12, 1993, less than a month after the vote that handed Banda a humiliating defeat, Chakufwa Chihana won his freedom.

"We welcome Brother Chihana's release," UAW President Bieber said in a press statement. "We maintained all along that he had been jailed solely for his peaceful activity on behalf of political democracy."

Bieber also gave credit to the Robert F. Kennedy Center, Amnesty International, Africa Watch, and other allies that had played important roles in the "Free Chihana" campaign along with the UAW.

On behalf of his father, Enoch Chihana told reporters after his release:

"Our family is deeply grateful to the UAW for all that it did to help win my father's freedom."

Within a year after Chihana's release, Banda had been swept from office in Malawi's first multiparty election. Bakili Muluzi's United Democratic Front (UDF) enjoyed strong support in the populous south of Malawi and outpolled Chihana's Alliance for Democracy.

Chihana later became Malawi's minister of agriculture and then served two terms as the country's vice president. He died of a brain tumor in 2006.

Enoch Chihana, the son with whom the UAW worked so closely on the "Free Chihana" campaign, went on to become a member of Parliament and Malawi's minister of sports and youth development.

UAW color guard at 2014 CAP Conference in Washington, D.C.
Photo by Chris Skelly.

CHAPTER FIFTEEN

UAW Waged Both War and Peace
Answered Call Of Duty, Fought Military Adventurism

The rich loam of Normandy will forever bear traces of UAW blood, sweat, and tears spilled in the battles to liberate France and all of Europe from Hitler's fascist oppression.

So, too, will the leech-infested rice paddies of the Mekong Delta in Vietnam, where UAW volunteers and draftees slogged with their M16s, flak jackets, and unanswered prayers.

More recently, UAW families sent their sons and daughters to the streets of Fallujah and Ramadi and elsewhere in Iraq, hoping against hope they would dodge the crude but effective roadside bombs and sniper fire.

While Americans at home posted selfies on Facebook, downloaded Beyoncé's latest, and watched Miguel Cabrera hit home runs, UAW members fought and died in the mountains and deserts of Afghanistan in a war that seemed to have no end.

In World War II, the Korean War, Vietnam, the first Gulf war, Iraq, and Afghanistan, the troops in harm's way, without fail, included UAW members and their families answering our nation's call. That patriotic heritage includes union locals caring for veterans and their families long after they have returned home to confront problems from joblessness to post-traumatic stress.

At the same time, the UAW for nearly 80 years also has been part of that army of Americans that waged peace, that opposed unchecked military adventurism, that fought bloated Pentagon budgets, that struggled to end the nuclear arms race, and that questioned whether politicians were robbing us of the very democracy and civil liberties we went to war to protect.

From Emil Mazey, who later became UAW secretary-treasurer, leading the demobilization protests at the end of World War II to UAW leaders opposing President George W. Bush's war in Iraq, the union has found itself in the streets and on the barricades with allies opposed to the primacy of militarism. It is an imperfect record, certainly, but one that stands up well overall.

Yes, while other top UAW leaders and many thousands of members opposed the Vietnam War, UAW President Walter Reuther came to that position late. But he also opposed the Cold War excesses of George Meany and the AFL-CIO, even to the point of withdrawing the UAW from the federation over issues that included foreign policy.

UAW Presidents Doug Fraser, Owen Bieber, and Steve Yokich also waged numerous battles with the Cold Warriors then in power in the AFL-CIO.

Fraser fought for labor to support cuts in excessive defense spending after the union reaffiliated with the federation. Bieber battled AFL-CIO President Lane Kirkland on Central America. And Yokich joined other progressive union presidents in helping to push Kirkland out in the mid-1990s, in part over the federation's prioritizing anti-communism over crucial bread-and-butter labor struggles on the organizing and bargaining front at home.

After the horrible events of September 11, 2001, the UAW backed military force against Osama Bin Laden and al-Qaeda for the "barbaric attack on innocent people" and supported an AFL-CIO executive council resolution that noted more than 600 of the 9/11 victims were union members. At the same time, Yokich strongly urged steps to protect the rights of people of Islamic faith and, more broadly, of all immigrants who feared hate crimes in the aftermath of the heinous attacks in New York City and Washington, D.C. Yokich and UAW Vice President Elizabeth Bunn also declared that the war on terrorism could not be won by military force alone and required a global offensive for equitable, sustainable, democratic development. The UAW's concern for the people of Afghanistan led the union to support the call for a massive effort to rebuild that country.

P hillip Serwinowski, a forklift driver at a General Motors plant in Tonawanda, New York, shared that concern for the people of Afghanistan. A deeply patriotic member of UAW Local 774, Serwinowski strongly opposed the wars in Iraq and Afghanistan.

With nearly 42 years of seniority at GM, he and his former wife, Sally Urban, had been regularly involved in supporting the troops as well. Their daughter, Kate, adopted three platoons in Afghanistan and, in just the first six months of 2011, their efforts resulted in about 250 packages of various items needed or requested by the troops, such as gloves, blankets, toiletries, and snacks, being sent overseas.

"It's the little things we take for granted," Kate Serwinowski told *UAW Solidarity* magazine. "For them, it's a luxury."[1]

Marine Lance Corporal Timothy Serwinowski wrote to his father, Phillip, in early 2010 from Afghanistan asking for advice on his future. He spelled out the options, which included a career in the Marine Corps, perhaps a job in border security, or becoming a police officer.

The blue-eyed 21-year-old graduate of North Tonawanda High School, who saw a future without bounds, closed his letter: "What do you think, Dad?"

Phillip Serwinowski had pondered his son's options as he worked at the GM Powertrain plant outside of Buffalo, but he never got to answer Timothy's question.

On June 21, 2010, Lance Corporal Serwinowski was the first to emerge from a tree line in Helmand Province. A sniper

Timothy Serwinowski photographed himself while on patrol in Helmand province in Afghanistan. A sniper's bullet killed the 21-year-old Marine—son of UAW member Phillip Serwinowski and his former wife, Sally Urban—in June 2010. Photo courtesy of the Serwinowski family.

fired, and the bullet that killed him hit just below his body armor.

Nathan McCormack, a fellow Marine, gave Timothy's parents the folded U.S. flag that had draped their son's coffin. He told the family that "Ski" was known as the platoon's "snack guy."

In addition to carrying all his heavy gear, including a SMAW—a shoulder-fired multipurpose artillery weapon—Timothy could "hold more food on his body than anybody else," his father recalled. "He had a knack for hiding snacks."[2]

Phillip Serwinowski, who had been politically active for many years, spent the weeks after his son's death writing letters to members of Congress urging that the United States withdraw from Afghanistan and bring the remaining troops home. The argument that fighting terrorists there and in Iraq would protect Americans at home never made sense to him.

"If that's the case, then we need to go into 50 other

nations and do the same thing," he told *UAW Solidarity*'s Vince Piscopo. "To me that is just bull, and let's stop it. I'm trying to get the politicians in the House and the United States Senate on board to stop this madness."

In his letters to lawmakers, Serwinowski enclosed photos of his son's funeral.

The Local 774 member argued the Iraq and Afghanistan wars needed to end in part because of the tremendous drain they had on the economic recovery by soaking up money that could have been spent on education, job creation, transportation infrastructure, and other vital needs. But the most important reason to bring the troops home was the futures of young Americans were being tragically cut short.

In addition to the letter-writing campaign, Sally Urban, Timothy's mother, began an effort to keep military recruiters from setting up shop at high schools. When not working on that, she joined Phillip and daughter Kate in the effort to raise money from UAW members and others for the packages to be sent to Timothy's platoon and other troops still in Afghanistan even as the war there winds down.

"They will be the best-supplied platoon in all of Afghanistan," Serwinowski said. "We will take care of them."

Seven years before Local 774's Serwinowski lost his son in Afghanistan, Bob King, then a UAW vice president, looked out at a crowd of more than 200 union activists in Dearborn, Michigan, on February 22, 2003. They were there at Local 600's hall to protest the likelihood that President George W. Bush would order U.S. forces to invade Iraq.

"We have a moral obligation to speak out against this war," King told the crowd.[3] He urged labor to join with allies to build an effective antiwar movement and called for vigorous United Nations inspections and enforcement to disarm Saddam Hussein's forces.

The Bush administration talked of "democratizing the

Middle East while they're destroying democracy here," King said at the rally.[4]

Other UAW activists supported King, including a leader of Local 909 who said "we won't be able to stop [this war] unless labor raises its mighty voice to stop it" and called for a dialogue with those who differed, including some veterans.

"We firmly stand in opposition to Bush's smokescreen that will end in our sons and daughters being brought home in body bags," said Millie Hall, a UAW clerical worker and OPEIU member who served as president of the Metro-Detroit chapter of the Coalition of Labor Union Women (CLUW).

James Settles Jr., a skilled union and political organizer and leader in the African American community who then served

Phillip Serwinowski (right), a member of UAW Local 774, opposed the Iraq and Afghanistan wars. He's shown here with his former wife, Sally Urban, and daughter, Kate. The photograph is of Timothy Serwinowski, a Marine Lance Corporal, who was killed in Afghanistan by a sniper's bullet. Photo courtesy of the Serwinowski family.

as UAW Region 1A director, joined the rally against the Iraq invasion.

King and Settles were not alone. A week earlier, on February 15, 2003, UAW Vice President Richard Shoemaker, who directed the union's General Motors Department, spoke out against the Iraq war at an antiwar event in Detroit. Elizabeth Bunn, UAW Secretary-Treasurer, also denounced President Bush and urged strong union opposition to the invasion of Iraq.

With King, Shoemaker, and Bunn speaking out against Bush's war, they seized leadership on the issue from the more reluctant Ron Gettelfinger, who was new to the UAW presidency and more focused on other issues.

The opposition to the Iraq war at the onset by King, Shoemaker, and Bunn and many UAW locals came at a time when much of the country supported the invasion.

Bush, Vice President Dick Cheney, Defense Secretary Donald Rumsfeld, National Security Advisor Condoleezza Rice, and others created much of that support through false public assertions. They argued that Iraq possessed weapons of mass destruction that posed a threat to the United States and the world and that Saddam Hussein had close ties to al-Qaeda, the terrorist force responsible for 9/11.

Years later, both arguments proved untrue. While various UAW leaders questioned those claims, many Democrats joined with a united Republican Party to support committing U.S. troops to invade Iraq. There was strong support among business leaders for the invasion as well. And many foreign governments, such as Great Britain (led at the time by the Labour Party's Tony Blair), embraced the war.

The initial enthusiasm in the aftermath of the invasion soon gave way to growing concern.

In February 2003, the same month UAW leaders spoke out against the invasion, the U.S. Army's top general, Eric Shinseki, said it would take several hundred thousand soldiers to secure Iraq. Defense Secretary Rumsfeld and his deputy, Paul Wolfowitz, blasted General Shinseki's analysis, and he soon retired from the Army—only later to be proven right.

As the invasion gave way to a violent occupation, a labor-based antiwar group called U.S. Labor Against the War (US-LAW) developed traction. The organization grew out of the National Labor Assembly for Peace that met in Chicago in October 2003.

"It is the mission of U.S. Labor Against the War to be the organized voice within the labor movement for peace and new priorities, better to secure human needs and to demilitarize U.S. foreign policy," its mission statement said. "USLAW also brings labor's voice and strength into wider movements for peace and new priorities in the U.S. and builds solidarity with labor movements around the world."

With increased activism by USLAW and various locals, including those of the UAW, as well as leaders from a number of AFL-CIO affiliated unions, there was pressure on the labor federation to speak out on the war. An early statement opposing use of military force had been followed by AFL-CIO positions that some believed undercut a broader antiwar push.

But by 2005, with UAW support, the labor federation adopted a resolution that called for withdrawal of U.S. troops from Iraq.[5]

With the preinvasion opposition of UAW leaders and the militant organizing activity by many locals against the war working independently and with USLAW, the labor movement became a growing force against the war. But by then Bush had been re-elected to a second term and, despite a discredited war strategy and growing public opposition, the war went on.

It would rest with Barack Obama, who opposed the Iraq war resolution, to bring an end to Bush's adventure that cost the lives of some 4,486 U.S. soldiers and more than 100,000 Iraqi lives, including many civilians.

Leo Abernathy, then a member of UAW Local 259, worked as a mechanic in an auto repair shop in Brooklyn, New York. He prided himself on doing high-quality repairs for his customers and enjoyed his weekends off.

But on a warm Saturday in June 1982, Abernathy chose to join a large delegation from UAW Regions 9 and 9A at a demonstration against the nuclear arms race.

He hopped the subway into Manhattan and, along with about 700,000 others, took a stand against the dangers posed by the then-growing stockpiles of nuclear weapons that were at the heart of the Cold War between the old Soviet Union and the United States.[6] In the early 1980s, during the Ronald Reagan presidency, the United States and the Soviet Union each possessed nuclear weapons that could have destroyed each country's population several times over. The two nations had stockpiles totaling about 16,000 strategic intercontinental bombs and missiles and about 50,000 nuclear warheads.

A U.S. congressional study during that time found that an all-out nuclear war would kill about two-thirds of the U.S. population. About 113 million Soviets and millions more in other countries would also die. Radiation would poison large portions of our planet, with no guarantees that earth would remain habitable for life as we know it.[7]

"I'm scared," said Local 259's Abernathy at the time. The deadly arms race "could mean an end to everything I hold dear."

The UAW International Executive Board in June 1982 discussed that arms race and adopted a resolution that stated:

"The greatest threat facing humanity today is the danger of nuclear holocaust. The greatest challenge facing us is to prevent the occurrence—whether by accident or by design—of nuclear war.

"We reject the notion advanced by the Reagan administration that a massive military buildup by the U.S. is necessary if there is to be meaningful arms control between our two countries," the UAW board stated. "More weapons, at this point in time, can only mean less security for the American people and the entire world."

UAW President Doug Fraser and other union leaders had a growing concern about President Reagan's massive budget increases for the Pentagon, which totaled $1.6 trillion over five years. U.S. military spending during this period was set to cost the country $234 million every hour for the following five years. Each American would be paying a tax bill of $15,800 (1982 dollars) just for the defense spending Reagan proposed.

For 1983, Reagan's defense hikes were roughly 50 percent larger than the combined federal outlays for health, education, job training, agriculture, energy, environment, transportation, natural resources, and law enforcement, according to *The Wall Street Journal.*

In May 1982, *The New York Times* reported on a secret Pentagon paper that argued that a limited, protracted nuclear war was possible and winnable.[8] Other military experts close to the Reagan administration began to argue that a first-strike nuclear response to Soviet conventional weapons use was no longer unthinkable.

UAW President Fraser testified before a congressional committee in the spring of 1982. He called for a cut in the military budget of $15–20 billion and said that it could be achieved without reducing national security. He cited a number of areas of savings, including ending the procurement of obsolete or useless equipment and budget controls that would prevent huge cost overruns by profit-hungry defense contractors.

Fraser's call for defense cuts was echoed by Herman Rebhan, a UAW member who served as general secretary of the International Metalworkers' Federation, a global union federation based in Geneva, Switzerland, with which the union was affiliated.

"Last year, world expenditures on arms broke all known records," Rebhan said. "It amounted to $550 billion—money that could have been so well spent on productive industry." He

Photo by David Bacon.

said halting the production of nuclear arms in itself would save the U.S. $20 billion or more each year.[9]

Fraser and Rebhan's efforts reflected long-time UAW policy emphasizing the importance of limits on runaway military spending, support for arms control and reduction of nuclear weapons, and opposition to unneeded armaments.

UAW President Walter Reuther played a lead role in advocating the retooling of auto factories in 1940 to build the tanks, warplanes, and other military equipment needed to mobilize for World War II. He met some resistance from short-sighted business leaders, but, after the Pearl Harbor attack, the retooling urged by the UAW became a priority for the nation.

After World War II, the UAW again urged conversion, but to civilian production in those same factories that had helped win the war against fascism. Reuther pressed to have the defense plants converted to produce civilian goods while keeping the same workforces, rather than mothballing those factories and displacing workers.

In 1969, Reuther again pressed for conversion of military production in the midst of the Vietnam War. In a speech that became known as "Swords into Plowshares," the UAW president urged the United States to impound part of each contractor's profits from defense production. That money would go to a fund to help convert military production to civilian uses.

Predictably, the big defense contractors saw little merit in the UAW proposal.

"Having found a sheltered and highly profitable berth, resting on the dangerous assumption of perpetual confrontation and conflict among major powers in a nuclear age, they are determined not to be dislodged from it," Reuther said.

"To say that millions of Americans want work and steady income is not to say they want perpetual war. What they really want is peace and full employment. To get them on the side of conversion, the government—and the defense contractors—

must offer them valid alternatives."

Shortly before Reuther's death in a plane crash in 1970, the UAW helped lead the fight against President Nixon's Anti-Ballistic Missile (ABM) System, which would have placed defensive nuclear missiles near heavily populated centers around the country.

"It is not time to put our money in new tactical weapons systems designed to assure an overkill capacity or to give the U.S. absolute military superiority for a few brief moments of history," the union stated in a resolution adopted on February 23, 1969.

"The UAW International Executive Board associates itself with [public] opposition to ABM," the resolution continued. "We urge the President to respond to the national protest with an order cancelling the ABM program. We urge him to turn away from the useless and unnecessary arms buildup and move vigorously towards the task of peace."

Nixon won the ABM fight by a single vote in Congress, but strong pressure from the UAW and its allies helped lead to a treaty in 1972 between the United States and the Soviet Union that limited the use of anti-ballistic missile systems. (President Reagan in 1983 proposed his "Star Wars" initiative, which would have violated the treaty, but his plan proved unworkable.) President George W. Bush withdrew the United States from the treaty soon after he took office—the first time in modern history our country has pulled out of a major international arms treaty.

At the same time the UAW fought Nixon's ABM deployment, the union also spoke out against the Vietnam War.

"The UAW will continue to press for an end to the United States involvement in Vietnam and will join with other responsible and nonviolent voices in the peace movement to bring about the total and earliest possible withdrawal of United States troops," the union said.[10] Many top UAW leaders and local union activists had been active in the anti-war movement in

We Take Our Stand for Peace
and
an End to the War in Vietnam

We take our stand with the millions of our fellow-Americans who call for an end to the war in Vietnam. We join the thousands of respected, responsible and patriotic national leaders in Congress, in the churches and synagogues, on campuses, in business, in civic organizations and in the professions in support of the peaceful, lawful, non-violent community activities of the October 15 Vietnam Moratorium.

We deplore the reprehensible activities of a small minority who burn the American flag and equate anti-Americanism with anti-war, for their actions are indefensible and counter productive.

We call upon our government to face up to the reality that there is nothing to be won in Vietnam that is worth one more drop of American blood.

No responsible person believes that the United States will continue indefinitely to sacrifice American lives in Vietnam. The only question remaining is not *whether* we will withdraw our troops but *how* and *when*. We take our stand with those who are for getting out quickly and completely.

We take our stand with the millions of our fellow-Americans who share the view that the support of efforts to disengage America from Vietnam is an act of the highest patriotism and a distinct service to our country. For as long as we are involved in Vietnam:

- America will be torn by serious division
- our youth will be alienated
- our urgent social problems will be neglected
- our resources will be wasted
- our moral credentials will be tarnished

Peace Can Unite America to Wage War Against Poverty, Hunger, Ignorance and Disease

Peace can unite America and enable us to use the resources being wasted in Vietnam:

- to rebuild our cities
- to solve the crisis in education
- to deal effectively with the problems of air and water pollution and the deterioration of man's living environment.
- to overcome the serious deficit in health care
- to provide security and dignity for our older citizens

Only peace will release the resources desperately needed to save America's cities.

Man Has Always Taken Risks in War
It Is Time We Take Risks in the Cause of Peace

Let us now put the sad Vietnamese chapter of our history behind us except to remember forever its lesson—that, of all political systems, democracy is the least capable of being transplanted at the point of a bayonet.

We call for bringing our troops home not only to save lives but in order to enable America to resume democracy's true work—to mobilize for peace and to turn our resources and the hearts, hands and minds of our people to the fulfillment of the democratic promise of liberty, equality, justice and brotherhood for all. For the only way to make democracy safe in the world and to promote the spread of its blessings to those now denied them — by every form of totalitarianism, whether communist, fascist or military dictatorship—is to make democracy work, to translate democracy's ideals into meaningful reality in the lives of people.

We support the peaceful, lawful and non-violent activities of the October 15 Vietnam Moratorium as a step toward that end.

ALLIANCE FOR LABOR ACTION

International Union, UAW	International Brotherhood of Teamsters
Walter P. Reuther, President	Frank E. Fitzsimmons, General Vice President
Emil Mazey, Secretary Treasurer	Thomas F. Flynn, General Secretary Treasurer

International Chemical Workers Union
Thomas E. Boyle, President
Marshall Shafer, Secretary Treasurer

The UAW joined with the Teamsters and International Chemical Workers to issue this appeal in 1969 for an end to the war in Vietnam.

the late 1960s, including Secretary-Treasurer Emil Mazey, who was involved with the Labor Assembly for Peace, as was Victor Reuther, the president's brother who ran the union's International Affairs Department in Washington, D.C. Paul Schrade, a UAW regional director based in California, also emerged as a leader of union opposition to President Lyndon Johnson's expansion of the war.

Walter Reuther's close ties to President Johnson, driven primarily by domestic political concerns, muted his voice on Vietnam for some time. Reuther's biographer, Nelson Lichtenstein, described a confrontation at a seder in 1967 where Barry Bluestone, the son of a UAW vice president, and Leslie Woodcock, the daughter of another UAW vice president, confronted Reuther on the war issue.

Barry, then a 22-year-old student, pressed the UAW president to get the union behind the end-the-war movement following a major speech by Dr. Martin Luther King Jr. in which he declared, "This madness must cease."

"Walter said that to be honest, he agreed that the war was wrong, but he added that he couldn't do it now while they were entering negotiations," Bluestone recalled.

In his excellent book, *The Most Dangerous Man in Detroit*, Lichtenstein wrote that "Reuther was unquestionably pained by this exchange . . . but the UAW president's dovish instincts were trapped within what [top Reuther aide] Jack Conway called an 'institutional personality' that Reuther thought mandated a public cordial relationship with the [Johnson] administration."[11]

Roy Reuther, who ran the union's political and legislative operations, had been a hawk on Vietnam, but by 1968 Roy, Walter's brother, saw the war as a disaster. In March of that year, Reuther told the UAW board the labor movement "has to have the youth. It has to have the student movement . . . the kind of forces that motivated guys to go to Mississippi to start the civil rights movement."[12]

A March 19, 1968, board meeting proved crucial. At the meeting, Walter Reuther sought to keep the union neutral in the Democratic presidential race during primary season. With both Senators Eugene McCarthy and Robert Kennedy seeking the nomination in opposition to the Johnson-Humphrey administration's war policies, the UAW board rejected Reuther's position. The pivotal moment came when Leonard Woodcock, generally viewed as hawkish on Vietnam, delivered a strong critique of the war and of President Johnson.

Most top UAW leaders then were free to campaign for Kennedy or McCarthy and to embrace their various criticisms of the Vietnam War.

With Richard Nixon's defeat of Vice President Hubert Humphrey in the general election in 1968, Walter Reuther strongly escalated his opposition to the war. He endorsed the Vietnam Moratorium antiwar demonstrations in the fall of 1969, the largest protests of the time, and the UAW helped fund them.

Having split in 1968 from the AFL-CIO in part over opposition to its staunch support of the war, Reuther pushed the union into a new relationship with the Teamsters union called the Alliance for Labor Action. Soon, the ALA, with the Teamsters' blessing, was echoing the UAW call for an end to the war in Vietnam.

In April 1970, President Nixon expanded the war into Cambodia and pushed America into even deeper polarization. College campuses quickly erupted in student demonstrations, which escalated after members of the Ohio National Guard shot into an antiwar crowd at Kent State University. Four students were killed, including the daughter of a UAW member.

Reuther sent a telegram to Nixon on May 7, 1970, attacking the "needless and inexcusable use of military force" at home. He also blasted the president for widening the war as "a moral defeat beyond measure among the people of the world." By the time the UAW message was sent, two more students had been killed at Jackson State College in Mississippi.[13]

That telegram opposing the killings of antiwar students at home and the expansion of the Vietnam War into Cambodia may have been Walter Reuther's last public statement.

Two days later, the UAW president, who had achieved so much for so many, boarded a two-engine Lear jet with his wife and two others on a trip to the union's brand-new Black Lake education center.

At 9:33 p.m. in fog and rain, the plane crashed into trees near the runway at Pellston, Michigan, and burst into flames, killing all the passengers, including Walter Reuther.

The UAW chose Leonard Woodcock to succeed Reuther. One of his first tasks as UAW president was to take Reuther's place before a Senate hearing chaired by Senator J. William Fulbright on the impact of the war on the economy.

Woodcock submitted a 75-page statement that argued that, at home, the heaviest human costs of the war had fallen on the working people of America. He told the senators that 9 million man-years had been squandered that could have gone into building the economy by producing goods and services to benefit the American public.[14]

He also criticized the contention that the Vietnam War had benefited labor by creating jobs. The new UAW leader described how, before the war, the economy had been growing and likely would have continued to create jobs meeting America's many civilian needs. And Woodcock argued for programs that would convert defense facilities to nondefense production and prevent layoffs.

The UAW leaders who followed Reuther and Woodcock would echo that "swords into ploughshares" theme.

UAW Secretary-Treasurer Ray Majerus spoke out frequently about the need for job security for defense-industry workers, who experienced spurts of employment and unemployment, depending on changes in the military budget.

"It's a terrible thing for workers to feel that their jobs and the health of their families are dependent on the continuation of the arms race," Majerus told a conference in Michigan that examined how to maintain an adequate national defense while achieving full employment.

"True national security for the people in the breadlines and unemployment lines of this nation will not be found by looking down the barrel of a gun, no matter how big it is, how fancy it is, or how fast it flies. This has never been the answer for the workers and the poor in the U.S. or around the world."[15]

When Owen Bieber became UAW president, he also continued to speak out on the issues of war and peace during and after the first Gulf War.

Bieber had argued for sufficient time for sanctions against Saddam Hussein to be allowed to work before the U.S. invasion in 1991. But with the onset of war, he told the UAW Community Action Program conference in Washington, D.C., "We stand united in support of our men and women in Operation Desert Storm."

"Our thoughts and prayers are with our troops and their families," Bieber said. "May they accomplish their mission with all due speed and, more importantly, with minimal loss of military and civilian life."

But Bieber also raised the issue of what kind of America the troops would return to:

"While the President [George H.W. Bush] has committed our sons and daughters to fight a war against Saddam Hussein, he refuses to join the fight here at home to secure America's economic future. Mr. President, you need to ask yourself what kind of America our troops will be coming home to.

"Will the same young Americans who mastered the most advanced technologies ever used in war come home only to find there is no place for them to use their skills and knowledge in rewarding jobs? Will they come home from the front lines

Carl Sagan (left), the noted astronomer and educator, spoke to the UAW International Executive Board in 1985 about the dangers of nuclear war and urged the union to continue its work opposing the arms race. Photo by Russ Marshall.

only to stand in the long lines at the unemployment offices?

"Thirty percent of the troops in Operation Desert Storm are members of minorities; six percent are women. Are you going to tell them that while they were risking their lives in the desert, you were using the power of the presidency to deny them the full protection of the laws against discrimination?"

The UAW president received a thundering ovation when he closed by saying, "Our nation has waited too long for attention to be paid to our needs here at home. We can wait no more."

Bieber's call sadly remained relevant as troops returned home from Iraq and Afghanistan to an economy racked by high unemployment, huge trade deficits, stagnating real wages, and massive inequality during the George W. Bush presidency.

After those early Iraq and Afghanistan veterans returned during UAW President Ron Gettelfinger's term, he spoke in 2006 to the Michigan Paralyzed Veterans of America.

Gettelfinger asked: "What more can we do for those who have served our country with such honor and dignity?

"We can stand tall and be counted by using the freedom that our veterans have preserved for all of us. . . . We can stand up and say it's time to end the insanity of giving away the opportunity for our children and grandchildren to have a better life.

"We can vote in every election to elect representatives . . . who will protect and improve veterans' benefits instead of reducing them. And for candidates who will stand up for increasing the minimum wage, providing healthcare for all of our citizens, and candidates who will insist on fair trade and not free trade."

UAW leaders sounded a similar theme in 2010 at the "Rebuild America: Jobs, Justice, and Peace" march that began at the UAW-Ford National Programs Center in Detroit.

The rally called for "ending the ongoing wars in Afghanistan and Iraq, saving lives, and redirecting the war budget to

Then UAW President Bob King and Secretary-Treasurer Dennis Williams, both veterans, joined Vice President Joe Ashton and Jim Taylor, chair of the UAW National Veterans Advisory Committee, in 2014 in laying a wreath at the Tomb of the Unknowns at Arlington National Cemetery. Photo by Jay Makled.

rebuilding America."

Among the lives too late to save was that of Marine Lance Corporal Timothy Serwinowski, son of UAW Local 774 member Phillip Serwinowski.

Cut down in Afghanistan by Taliban sniper fire, Timothy did not get a chance to return home to join his union family around the dinner table, or to marry and have children, or to see himself honored by UAW veterans committees.

Timothy is gone, but his UAW family fights on to stop the madness of wars that have no end.

REPRESSION IS NOT AN OLYMPIC SPORT

釋放所有工人活動家

FREE CHINA'S LABOR ACTIVISTS

The Chinese people deserve to host the 2008 Olympic games. But the Chinese government does not. China has jailed hundreds of labor activists for exercising internationally recognized worker rights. You can support the Olympic spirit by sending a message to the Chinese government demanding the release of imprisoned labor activists.

Write today to President Jiang Zemin, People's Republic of China, c/o P.O. Box 1800, Washington, DC 20034, USA. LABOR RIGHTS NOW! has launched an international campaign seeking the release of China's jailed labor activists. Labor Rights Now! is a project of the UAW working with the AFL-CIO on behalf of imprisoned and endangered trade unionists around the world. Please contact us at the project coordinator, Labor Rights Now, c/o UAW, 1757 N Street, N.W., Washington, DC 20036, USA. Or email us at laborrights.org, or visit our website at www.LaborRightsNow.org. Poster produced by Don Munoz and Kristyne Peter, Bar One Media. Illustration: Byron Gonzalez, Calligraphy by Chen Wing.

CHAPTER SIXTEEN

UAW Fights Labor Abuses In China
Repression There Costs Jobs Here

Yao Fuxin, a former steelworker, ran a small convenience store in Liaoyang, China, with his wife, who worked at the Ferroalloy factory, where layoffs and unpaid wages had resulted in repeated protests.

On March 17, 2002, Yao rose early and went out to get tobacco and other items needed to restock the store. He didn't come back.

A friend, Xiao Yunliang, searched the neighborhood because Yao's family feared the ties local Communist Party officials had to organized crime. Yao and Xiao had led earlier protests of factory workers that had angered those officials.

Xiao soon found Yao's moped in a ditch and talked to a local resident nearby, who said three men grabbed Yao and took him away in a car. Although no officials would confirm that Yao had been arrested, Xiao and his fellow workers believed that was what had happened.

The next day, more than 30,000 protesters marched down Democracy Road to the local party headquarters. While it was another in a series of demonstrations over layoffs, unpaid wages, and corruption, the crowd now angrily demanded the release of Yao Fuxin. He had become one of China's most outspoken labor activists during the time of the Liaoyang upheaval.[1]

Yao's daughter addressed the crowd through a megaphone and demanded that the authorities tell them where her father was being held. In addition to Ferroalloy workers, many from more than 20 factories in the Liaoyang area carried signs calling for Yao's release.

Two days later, authorities went to Xiao Yunliang's home and took him to a meeting of government officials. They told him they had purchased airline tickets for him and his family to take a vacation in Yunnan Province thousands of miles away.[2]

"As long as you take the trip and forget about Yao, we'll let bygones be bygones," one of the officials told Xiao, who immediately rejected the offer. "We're going to squash you if you don't go," came the response, according to Philip P. Pan in his excellent book *Out of Mao's Shadow*.

Soon, the authorities arrested Xiao, and he joined Yao in prison for participating in labor protests in the northwestern Chinese city.

UAW President Steve Yokich protested the arrests shortly after they occurred and demanded that China's top leaders intervene. It was the beginning of a seven-year campaign waged by the union to win freedom for Yao and Xiao and to stand in solidarity with workers in China.

The UAW took up these cases because they vividly illustrated the Chinese government's harsh repression of worker activists who sought to exercise internationally recognized labor rights.

For millions of Chinese workers to have a better life, the UAW argued, they should have the right to form unions independent of government or party control. Those independent unions should have leaders democratically chosen by workers and should vigorously advocate for wage increases, expanded benefits, and workplace rights.

Beginning in the 1990s, with China's labor costs just a small fraction of those in the United States and workers regularly putting in extremely long hours in harsh and often unsafe factories, U.S. imports of Chinese production had rapidly be-gun to cost good-paying American jobs.

The revolt in Liaoyang in 2001–2002 stood out as one of the clearest examples of workers paying a heavy price for the massive privatization that occurred as the country shifted away from state-owned enterprises toward its own brand of authoritarian capitalism.

Yao Fuxin did not seem particularly suited to emerge as a labor leader. After his wife was laid off at Ferroalloy, other unhappy workers would gather at night in their convenience store and discuss developments at the factory. They focused much of their anger on Fan Yicheng, the party official who had risen to become plant manager in 1993.[3]

Fan privatized certain segments of production, and workers suspected the new independent firms included the most profitable elements of Ferroalloy's business. By the mid-1990s, Fan had begun to miss payroll and to lay off workers. In the years that followed, Ferroalloy failed to pay for workers' health insurance premiums and to set aside money for their pensions.

One of the accountants for the factory began joining the group at Yao's store. She soon revealed that the plant manager and other party officials indeed reaped huge windfalls by transferring Ferroalloy assets to private companies they owned or controlled. The accountant had tried to report the crimes, but authorities had jailed her for 19 days and made it clear the factory manager's party status made him untouchable.[4]

Yao, Xiao, and another worker, Pang Qingxiang, soon led a group of Ferroalloy employees who drafted letters outlining their grievances and demanding a meeting with government officials.

"The official trade union controlled by the party—the only union allowed under law—rebuffed them," Pan wrote. "The labor arbitration bureau refused to accept their case. The state media, the police, the courts, the prosecutors, the party's discipline office—they all turned them away, too."[5]

Protests broke out in 2000 after Ferroalloy workers had gone two years without pay and up to 4,000 retirees and laid-off workers had not received the benefit payments owed them for as long as six months. Anti-riot police attacked the demonstrators, who had blocked Zhenxing Road, which connected Liaoyang and the provincial capital of Shenyang.[6]

"What I saw was the despotism of the Communist Party," Xiao said later. "I saw workers begging for food, and the party respond with armed force."[7]

In addition to protesting the nonpayment of wages and benefits, the workers in Liaoyang continued to demand investigations into corruption by factory managers, government officials, and party leaders. Their appeals had been fueled in part by revelations of corruption on the part of the mayor of Shenyang.

"When investigators searched two country houses belonging to Shenyang's mayor, they found $6 million worth of gold bars hidden in the walls, 150 Rolex watches, [and] computer files documenting years of illegal activities," according to John Pomfret, a journalist who covered China for *The Washington Post*.[8] And Shenyang's deputy mayor had gambled away about $5 million of public funds in Macao and Las Vegas.[9]

The workers in Liaoyang saw the corruption as even more widespread and believed factory closings and bankruptcies occurred as part of a broader pattern of malfeasance. The Communist Party itself regularly condemned corruption, so Yao and Xiao sought to rally protesters on that issue in hopes their actions would not be crushed.

"We were trying to promote democracy, but we couldn't say it," Xiao said later. "So we decided to protest against corruption. We wanted to use the corrupt behavior of factory and city officials to motivate people and wake them to the cause."[10] The strategy sought to split national party leaders from those in Liaoyang.

Yao and Xiao also knew that in the past, officials would divide the workers at different factories by giving in on a wage demand here or a reinstatement there. The tactic made it hard to sustain a broader fight because workers would end their protests once their own plant issues had been resolved, even when their colleagues at other factories still tried to fight on.

On March 11, 2002, a misstep by a top party official who led Liaoyang's delegation to the National People's Congress meeting in Beijing fueled the workers' anger even more. Gong Shangwu told a television reporter "there are no unemployed in Liaoyang."[11] He also said laid-off workers received a living stipend of 280 yuan per month.

The statements stirred up many in Liaoyang, and they took to the streets in protest, led by Yao and Xiao. On March 12,

释放中国的劳工积极份子

FREE CHINA'S
LABOR ACTIVISTS

In China, supporting a trade union
can get you a long sentence in prison.

Yao delivered a rousing speech in front of City Hall. His arm cradled an elderly widow of one of the workers as he told the angry crowd: "We devoted our youth to the party, but no one supports us in old age," Pan wrote in *Out of Mao's Shadow*.[12]

The next day, government officials invited Yao and Xiao to negotiate on the second floor of City Hall and promised to address the workers' complaints if the protest ended. They discussed the back wages due the workers at Ferroalloy and other factories and the unpaid benefits. It seemed like a good start, so Yao and Xiao called off the protests.

Nothing happened for three days, but on the fourth the deputy mayor called in Xiao and Yao and demanded they "put the brakes on this movement."

"Don't push it any further," he ordered. "Your problem is already an international one now. Overseas, they're calling you labor leaders."[13]

Lacking any concessions that addressed the workers' demands, Yao and Xiao thanked the deputy mayor. As they departed, Xiao told him: "We can't rush out and tell everyone not to protest just because you told us not to."

It was the next morning that Yao went out to buy items to restock his store and plainclothes police grabbed him.

The protests continued with thousands of workers in the streets. Yao's family learned from officers of the Public Service Bureau that he was in custody. On March 21, he was allowed to phone his wife from the Tieling city police lockup, about 60 miles from Liaoyang.[14]

The *Liaoyang Daily* described Yao's actions as "putting up posters in public places and making links of cooperation among workers from different factories" and reported these actions as criminal activities. Government officials also blamed "outside agitators" from Hong Kong and foreign "black hands," including overseas media, for fanning the unrest.[15]

While Yao and Xiao faced the possibility of long jail sentences, Ferroalloy workers reportedly received half their back wages and part of their severance pay. Authorities once again decided to make tactical concessions to deflate the protests rather than risk broader insurrection.

As the protests petered out, Yao's wife finally saw him in jail and found the right side of his body was numb. He had been kept in leg irons and seemed in poor health.

Yao's daughter helped lead some additional rallies calling for the release of her father and Xiao. But police had visited many of the other leaders of the workers and threatened them. They also demanded that those activists spy on their colleagues and, in return, "your financial problems will go away."[16]

The government paid out more money in back wages and benefits to the Ferroalloy and other workers. They did not get all they were owed, but enough to dampen further protests.

In addition, authorities pursued Fan Yicheng, the factory manager, on corruption charges after the workers' claims were investigated. Government-controlled media reported about $12.5 million was unaccounted for at Ferroalloy.

Despite relative calm, the Liaoyang workers soon found themselves under attack by the very institution that should have protected them. The All-China Federation of Trade Unions (ACFTU), the government-controlled official union federation, blasted the workers during the annual conference of the International Labor Organization (ILO) in Geneva, Switzerland.

An ACFTU spokesperson said Yao and Xiao had been arrested not only for "illegally demonstrating," but also because they had "burned cars and destroyed public property."[17]

The UAW and the AFL-CIO had supported a formal complaint on behalf of Yao and Xiao filed by the International Confederation of Free Trade Unions (ICFTU) with the ILO's Committee on Freedom of Association. The Chinese government responded in September 2002, just a year after the 9/11 attacks

in the United States, that Yao and Xiao had "jointly carried out planned activities of terrorism and sabotage."[18]

"Such arbitrary smear tactics have long been the hallmark of legal proceedings in China against dissidents of all kinds," said a report on the Liaoyang protests by the *China Labour Bulletin*, with which the UAW worked closely. "In this case, they were clearly an effort by desperate officials eager to destroy the public reputation of Yao Fuxin and his fellow detainees and to dissuade the international community from any further condemnation of the authorities' repressive tactics against the Liaoyang workers' movement as a whole."[19]

UAW President Steve Yokich continued to demand freedom for Yao and Xiao despite the charges of violence and terrorism from the ACFTU and the Chinese government. Yokich dismissed those claims as a heavy-handed and failed attempt to invoke public fears in the aftermath of 9/11 that had no relevance to what had occurred in Liaoyang.

The credibility of the claims was shredded further in November 2002 when the ACFTU's local leader denied them. A Mr. Su was chairman of the Liaoyang Municipal Trade Unions. In a recorded telephone interview with Han Dongfang, *China Labour Bulletin* director, Su denied there was any violence during the Liaoyang protests.

"No, everything was peaceful," the ACFTU local leader said. "There is no way that Yao Fuxin was involved [in burning cars]. . . . Nothing was especially serious. [Protesters] were just going to the government to petition and voice their views. Nothing more than that. There was no violence or extreme behavior of any sort."[20]

A second interview by Han Dongfang with an official from the Liaoyang Government's Security Office, reported in the *Bulletin*, confirmed that no violence had occurred.[21]

When Yao and Xiao faced trial in January 2003, the government dropped the false terrorism claim. Both men

10

were charged with "illegal assembly and demonstration" and a far more serious charge of "subversion."

The Chinese government failed to honor its own laws on access to lawyers and the specific charges in the indictment. Yao's lawyer, Mo Shaoping, had sought to meet with him beginning in July 2002, but the authorities repeatedly denied his request. Finally, five days before the trial, Yao got access to his lawyer.

When the trial began, several hundred Liaoyang workers protested in front of the Liaoyang Intermediate People's Court. "How is it a crime to ask for our wages?" one worker asked. "How can that be subverting state power?"[22]

Inside the courtroom, prosecutors did not call any witnesses to support the charges against Yao and Xiao, thereby preventing any cross-examination by the defense.

Xiao testified that he had helped organize demonstrations at which his fellow workers could express the grievances they experienced, including failure to be paid back wages and benefits owed them. Xiao himself had not received wages for the 23 months prior to the demonstrations, he testified.

Yao admitted he had gone to several rallies of the China Democracy Party but said he did not join the party. He said the protests occurred because workers were suffering, including those who were old and sick. Some Ferroalloy workers had not been paid in more than 20 months, Yao testified, and then broke down in tears.[23]

After only four hours, the court adjourned without delivering a verdict, and the two defendants remained in jail.

After the trial, the home telephones of Yao and Xiao no longer could receive incoming calls, presumably to prevent their families from talking with foreign news media covering the situation. Yao's family tried to have a new phone line installed, but the technician who came to the house refused to proceed once he realized the situation.

In February 2003, the two labor leaders' homes were placed under 24-hour surveillance by police, and family members were prevented from leaving without approval. Authorities likely hoped to intimidate them from organizing protests on the one-year anniversary of the Liaoyang uprising.

The campaign to free Yao and Xiao got a boost in March 2003, when the International Labor Organization upheld the complaint against the Chinese government over the detention and prosecution of Yao and Xiao. The ILO demanded that China release them and drop all charges.

Instead, on May 9, 2003, the Liaoyang Intermediate Court announced that Yao and Xiao had both been found guilty. Yao received a seven-year prison sentence and Xiao got four years imprisonment.

UAW President Ron Gettelfinger blasted China for the shameful verdicts and lengthy prison terms.

UAW President Dennis Williams met with reporters at the union's headquarters. Behind him are the union's posters that called for the release of labor prisoners in China (see next page for larger version).

The UAW produced this poster calling for the release of Yao and Xiao.

In a letter to Jiechi Yang, the Chinese ambassador to the United States, Gettelfinger wrote: "With this decision, China has sent a chilling message to millions of workers that peaceful labor protest will end in subversion trials."

The UAW president also questioned China's legitimacy as a member of the International Labor Organization and the World Trade Organization.

"I strongly urge China to halt the outrageous and continuing repression of its workers," Gettelfinger told the Chinese ambassador.

Yao and Xiao appealed their guilty verdicts and prison sentences, but predictably the appeals were rejected.

Yao ended up in Lingyan No. 2 Prison, where his health deteriorated quickly. He suffered from heart disease and high blood pressure that went untreated.

Authorities feared that Yao maintained his influence in the outside world. As a result, they treated him harshly.

"He is not allowed to talk with other prisoners, go outside for fresh air, or to dry his clothes outside of his tiny prison cell," reported Human Rights in China in December 2004. "Two prisoners have been assigned to monitor Yao's every movement, even his brief toilet breaks. He is not allowed to read books or newspapers or telephone his family."[24]

Human Rights in China also revealed that prison officials threatened Yao by telling him that visits from his family would be curtailed or ended if reports of his treatment and condition circulated outside the prison.

Gettelfinger continued to raise Yao and Xiao in speeches and testimony. China's rulers knew the UAW quite well, largely due to the time former UAW President Leonard Woodcock spent in Beijing as the first United States ambassador to the People's Republic of China.

President Carter appointed Woodcock to that crucial position where the retired union leader served from 1979 to 1981. Despite the lines of communication between the UAW and

China's leaders that developed during that period, the union became increasingly critical of Beijing's repeated abuses of labor rights during the last 25 years.

"The Chinese government's behavior in the [Yao and Xiao] cases, and countless others, is shameful and inexcusable," UAW President Gettelfinger said in testimony before the U.S.-China Economic and Security Review Commission on September 23, 2004. "Both men suffer from serious illnesses and should be released from prison on medical grounds.

"The large profits reported by many of the automotive joint venture companies in China are the result, in part, of the inability of Chinese workers to form organizations that can represent the interests of workers in receiving a fair share of the value of their contribution to the production process."[25]

The UAW repeatedly asked China to release Yao and Xiao on humanitarian grounds, as did other labor groups and human rights organizations. We hoped arguing for medical parole might provide Chinese authorities with a face-saving path to freedom for the two men.

We worked closely with NGOs and the U.S. State Department to get Yao and Xiao included on lists of political prisoners so their cases would be raised in official meetings between the two governments.

In the end, despite all the pressure, Yao served his full seven-year sentence, and Xiao served nearly all of his four-year term.

The UAW work on behalf of Yao and Xiao did help to publicly highlight the abuses of labor rights by China at a time when its government sought global legitimacy.

The union had waged similar campaigns on behalf of other jailed worker activists in China. We opened a new front in such efforts shortly after the 2000 Olympic Games.

The city of Beijing had lost its bid in 1993 to host the 2000 Summer Games. China resolved then to win the right to host the 2008 Olympics. It promised to improve its human and labor rights record as part of the overall pitch.

In February 2001, I wrote to Hein Verbruggen, who chaired the Evaluation Commission of the International Olympic Committee, to express fears about Beijing's application to host the games.

"The UAW is particularly concerned about the application of Beijing because of the deterioration in the human and labor rights record of the government of the People's Republic of China," my letter stated. "Hundreds of worker activists currently are imprisoned in China for exercising internationally recognized labor rights as defined by the International Labor Organization.

"There are those who attempt to argue that Olympic competition should occur without regard to the world's political problems," I wrote. "That wasn't true in 1936 when Jesse Owens won the Gold in Berlin. It isn't true today. And it won't be true in 2008, particularly if Beijing hosts the Games while many Chinese citizens languish in prison merely for attempting to exercise basic human and labor rights."

Along with my letter, I enclosed one sent by UAW President Yokich to Jiang Zemin, China's president, detailing the cases of a number of labor activists who had been imprisoned by his government.

"The UAW asks that the IOC Evaluation Commission raise these cases with officials of the Chinese government during your visit to Beijing this month," my letter stated. "If this cannot be done publicly, we hope you will do so privately."

Paris, Toronto, Istanbul, and Osaka also sought to host the 2008 games. All appeared to be good possibilities, so we believed our pressure might cause China to release some of the worker activists to boost Beijing's candidacy. In the past, Chinese leaders often orchestrated such releases to occur before global summits and other important international gatherings.

Despite modest lip service about concern for human rights, the International Olympic Committee totally failed to raise our cases or any others. With its tremendous leverage,

the IOC abandoned its ideals and awarded the 2008 Summer Games to Beijing.

While this was a defeat, we still hoped China might respond to Beijing's successful bid by reducing its violations of labor and human rights.

In 2002, we produced a poster headlined "Repression Is Not an Olympic Sport." The art portrayed workers' arms chained by the five Olympic "rings" in front of the Olympic torch.

"The Chinese people deserve to host the 2008 games," the poster stated. "But the Chinese government does not. China has jailed hundreds of labor activists for exercising their internationally recognized worker rights."

The UAW also highlighted specific cases in an attempt to put a human face on China's abuses of labor rights. Among the individuals we focused on were:

- Peng Shi, an electrical worker, who was sentenced to life imprisonment for leading a worker protest at the Xiangtan Electrical Machinery Plant in China;
- Yue Tianxiang, who received a 10-year prison term for helping workers who sought unpaid wages from Tianshui Auto Transport Co. and for publishing a newsletter, the *Chinese Workers' Monitor*;
- Hu Shigen, who was the founding member of the "China Free Labor Union" and received a 20-year prison sentence;
- Kong Youping, a former official trade union leader, who got a 15-year sentence for his labor activism, which the government called "subversion";
- Li Wangyang, who served a 13-year prison term in the 1990s for organizing workers and a second sentence of 10 years for "incitement to subvert state power" in 2001; and
- Hu Mingjun, a labor organizer who helped workers at Dazhou Steel Mill in their campaign to win unpaid wages and got an 11-year prison sentence.

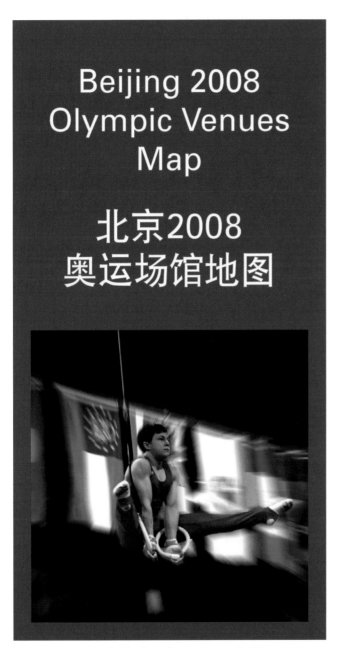

Labor Rights Now produced a "tourist" map of venues for the 2008 Olympic Games in Beijing. On the inside, the map highlighted the cases of 11 Chinese worker activists imprisoned by the government (see map on next two pages).

All of the UAW materials on China's repression of its workers urged union members to send letters, faxes, or e-mails to China's president and premier. Many UAW locals took up the labor rights cases and raised the profile of China's repression as the Olympics approached.

I also wrote to Jacques Rogge, who had become president of the International Olympic Committee.

"China deserves a gold medal for labor repression," my letter stated. "China's leaders have reneged on their promise to the world that they would improve their abysmal human rights record in order to win the right to host the Olympics."

I urged Rogge to appoint a blue-ribbon commission to go to China to examine the failure of China to honor promises it made to the IOC to improve its human and labor rights record.

"I ask that the International Olympic Committee press the Chinese government for the release of Yao Fuxin and other imprisoned worker activists," the letter said.

Rogge was born in Belgium under Nazi occupation. He participated in the Olympics in yachting in 1968, 1972, and 1978. He not only failed to raise labor rights with Beijing officials but also secretly agreed to allow Chinese authorities to censor the Internet during the 2008 games.

Our final effort to leverage the Beijing games to win freedom for worker activists came in the month leading up to the games, July 2008.

We produced what appeared to be a run-of-the-mill tourist map of Beijing with the Olympic venues marked. The map had old Olympic posters on the back and details of the medal counts from past games.

But when you opened the map, there was a surprise. While the various venues for the different Olympic events were shown on the map, so were 11 boxes, each of which called for the release of a specific worker activist who was in prison.

Our goal was to get the map in the hands of tourists headed to Beijing for the Olympics. We mailed thousands of maps

Free Ning Xianhua (Liaoning) 宁先华

Labor activist and political organizer sentenced in the same trial as Kong Youping. Convicted by the Shenyang Intermediate People's Court and sentenced to 12 years' imprisonment on September 16, 2004. Co-defendant with Kong Youping at the September 2004 trial. Kong Youping and Ning Xianhua were convicted of "subversion" at their trial.

Status: Due for release on December 12, 2015.

Free Hu Shigen (Beijing) 胡石根

Founding member of "China Free Labor Union." Academic at Beijing Foreign Languages Institute and leader of China Liberal Democratic Party. Arrested with 15 other activists from unofficial trade union and party who made up "Beijing Sixteen." Convicted of "organizing and leading a counterrevolutionary group" and "counterrevolutionary propaganda and incitement" by the Beijing Intermediate People's Court and sentenced on June 14, 1995 to 20 years' imprisonment. He received sentence reduction of 7 months on Dec. 16, 2005 and of 17 months on Feb. 5, 2007.

Status: Due for release from Beijing No. 2 Prison on May 26, 2010.

Free Li Xintao (Shandong) 李信涛

Garment worker who, with Kong Jun, led workers in petition protest against a Yantai factory's failure to make wage and insurance payments. Convicted of "gathering a crowd to attack an organ of the state" by Mouping District People's Court and sentenced in May 2005 to five years' imprisonment.

Status: Due for release in November 2009.

Free Kong Youping (Liaoning) 孔佑平

A former official trade union leader in Liaoning P... sentenced to 15 years' imprisonment on Sep... Intermediate People's Court. Kong's co... 2004 trial, Ning Xianhua, was s... years old, originally work... in Liaoning. Kong ... their trial.

Free Wang Sen

Political activist and labo... in Sichuan. Convicted o... and sentenced on May 3... has deteriorated and he...

Status: Due for release...

Beijing Olympic Green Tennis Court

Beijing Olympi... Green Hocke... Stadium

China Agricultural University Gymnasium

Beijing Science and Technology University Gymnasium

Peking University Gymnasium

Beijing University of Aero & Astronautics Gymnasium

Beijing Institute of Technology Gymnasium

Qinghua Xilu

Qinghua Donglu

Beijing University

Tsinghua University

Chengfu Lu

Chengfu Lu

Beisihuan Xilu

Beisihuan Xilu

Huayuan Beilu

Beituchengxilu

Great Bell Temple

Beijing Art Museum

Beijing North Railway Station

Beijing Zoo

Shuangqing Lu

Xueyuan Lu

Changping Lu

Zhongguancun Beidajie

Suzhoujie

Kunminghu Lu

Wangu

Zhongguancun Nadajie

Suzhoujie Lu

Landianchang Beilu

Xisihuan Beilu

Xisihuan Beilu

Zizhuyuan Lu

Zongguancun Nadajie

Xinjiekou Waid

Deshengm

WORKER ACTIVISTS

工运人士

Free Yao Fuxin (Liaoning) 姚福信

Leader of large-scale worker demonstrations after Liaoyang Ferro-Alloy Factory declared bankruptcy and failed to make wage/benefit/pension payments to workers. Leader of "All-Liaoyang Bankrupt and Unemployed Workers' Provisional Union." Convicted of subversion by Liaoyang Intermediate People's Court and sentenced on May 9, 2003 to seven years' imprisonment. Appeal was rejected by Liaoning Higher People's Court on June 27, 2003. Serving sentence in Lingyuan No. 2 Prison, where he suffered a heart attack in August 2005.

Status: Due for release on March 19, 2009.

Free Liu Zhihua (Hunan) 刘智华

Member of Xiangtan Workers' Autonomous Federation involved in a large-scale strike in 1989. Convicted of "hooliganism" and aggravated assault by Xiangtan Intermediate People's Court and sentenced in October 1989 to life imprisonment. Sentence commuted to 15 years' imprisonment in 1993, extended by five years in 1997, and reduced by two years in 2001.

Status: Due for release from Longxi Prison on January 16, 2011.

Free Hu Mingjun (Sichuan) 胡明军

Political activist and labor organizer who communicated with workers on strike at Dazhou Steel Mill over unpaid wages. Led Sichuan unit of China Democratic Party (CDP). Convicted of subversion by the Dazhou Intermediate People's Court and sentenced on May 30, 2002 to 11 years' imprisonment.

Status: Due for release from Chuanzhong Prison on May 28, 2012.

Free the Sanming 3

Li Jianfeng, Lin Shun'an, and Huang Xiangwei were accused of organizing the "Labor and Employment Research Association," of downloading labor union-related materials from the Internet, and of allegedly trying to form labor unions. Convicted by the Sanming Intermediate People's Court and sentenced in 2003.

Status: Li Jianfeng is due for release April 2, 2018. Lin Shun'an is due for release in April 2010, and Huang Xiangwei is due for release in 2008.

3, 2001 for organizing workers
u Intermediate People's Court
onment. Reportedly, his health

ng) Prison on May 2, 2011.

y Don Stillman, Big Oak Media, for Labor Rights Now.
Doe Bay Institute. Design by Katerina Barry.

to travel agents. In addition, we placed the maps in the airport waiting areas where passengers boarded flights from the United States to Beijing in the 10 days preceding the Olympics.

The hope was travelers would pick up the map thinking it would be useful at the Olympics. Upon opening it, they would be exposed to China's offensive violations of labor rights. Given the controversial nature of the map, we knew also that Chinese officials soon would see that labor rights advocates had penetrated the glitter of the Olympics with the sad truths about Beijing's abysmal labor rights record.

In addition to standing in solidarity with jailed worker activists and others who sought independent unions to improve the living standards in China, the UAW took on China regarding an important environmental issue.

The Chinese government launched a project to build Three Gorges Dam in Hubei province in the mid-1990s. The hydroelectric project displaced about 1.4 million Chinese citizens who lived along the Yangtze River in areas that now are underwater.

Friends of the Earth, a prominent environmental group, strongly opposed the Three Gorges Dam project, as did other green organizations the UAW worked with on various issues over the years.

The UAW had been in a five-year series of disputes with Caterpillar, the heavy-equipment manufacturer that began when the company locked out UAW members in 1991. Strikes occurred in 1992 and 1994, and Caterpillar committed numerous unfair labor practices. The National Labor Relations Board (NLRB) repeatedly found Caterpillar had violated federal labor law.

Caterpillar had sought $200 million in tax-subsidized funding to provide heavy-duty construction equipment and machinery to China for use in the Three Gorges Dam project.

We reached out to Friends of the Earth and began to learn more about the damaging impact the dam would have on the Chinese people who lived nearby and on the broader environment.

Soon, the UAW and Friends of the Earth began working to deny Caterpillar the subsidized financing it sought from the Export-Import Bank of the United States.

"We believe Three Gorges Dam will go down in history as an environmental disaster—a Chernobyl, Love Canal, and Three Mile Island rolled into one," said UAW President Steve Yokich and Vice President Dick Shoemaker. Shoemaker, among his other responsibilities, then directed the union's Caterpillar Department.

Human Rights Watch revealed that Chinese government officials planned to use forced prison labor from the notorious Shayang Farm, the biggest prison labor camp in China, to work on the dam. About 70,000 prisoners were held there, just 75 miles from the dam site.

Friends of the Earth argued the dam could cause the water quality of the Yangtze's tributaries to deteriorate, as the dammed river would be less able to disperse pollutants effectively. The rising water also could cause rampant soil erosion and result in riverbank collapses and landslides.

The UAW began an intensive lobbying campaign with the Export-Import Bank to deny Caterpillar the funding it sought for the Three Gorges Dam construction.

Yokich and Shoemaker argued the bank would be contributing to an environmental disaster if it provided Caterpillar with funding. With help from Friends of the Earth and International Rivers, another green organization, we described how the dam would worsen the sediment problem and cause toxic contamination from the 1,600 factories and mines in the area to be flooded by the dam's reservoir.

In May 1996, the Export-Import Bank announced it would not support loans to U.S. companies pursuing Three Gorges Dam contracts. The decision resulted in Caterpillar being denied its $200 million funding.

"The Bank's decision is the right one for American workers," Yokich and Shoemaker said in a statement after the decision. "We don't want to see U.S. taxpayer funds go to projects that use slave labor, such as the Three Gorges Dam in China."

In 1997, UAW President Yokich and I went to Hong Kong with AFL-CIO President John Sweeney to meet with unions there that were deeply worried about what would happen when the United Kingdom handed over control of Hong Kong to China.

British Prime Minister Margaret Thatcher, a right-wing conservative, agreed to return control of Hong Kong to the Chinese government in the mid-1980s. Negotiators accepted a principle of "One Country, Two Systems," yet unions in Hong Kong feared that, once China had control, it would impose harsh limits on labor.

Lee Cheuk Yan, the general secretary of the Hong Kong Confederation of Trade Unions (HKCTU), described how independent unions in Hong Kong had won higher wages and better working conditions through negotiations and occasional work stoppages. Now, he feared Beijing would crack down on the freedom Hong Kong workers enjoyed, rather than risk Chinese workers demanding similar rights.

"Our goal was to express the support of the American labor movement for Hong Kong workers and their unions during a period in which their gains appeared correctly to be in jeopardy," Yokich later reported to delegates to the UAW's convention in 1998.

"Unfortunately, worker rights there were the first to be attacked after China took over Hong Kong," the UAW president stated.

The new Beijing-controlled government in Hong Kong quickly suspended three important labor laws:

- The first gave workers the right to collective bargaining if a union has the support of more than 50 percent of the workers and if it has 15 percent of them as members.
- The second law protected Hong Kong workers in the event they were fired or victimized because of union activity, and it detailed their right to reinstatement.
- The third law limited the ability of government to interfere in trade union activities and gave Hong Kong workers the right to affiliate with international union organizations without government approval.

While in Hong Kong, we met with Tung Chee-Hwa, whom Beijing had installed to run Hong Kong. Yokich and Sweeney warned him that repression of Hong Kong unions and workers would result in international condemnation.

By suspending Hong Kong's labor laws just two weeks after the handover from the British, China's rulers made it clear they cared little about honoring the "One Country, Two Systems" commitment they had made to the United Kingdom and the world.

UAW President Steve Yokich joined AFL-CIO President John Sweeney at a Capitol Hill rally in 2000. Yokich strongly opposed admission of China to the World Trade Organization while it continued to deny its workers internationally recognized labor rights.

The UAW's strong support for worker activists in China who seek independent unions has been an important ele-

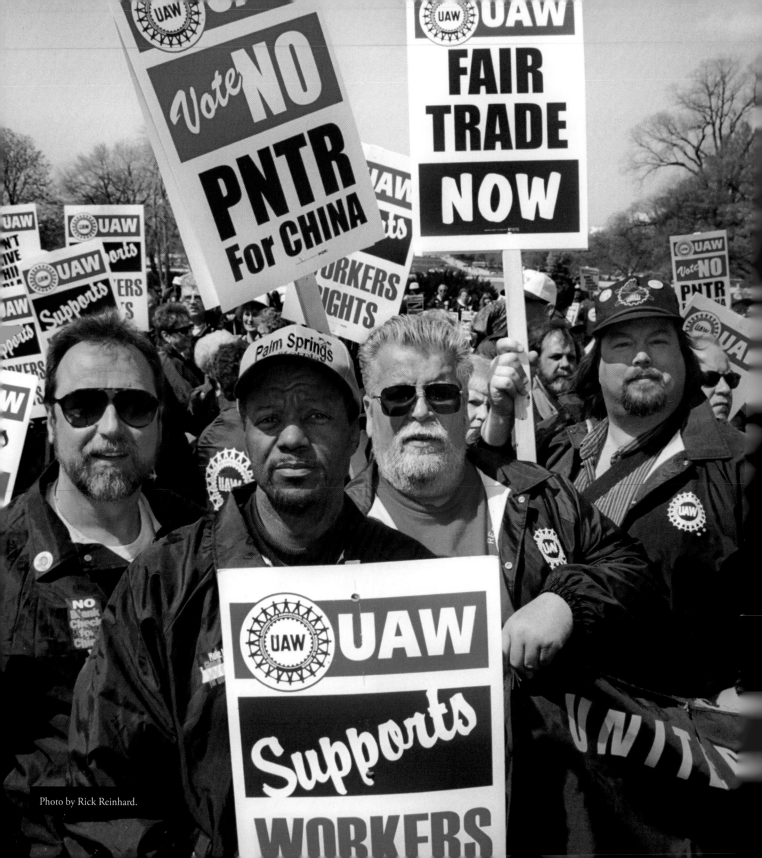

Photo by Rick Reinhard.

ment of the union's global solidarity program for years.

The union has pressed for labor rights in China for two reasons. First, we hope to see Chinese workers and their families improve their lives through winning higher wages and better working conditions. Second, the huge gap in labor costs between China and the United States threatens good-paying American jobs as more goods made with cheap labor are imported into the United States.

The Economic Policy Institute reported in 2012 that between 2001 and 2011, the trade deficit with China eliminated or displaced more than 2.7 million U.S. jobs. About 2.1 million of those lost jobs were in manufacturing.[26]

Chinese auto-parts exports increased more than 900 percent from 2000 to 2010. In addition to low wages in China, the central and local governments there provided $27.5 billion in subsidies to the country's auto-parts industry. In addition, China illegally manipulates its currency, which reduces the costs of Chinese auto parts by 25 percent to 30 percent.[27]

"It is fair to say that every one of the United States' auto-parts jobs is individually at risk from China's unfair labor practices," wrote Robert E. Scott and Hilary Wething in a 2012 report for the Economic Policy Institute.

Motor vehicle manufacturing is the second-largest employer among all U.S. manufacturing industries. The combination of labor repression in China and that country's unfair trading practices gives it a huge competitive advantage.

In the late 1990s, the UAW repeatedly warned U.S. politicians about the dangers of giving China special trade benefits, such as those provided under what was called Permanent Normal Trade Relations (PNTR). When America accords a nation PNTR status, it gets trade advantages such as low tariffs that are enjoyed by our best trading partners.

The UAW strongly opposed President Clinton's effort to give PNTR to China. The union also fought against allowing China to join the World Trade Organization (WTO).

"These trade proposals do not contain any provisions requiring China to abide by internationally recognized human and worker rights," UAW President Yokich said in a letter to President Clinton. "Thus, we turn a blind eye to China's egregious record of using child and prison labor, and denying workers the right to organize independent trade unions."

Yokich also expressed concern that if China was admitted to the WTO, it would be able to block any future effort to include basic worker rights and labor standards in the rules governing international trade.[28]

President Clinton pushed hard to win China's admission to the WTO, and he had the support of most Republicans and of many multinational corporations that saw the chance to expand outsourcing to China.

China's supporters rejected the UAW's concerns and argued that China's WTO membership would bring a vastly improved labor and human rights record there. They also promised that China would improve adherence to the rule of law, reduce trade barriers and open markets, increase transparency, protect intellectual property rights, and expand freedoms of speech, religion, and assembly.

Years later, it's clear that those promises remain unfulfilled.

"Not only did WTO not bring freedom and democracy to China, it didn't bring fair trade either," said U.S. Senator Sherrod Brown, who chaired the Congressional-Executive Commission on China. "Instead, China has flouted WTO rules and gamed the system to its advantage.

"American workers and American manufacturers can compete with anyone," Senator Brown stated. "But they'll never be able to compete on a level playing field as long as we continue to let China do what it wants, without any repercussions."[29]

Just as time has proven the UAW correct in its opposition to China's WTO accession and to NAFTA, free-trade cheerleaders ignore the huge trade deficits that have resulted from those deals and the massive American job losses.

Sadly, they also ignore the plight of Chinese workers such as Yao Fuxin, who was arrested just months after his country won admittance to the WTO following promises that it would improve its abysmal labor and human rights record.

A tighter labor market in China has meant wages improved in 2013–14. There also are positive signs that some activists in the All-China Federation of Trade Unions at the regional and local level want the government-controlled union to represent workers more aggressively.

In recent years, the AFL-CIO, UAW, and other U.S. unions have engaged with the ACFTU to better understand industrial and labor-relations issues in China while acknowledging the very different union cultures in both countries.

U.S. unions and the ACFTU have begun to share information on subjects such as collective bargaining, health and safety, and organizing.

Still, there remain many workers targeted by China's government for their labor activism, and wages there remain so low many American jobs continue to be lost to China.

So the UAW presses on.

We don't quit.

Resources On Global Labor Issues

Top Sites

International Union, UAW

uaw.org

AFL-CIO

aflcio.org

LabourStart

The premier source for daily labor news and how to get involved in international solidarity campaigns. "LabourStart is an online news service maintained by a global network of volunteers which aims to serve the international trade union movement by collecting and disseminating information—and by assisting unions in campaigning and other ways. Its features include daily labor news links in more than 20 languages."

labourstart.org

IndustriALL Global Union

UAW's primary global affiliate, their website features up-to-date news and campaigns. "IndustriALL Global Union represents 50 million workers in 140 countries in the mining, energy, and manufacturing sectors and is a force in global solidarity taking up the fight for better working conditions and trade union rights around the world. IndustriALL fights for another model of globalization and a new economic and social model that puts people first, based on democracy and social justice."

industriall-union.org

Union Solidarity International

"USi is an organization supported by major U.K., Irish, and trade unions in countries such as Brazil, Greece, Austria, North America, Europe, South Africa, and Australia that aims to build grassroots international union solidarity using the latest technology."

usilive.org

Global Union Federations (GUFs)

Global Union Federations are alliances of unions in related work sectors.

Building and Wood Workers' International (BWI)

bwint.org

Education International (EI)

ei-ie.org

International Arts and Entertainment Alliance

iaea-globalunion.org

International Federation of Journalists (IFJ)

ifj.org

International Transport Workers' Federation (ITF)

The International Transport Workers' Federation (ITF) is a global union federation with 700 affiliates—including the UAW—in transport, shipping, logistics, and allied industries.

"The ITF organizes international solidarity when transport unions in one country are in conflict with employers or government and need direct help from unions in other countries."

itfglobal.org

International Union of Food, Agricultural, Hotel, Restaurant, Catering, Tobacco, and Allied Workers' Associations (IUF)

"From the planting of seeds through the sowing of crops, the processing and manufacture of food, beverages, and tobacco products through to the catering and tourism sectors, no worker in the IUF sectors is unaffected by globalization. The process is being driven by the transnational companies which increasingly dominate world production, trade, and investment and set the international social and political agenda. The IUF seeks to create an international union counterweight to the power of the TNCs. We fight for union recognition at every level, including the international level."

iuf.org

Public Services International (PSI)

world-psi.org

UNI Global Union

UNI Global Union "represents more than 20 million workers from over 900 trade unions in the fastest-growing sectors in the world—skills and services. A total of 90 percent of new jobs are expected to be in these sectors in the next decade. UNI and our affiliates in all regions are driven by the responsibility to ensure these jobs are decent and workers' rights are protected, including the right to join a union and collective bargaining."

union-network.org

International and Regional Labor Groups

Council of Global Unions (CGU)

A forum to unite the Global Union Federations and the International Trade Union Confederation

global-unions.org

International Domestic Workers Federation

"We are a membership-based global organization of domestic/household workers… We believe domestic work is work and all domestic/household workers must enjoy the same rights as all other workers."

www.idwfed.org

International Trade Union Confederation (ITUC)

The ITUC is the largest trade union organization in the world, uniting national federations and unions from all sectors. "The ITUC's primary mission is the promotion and defense of workers' rights and interests, through international cooperation between trade unions, global campaigning, and advocacy within the major global institutions."

ituc-csi.org

Regional Affiliates of the International Trade Union Confederation

- ITUC Africa: ituc-africa.org
- ITUC Asia-Pacific: ituc-ap.org
- Trade Union Confederation of the Americas: csa-csi.org
- European Trade Union Confederation: etuc.org

International Union League for Brand Responsibility

"A global organization of workers who make products for multinational brands, such as clothing, footwear, and textiles. Our workers and our unions are uniting to demand that the multinational brands take responsibility and guarantee living wages, safe factories, and stable jobs."

union-league.org

Tri-National Solidarity Alliance

"We recognize that the structural causes of our oppression are the same in Mexico, Canada, and the United States. Together with the Global Union Federations and the ITUC, we denounce the attack on the working class, and strive to resist and repel the forces that are working against our interests and to promote a decent standard of living and work with dignity for working people in all of our countries."

trinationalsolidarity.org

Workers Uniting: The Global Union

"Workers Uniting is the name of the new international union created by Unite—the biggest union in the U.K. and Republic of Ireland and the United Steelworkers (USW)."

workersuniting.org

International Labor Rights Organizations

Labor Rights Now

"Labor Rights Now is an independent human rights group founded by the UAW based in Washington, D.C. We campaign for the release of imprisoned worker activists in other countries and fight against labor repression worldwide."

laborrightsnow.org

Asia Monitor Resource Center

"The mission of AMRC is to support and contribute towards the building of a strong, democratic, and independent labor movement in Asia by understanding and responding to the multiple challenges of asserting workers' rights to jobs, decent working conditions, and gender consciousness, while following a participatory framework."

amrc.org.hk

Clean Clothes Campaign

"The Clean Clothes Campaign is dedicated to improving working conditions and supporting the empowerment of workers in the global garment and sportswear industries. Since 1989, the CCC has worked to help ensure that the fundamental rights of workers are respected. We educate and mobilize consumers, lobby companies and governments, and offer direct solidarity support to workers as they fight for their rights and demand better working conditions."

cleanclothes.org

China Labour Bulletin

"A proactive outreach organization that seeks to defend and promote the rights of workers in China. We support the development of democratically-run trade unions, encourage respect for and enforcement of the country's labor laws, as well as the full participation of workers in the creation of civil society."

clb.org.hk/en

Friedrich-Ebert-Stiftung: International Trade Union Policy

"Our international trade union work fosters social democracy worldwide. We act in close coordination with the unions affiliated to the German Confederation of Trade Unions (DGB). For the global trade union movement, our Foundation is a unique partner, thanks to decades of experience and a worldwide network of field offices."

fes.de/gewerkschaften/index_en.php

Global Labour University

"The Global Labour University is a new approach to increase the intellectual and strategic capacity of workers organisations and to establish stronger working relationships between trade unions, the ILO, and the scientific community. It strengthens trade union capacity and competence to advocate for social justice and decent work at the workplace nationally and internationally."

global-labour-university.org

Institute for Global Labour and Human Rights

"Founded in 1981 as the National Labor Committee, the Institute's research, in-depth reports, high profile public campaigns, and widespread media coverage have been instrumental in creating the anti-sweatshop movement in the United States and internationally."

globallabourrights.org

International Labor Rights Forum

"ILRF works with trade unions, faith-based organizations, and community groups to support workers and their families. We lead on initiatives such as making apparel factories safe in Bangladesh; stopping the exploitation of children in the cotton fields of Uzbekistan; increasing the income of farm workers in the cocoa fields of West Africa; developing labor law clinics in China; and supporting threatened union leaders in Latin America's banana sector."

laborrights.org

Labor is Not a Commodity blog

laborrightsblog.typepad.com

U.S Labor Education in the Americas Project

usleap.org

International Center for Trade Union Rights

ICTUR "has a unique and valuable skills set as the only organization of its kind, not only as an organization that is firmly

rooted in and supported by international trade union networks but also well-known and respected among lawyers and academics in the human rights sphere. ICTUR bridges these realms of expertise, which are each relevant to union rights."

ictur.org/Eng/Lawyers.html

Labour Research Service

Based in South Africa, "the Labour Research Service (LRS) was established in 1986 as a nonprofit labor service organization. The LRS specializes in research, dialogue-building, and developmental projects with the broad aim of strengthening civil society and a particular focus on the world of the work."

lrs.org.za

New Unionism Network

"New unionism is about seeking creative ways to organize internationally to democratize work. Together, these four principles (organizing, internationalism, creativity, and workplace democracy) unite us as a network of union activists."

newunionism.net

newunionism.wordpress.com

Solidarity Center

Affiliated with the AFL-CIO, "the Solidarity Center is a nonprofit organization that assists workers around the world who are struggling to build democratic and independent trade unions. We work with unions and community groups worldwide to achieve equitable, sustainable, democratic development and to help men and women everywhere stand up for their rights and improve their living and working standards."

solidaritycenter.org

Students and Scholars Against Corporate Misbehaviour

Based in Hong Kong, "SACOM aims at bringing concerned students, scholars, labor activists, and consumers together to monitor corporate behavior and to advocate for workers' rights. We believe that the most effective means of monitoring is to collaborate closely with workers at the workplace level. We team up with labor NGOs to provide in-factory training to workers in South China. Through democratic elections, we support worker-based committees that can represent the voices of the majority of workers."

sacom.hk

United Students Against Sweatshops

"United Students Against Sweatshops (USAS) is the nation's largest youth-led, student labor campaign organization, with affiliated locals on more than 150 campuses. USAS affiliates run both local and nationally-coordinated campaigns for economic justice in partnership with worker and community organizations... USAS seeks to hold accountable multinational companies that exploit people who work on university campuses, in our communities, and in the overseas factories where collegiate apparel is produced."

usas.org

Women in Informal Employment: Globalizing and Organizing

"WIEGO is a global action-research-policy network that seeks to improve the status of the working poor in the informal economy, especially women."

wiego.org

Worker Rights Consortium

"The Worker Rights Consortium (WRC) is an independent labor rights monitoring organization, conducting investigations of working conditions in factories around the globe. Our purpose is to combat sweatshops and protect the rights of workers who make apparel and other products. The WRC conducts independent, in-depth investigations; issues public reports on factories producing

for major brands; and aids workers at these factories in their efforts to end labor abuses and defend their workplace rights."

workersrights.org

Human Rights Organizations

Amnesty International

"Amnesty International is a global movement of more than 3 million supporters, members, and activists in more than 150 countries and territories who campaign to end grave abuses of human rights. Our vision is for every person to enjoy all the rights enshrined in the Universal Declaration of Human Rights and other international human rights standards."

amnesty.org

Centre for Research on Multinational Corporations

The Centre "strives toward global economic development that is sustainable and fair and toward the elimination of the structural causes of poverty, environmental problems, exploitation, and inequality. Through research targeted at achieving sustainable change and strengthening cooperation, the Centre seeks to offer social organizations worldwide, especially those in developing countries, the opportunity to promote sustainable alternatives and to provide a counterweight to unsustainable strategies and practices of multinational corporations."

somo.nl

Committee in Solidarity with the People of El Salvador

"We are a grassroots organization dedicated to supporting the Salvadoran people's struggle for self-determination and social and economic justice...We focus our work on El Salvador because of the U.S. government's continuing military, economic, and political intervention on behalf of U.S. corporate interests, and because of the Salvadoran people's tenacious and inspiring struggle to build social justice."

cispes.org

Global Witness

"Global Witness investigates and campaigns to change the system by exposing the economic networks behind conflict, corruption, and environmental destruction."

globalwitness.org

Grassroots Global Justice

"Grassroots Global Justice is an alliance of U.S.-based grassroots groups who are organizing to build an agenda for power for working and poor people. We understand that there are important connections between the local issues we work on and the global context, and we see ourselves as part of an international movement for global justice."

ggjalliance.org

Human Rights Watch

"Human Rights Watch defends the rights of people worldwide. We scrupulously investigate abuses, expose the facts widely, and pressure those with power to respect rights and secure justice. Human Rights Watch is an independent, international organization that works as part of a vibrant movement to uphold human dignity and advance the cause of human rights for all."

hrw.org

Institute for Policy Studies

"IPS is a community of public scholars and organizers linking peace, justice, and the environment in the United States and globally. We work with social movements to promote true democracy and challenge concentrated wealth, corporate influence, and military power."

ips-dc.org

SOA Watch

"SOA Watch is an independent organization that seeks to close the U.S. Army School of the Americas, under whatever name it is called, through vigils and fasts, demonstrations and nonviolent protest, as well as media and legislative work."

soaw.org

Washington Office on Latin America (WOLA)

wola.org

International Agencies and Forums

European Works Councils (EWC)

"The purpose of a European Works Council (EWC) is to bring together employee representatives from the different European countries in which a multinational company has operations. During EWC meetings, these representatives are informed and consulted by central management on transnational issues of concern to the company's employees."

worker-participation.eu/European-Works-Councils

International Labor Organization (ILO)

A specialized agency of the United Nations, "the International Labor Organization (ILO) is devoted to promoting social justice and internationally recognized human and labor rights, pursuing its founding mission that labor peace is essential to prosperity. Today, the ILO helps advance the creation of decent work and the economic and working conditions that give working people and business people a stake in lasting peace, prosperity and progress."

ilo.org

ILO Bureau of Workers' Activities

ilo.org/actrav/lang--en/index.htm

Trade Union Advisory Committee to the Organization for Economic Cooperation and Development (TUAC)

"TUAC's origins go back to 1948 when it was founded as a trade union advisory committee for the European Recovery Programme—the Marshall Plan. When the OECD was created in its current form in 1962 as an intergovernmental policymaking body, TUAC continued its work of representing organized labor's views to the new organization…TUAC's role is to help ensure that global markets are balanced by an effective social dimension."

tuac.org

International Labor Standards

- The OECD Guidelines for Multinational Enterprises: www.oecd.org/daf/investment/guidelines/index.htm
- United Nations Guiding Principles on Business and Human Rights: http://www.ohchr.org/Documents/Publications/Guiding-PrinciplesBusinessHR_EN.pdf
- Universal Declaration of Human Rights, Article 23(4), 1948: http://www.un.org/en/documents/udhr/#atop
- International Covenant on Civil and Political Rights, Article 22(1), 1966 http://www.ohchr.org/en/professionalinterest/pages/ccpr.aspx
- International Covenant on Economic, Social and Cultural Rights, Article 8, 1966 http://www.ohchr.org/EN/ProfessionalInterest/Pages/CESCR.aspx
- ILO Convention No. 87- Freedom of Association and Protection of Right to Organize, 1948 http://www.ilo.org/dyn/normlex/en/f?p=NORMLEXPUB:12100:0::NO::P12100_ILO_CODE:C087

- ILO Convention No. 98- Right to Organize and Collective Bargaining, 1949.: http://www.ilo.org/dyn/normlex/en/f?p=NORMLEXPUB:12100:0::NO:12100:P12100_INSTRUMENT_ID:312243:NO
- ILO Core Labor Standards
  - ILO core labor standards derive from eight fundamental ILO conventions identified as basic to the rights of human beings at work, irrespective of the development of individual member states within the ILO. These conventions promote freedom of association and the right to organize and collective bargaining (No. 87, No. 98), the elimination of forced labor (No. 29, No. 105), the abolition of child labor (No. 138 and No. 182) and the elimination of discrimination with respect to employment (No. 100, No. 111).
  - The United States and Burma (Myanmar) are the only two ILO member states to have ratified only two of the eight core labor standards. The U.S. has ratified ILO Convention No. 105 on forced labor and ILO Convention No. 182 on the elimination of the worst forms of child labor. By contrast, 127 members have ratified all eight fundamental core labor standards, including most of Western Europe: Great Britain, Austria, Belgium, Denmark, Finland, France, Germany, Italy, Spain, Norway, Sweden, and Switzerland. Unfortunately, given that China, India, the United States, and Brazil have failed to ratify ILO Convention No. 87 (Right to Organize), almost half of the world's population remains outside its scope.

Endnotes

Chapter 1

1   "UAW Will Withdraw Funds from Banks Making Loans to Racist South African Regime." *News from UAW*, March 3, 1978.

2   Ibid.

3   Ibid.

4   Ibid.

5   "Pulling Our Money Out of Racist South Africa." *UAW Solidarity*, 1983.

6   "Union Condemns Apartheid, Seeks Halt to New Chrysler Pension Fund Investments in South Africa." *UAW Solidarity*. July 1981.

7   UAW President's Report, Part 1, 1986.

8   Isikoff, Michael. "Boycott in U.S., Europe Vexes Royal Dutch Shell." *Washington Post*, November 29, 1986.

9   "The Royal Dutch/Shell Group of Companies Alternative Corporate Report 1987," a counter annual report prepared by Don Stillman/John Bell for the Shell Boycott campaign.

10 Walker, Matthew. "The Cost of Doing Business in South Africa." *Multinational Monitor*, April 15, 1986.

11 Ibid.

12 Sparks, Samantha. "South Africa: U.S. Clergy Group Linked to Shell Oil." Inter Press Service (IPS), October 7, 1987.

13 Horn, Steve. "Divide and Conquer: Unpacking Stratfor's Rise to Power." *Mint Press News*, July 25, 2013.

14 Minter, William, and Sylvia Hill. Chapter in *The Road to Democracy in South Africa*, Vol. 3, *International Solidarity*, Part II, ed. South African Democracy Education Trust (SADET). Unisa Press, 2008.

15 Ibid.

16 UAW President's Report, 1989.

17 "UAW to Conduct a Series of 48-Hour Fasts in Support of Black South African Detainees." *News from UAW*, February 17, 1989.

18 Barbee, Bobbie. "UAW Backs Struggle of South African Workers." *UAW Solidarity*, December 1984.

19 "How African Americans Helped Free South Africa." *Ebony*, August 1994.

20 South Africa Advisory Committee Report, Dissenting Opinion by Owen Bieber, 1987.

21 "Mandela Hails UAW Effort Against Apartheid." *UAW Washington Report*, July 6–13, 1990.

22 Ibid.

23 Ibid.

24 "Recalling Nelson Mandela." *USA Today*, December 5, 2013.

25 Karimi, Faith, and Marie-Louise Gumuchlan. "Mandela Laid to Rest in Qunu." CNN, December 15, 2013.

26 www.detroitbadboys.com/2013/12/6/5182516/nelson-mandela-detroit-pistons-uaw-organized-labor.

Chapter 2

1   In 1989 I won the Samuel Gompers Union Leadership Award given by the Center for Labor-Management Policy Studies of the City University of New York (CUNY) Graduate School and University Center led then by Victor Gotbaum. I gave a presentation on the UAW effort on behalf of Moses Mayekiso at CUNY. Later, I wrote up that talk, which became a chapter in a book entitled *Union Voices: Labor's Responses to Crisis*, which was edited by Glenn Adler and Doris Suarez and published by State University of New York Press. I relied heavily on my book chapter and talk for this account of the solidarity campaign on behalf of Mayekiso. I want to credit Mongane Wally Serote, *To Every Birth Its Blood* (1981) quoted in M. Sarakinsky, *From 'Freehold Township' To 'Model Township'—A Political History of Alexandra: 1905-1983* (Dissertation, University of the Witwatersrand, 1984). I also credit Steven Friedman, *Building Tomorrow Today—African Workers in Trade Unions, 1970-1984*. Raven Press, 1987. Thanks to Glenn Adler for reviewing this chapter.

Chapter 3

1   In this chapter, we use Burma for that country's name. But the ruling military junta changed the official name from Burma to Myanmar in 1989, just a year after the regime killed large numbers of protesters. Campaigners against the government preferred Burma over Myanmar for many years. The U.S. government uses Burma, while the United Nations calls the country Myanmar.

2   *Associated Press*, Fort Wayne, Indiana, September 5, 2001.

3   Wikipedia: citing Martin Smith, *Burma—Insurgence and the Politics of Ethnicity*. London and New Jersey: Zed Books 1991.

4   BBC. "Burma's 1988 Protests," September 25, 2007, http://news.bbc.co.uk/2/hi/asia-pacific/7012158.stm.

5   U.S. State Department, Country Reports on Human Rights Practices, February 23, 2001, www.state.gov/j/drl/rls/hrrpt/2000/eap/index.cfm?docid=678.

6   Ibid.

7   World Movement for Democracy. "Trade Unionist Continued Imprisonment by Burmese Dictatorship," June 16, 2000, www.wmd.org/alerts/trade-unionists-continued-imprisonment-bur-mese-dictatorship.

8   Schilling, Sara. "Political Prisoner Returns to Family After 16 Years." *Tri-City (WA) Herald*, May 24, 2013, www.tri-cityherald.com/2013/05/24/2408046/political-prisoner-returns-to.html.

9   Jailing of U Myo Aung Thant letter from Bill Jordan to General Than Shwe on August 21, 1997, www.burmalibrary.org/reg.burma/archives/199708/msg00256.html.

10   ICFTU Annual Survey of Violations of Trade Union Rights, 2003, www.newunionism.net/library/internationalism/ICFTU%20-%20Annual%20Survey%20of%20Violations%20of%20Trade%20Union%20Rights%20-%202003.pdf.

11   Martin, Michael F. "U.S. Sanctions on Burma." Congressional Research Service, October 19, 2012.

12   Labor Rights Now website, June 29, 2006, www.laborrightsnow.org.

13   Schilling, Sara. "Political Prisoner Returns to Family After 16 Years." *Tri-City Herald*, May 24, 2013.

Chapter 4

1   U.S. Department of Labor Bureau of Labor Statistics news release, "Union Members Summary," January 23, 2013, www.bls.gov/news.release/union2.nr0.htm.

2   Kirkland, Sam, and Dave Elsila. "Help from Our Friends." *UAW Solidarity*, January–February 1992.

3   Ibid.

4   Ibid.

5   "Freightliner Time Line," *UAW Solidarity*, March–April 2012.

6   Kirkland and Elsila, "Help from Our Friends."

7   Ibid.

8   UAW President's Report, Part 1, 1992, p. 159.

9   Kirkland and Elsila, "Help from Our Friends."

10   Ibid.

11   "Freightliner Time Line."

12   Ibid.

13   Ibid.

Chapter 5

1   Thanks to Dan La Botz, whose insightful account of the Indonesia labor struggle during this period I relied on in this chapter: *Made in Indonesia: Indonesian Workers Since Suharto*. South End Press, 2001, p. 16.

2   "Indonesia: Suharto's Death a Chance for Victims to Find Justice." Human Rights Watch news release, January 28, 2008.

3   La Botz, *Made in Indonesia*, p. 14.

4   Ibid., p. 15.

5   Ibid., p. 16; Vedi R. Hadiz, *Workers and the State in New Order Indonesia*. New York: Routledge and Asia Research Centre, Murdoch University, 1997, p. 113.

6   La Botz, *Made in Indonesia*, p. 18.

7   *Japan Press*, July 6, 1999.

8   *UAW Solidarity*, March–April 1998.

9   La Botz, p. 18.

10 "Dita Sari—Jailed for Her Union Organizing in Indonesia." "UAW/Labor Rights Now" pamphlet, ca. 1997.

11 La Botz, pp. 20–21.

12 Bresnan, John, ed. *Indonesia: The Great Transition*. Studies of the Weatherhead East Asian Institute, Columbia University. Lanham, MD: Rowman and Littlefield, 2005, p. 261.

13 La Botz, pp. 21–22.

14 "Labor Activist Dita Released from Prison." *Japan Press*, July 6, 1999.

15 La Botz, p. 22.

16 "Labor Activist Dita."

17 La Botz, p. 22.

18 *Green Left Weekly*, May 31, 1995, issue 189.

19 UAW President's Report, 1998.

20 *UAW Solidarity*, January-February 1997.

21 *UAW Solidarity*, December 1996.

Chapter 6

1 Gacek, Stanley A. "Repression in Brazil." *Dissent*, Spring 1982.

2 "Twelve Unionists Jailed in Brazil." *UAW Solidarity*.

3 Bourne, Richard. *Lula of Brazil: The Story So Far*. University of California Press, 2008.

4 Ibid.

5 Ibid.

6 Ibid.

7 Ibid.

8 Ibid.

9 Ibid.

10 Ibid.

11 Ibid.

12 Goertzel, Ted. *Brazil's Lula: The Most Popular Politician on Earth*. Brown Walker Press, 2011.

13 Ibid.

14 Bourne, *Lula of Brazil*.

15 Ibid.

16 "World of Work." *UAW Solidarity*, April 16, 1979.

17 Bourne, *Lula of Brazil*.

18 Ibid.

19 Ibid.

20 Ibid.

21 Ibid.

22 Ibid.

23 Gacek, "Repression in Brazil."

24 "Eleições 2006—Com votação recorde, Lula chega ao segundo mandato".G1.globo.com; http://en.wikipedia.org/wiki/Luiz_In%C3%A1cio_Lula_da_Silva#cite_note-16.

25 www.cnn.com/2013/10/01/world/americas/2016-rio-de-janeiro-summer-olympics-fast-facts/.

Chapter 7

1 MacShane, Denis. *Solidarity, Poland's Independent Trade Union*. Spokesman, 1981.

2 Ibid.

3 Ibid, 17.

4 Weschler, Lawrence. "A Reporter in Poland: And There Was Light." *The New Yorker*, November 9, 1981. I relied on Weschler's reporting both at the time to help us know what was happening from afar and also for this chapter. His wife, Joanna Weschler, also helped the UAW directly. She was both Polish and a human rights campaigner who provided us with her insights. The UAW owes thanks to both Joanna and Lawrence Weschler.

5 "100 Most Influential People: Leaders and Revolutionaries: Lech Wałęsa." *Time*, April 18, 1998.

6 Weschler.

7 Ibid.

8 "100 Most Influential People: Leaders and Revolutionaries: Lech Wałęsa." *Time*, April 18, 1998.

9 Weschler.

10 Ibid.

11   Wikipedia, "Gdańsk Agreement," http://en.wikipedia.org/wiki/Gda%C5%84sk_Agreement.

12   MacShane.

13   Ibid.

14   Ibid.

15   Ibid.

16   Ibid.

17   Ibid.

18   UAW President's Report, 1983.

19   Letter from Lech Wałęsa to Otto Kersten, ICFTU. From archived files of UAW President Doug Fraser at the Walter P. Reuther Library, Wayne State University.

20   Memo from UAW Secretary Treasurer Ray Majerus to UAW President Doug Fraser, August 28, 1981. From Fraser archives at Walter P. Reuther Library, Wayne State University.

21   MacShane.

22   Ibid.

23   Ibid.

24   Ibid.

25   Ibid.

26   Ibid.

27   Ibid.

28   Ibid.

29   Weschler, Lawrence. "A Reporter in Poland: And There Was Light," Part II. *The New Yorker*, November 16, 1981.

30   Ibid.

31   Ibid.

32   Ibid.

33   Ibid.

34   "UAW Opens Fund Drive for Food for Poland." *UAW Solidarity*, 1981.

35   Letter to UAW President Fraser from Bishop Czeslaw Domin, May 12, 1982. From the Fraser files at the Walter P. Reuther Library, Wayne State University.

36   "Poland Remembers 1981 Martial Law Victims." Polskie Radio, December 13, 2012. www.thenews.pl/1/9/Artykul/121354,Poland-remembers-1981-martial-law-victims.

37   MacEachin, Douglas J. "U.S. Intelligence and the Polish Crisis, 1980–1981." Central Intelligence Agency, www.cia.gov/library/center-for-the-study-of-intelligence/csi-publications/books-and-monographs/us-intelligence-and-the-polish-crisis-1980-1981/index.htm.

38   Ibid.

39   Ibid.

40   Weschler, Lawrence. "A Reporter at Large: A State of War." *The New Yorker*, April 11-18, 1983.

41   "Poland," IMF press release, Geneva, December 14, 1981.

42   Weschler, "A Reporter at Large."

43   Ibid.

44   Ibid.

45   Ibid.

46   Ibid., Weschler, quoting the *Uncensored Polish News Bulletin*.

47   Letter to UAW President Doug Fraser from Julian Dziura, translated by Wallace Witkowski, September 16, 1982. From Fraser files at the Walter P. Reuther Library, Wayne State University.

48   "UAW Supports Polish Strikers." UAW *Washington Report*, May 13, 1988.

49   "UAW Backs Poland's Solidarność Union." UAW *Washington Report*, May 26, 1989.

50   Ibid.

51   Stillman, Don. "Report from Poland, After Euphoria." UAW *Washington Report*, October 10, 1989.

52   Ibid.

53   Wałęsa made statements on LGBT issues that were totally unacceptable.

Chapter 8

1   *Oil & Gas Journal*, January 2007, cited by Wikipedia, http://en.wikipedia.org/wiki/Kuwait.

2   "CIA—The World Factbook—Rank Order—GDP—Per Capita PPP." Cia.gov, cited by Wikipedia, http://en.wikipedia.org/wiki/Kuwait.

3   http://www.hrw.org/reports/1995/WR95/MIDEAST-08.htm0.

4   Ibid.

5   http://www.industriall-union.org/kuwait-oil-workers-win-after-strike.

Chapter 9

1   *UAW Solidarity*, May 1996.

2   Ibid.

3   Ibid.

4   Noel Saleh, phone interview, January 2, 2014.

5   Parsons, David. "UW Researchers Need Comprehensive Immigration Reform." *Seattle Times*, April 15, 2013.

6   "Immigrants: Building the Union Yesterday and Today." *UAW Solidarity*, December 1994.

7   Pilkington, Ed. "Alabama Red-Faced as Second Foreign Car Boss Held Under Immigration Law." *Guardian*, Dec. 2, 2011.

8   "Immigrants Help Beat De-Cert." *UAW Solidarity*, December 1994.

9   Neather, Andy. "The Pizza Parlor Plantation." *UAW Solidarity*, December 1994.

10 Funke, Michael. "UAW Members Defend the Rights of Immigrant Workers." *UAW Solidarity*, December 1994.

11 Marshall, Ray. "Immigration for Shared Prosperity." Economic Policy Institute, 2009.

12 Funke, Michael. "Mario & Gabie Rivera: When Citizenship's Not Enough." *UAW Solidarity*, December 1994.

13 Stark, Sam. "Do Not Stand Idly By: UAW Supports Rights of Immigrant Workers." *UAW Solidarity*, October 2003.

14 Ibid.

Chapter 10

1   Funke, Michael. "Solidarity with El Salvador." *UAW Solidarity*. 1991.

2   Ibid.

3   Dear, Rev. John, S.J. "The Life and Example of Jean Donovan," *Common Dreams*, December 2, 2005.

4   "From Madness to Hope: The 12-year War in El Salvador." Commission on the Truth for El Salvador. United Nations, March 1993.

5   http://dwkcommentaries.com/2011/12/14/the-december-1980-murders-of-the-four-american-churchwomen-in-el-salvador/.

6   http://en.wikipedia.org/wiki/Jean_Donovan.

7   Goldston, James, and Jemera Rone. "A Year of Reckoning." Americas Watch Report, March 1990. Americas Watch was founded in 1981 during the conflicts in Central America. In 1988, Americas Watch and other groups, including Asia Watch and Africa Watch, joined to become what is known today as Human Rights Watch. Human Rights Watch shared the Nobel Peace Prize in 1997.

8   *Diario de Hoy*, November 7, 1989.

9   McGrory, Mary. "Why Do We Keep on Aiding El Salvador?" Universal Press, *Spokane Chronicle*, Feb. 1, 1990.

10 Goldston and Rone, "A Year of Reckoning."

11 "Labor Rights in El Salvador." Americas Watch Report, March 1988.

12 This section is based on my own notes and, more importantly, a diary kept by Dave Dyson of the trip on October 14–16, 1984. My thanks to both Dyson and Janet Shenk for their help.

13 Battista, Andrew. *The Revival of Labor Liberalism*, p. 126. University of Illinois Press, 2008.

14 Ibid., p. 128.

15 Ibid., p. 135.

16 Ibid., p. 140.

17 "CAP Report on Central America," *UAW Washington Report*, 1986.

18 "Central America: Can We Keep the U.S. Out of War?" *UAW Solidarity*, June 1985.

19 http://en.wikipedia.org/wiki/Ben_Linder.

20 Lewis, Anthony. "Abroad at Home: The Most Cruel," *The New York Times*, May 15, 1987.

21 http://en.wikipedia.org/wiki/Chapultepec_Peace_Accords.

Chapter 11

1   www.wmnf.org/news_stories/9090

2   List of Military Officers in the Guatemalan Army, document in the National Security Archive at George Washington University.

3   BBC News: www.bbc.co.uk/news/world-latin-america-22490408.

4   Ibid.

5   Rohter, Larry. "Ford Motor Is Linked to Argentina's Dirty War." *The New York Times*, November 27, 2002.

6   Ibid.

7   Gill, Lesley. *The School of the Americas: Military Training and Political Violence in the Americas*. Duke University Press, 2004.

8   Quigley, Bill. "The Case for Closing the School of the Americas." *Brigham Young University Journal of Public Law*, 2005.

9   Ibid.

10   Ireland, Doug. "Teaching Torture in the USA." *Human Quest* 218, no. 5 (Sept. 1, 2004). www.findarticles.com/p/articles/mi_qa3861/is_200409/ai_n944113.

11   Dean, Heather. "Notorious Haitian School of the Americas Graduates." http://derechos.org/soa/ha-not.html.

12   Bullard, Alice, ed. *Human Rights in Crisis*. Ashgate Publishing, 2008, p. 95.

13   Gill, *The School of the Americas*.

14   Quigley, *The Case for Closing*, p. 6.

15   Faiola, Anthony. "Many Allies in Peru Apparently Were Corrupt." *Seattle Times*, May 20, 2001, p. A19.

16   Dean, Heather. "Notorious Venezuelan School of the Americas Graduates." http://derechos.org/soa/uynot.html.

17   www.uawregion8.net/feedback/fd-01.htm.

18   Priest, Dana. "U.S. Instructed Latins on Executions, Torture." *Washington Post*, September 21, 1996.

19   www.soaw.org/index.php?option=com_content&view=article&id=98.

20   Dwyer, Katherine. "School of the Assassins." *International Socialist Review*, no. 9 (Fall 1999).

21   Temple, Kathryn. "Exporting Violence Against Women." *Yale Manifesta*, Spring-Summer 2005.

22   Ibid.

23   Silvi, Joan. "You Can Only Oppress People For So Long." *UAW Solidarity*, September–October 2010.

24   Nelson, Sarah. "The School of the Americas Tries to Hide with a Name Change." www.greens.org/s-r/23/23-08.html

25   www.soaw.org/take-action/legislative/background-info/3999-soa-watch-meets-with-white-house-deputy-national-security-adviser-lessons-learned.

Chapter 12

1   Adler, Glenn. "Labor Rights and Democracy in Nigeria." UAW Labor Rights Now *Issues Brief*, 2000.

2   Drainville, Andre. "Contesting Globalization: Space and Place in the World Economy." London: Routledge, 2004, p. 79.

3   www.trilliuminvest.com/news-articles-category/advocacy-news-articles/speaking-truth-to-powerarchive/.

4   Adler, "Labor Rights."

5   http://en.wikipedia.org/wiki/Sani_Abacha, citing Jyoti Malhotra, "Did Indian Girls See Nigerian Dictator Die?" *Indian Express*.

Chapter 13

1   Shorrock, Tim. "UAW Protests Mexico's Arrest of Labor Leader." *Journal of Commerce*, February 5, 1992.

2   "UAW-Backed Strikes Win Wage Hikes in Border Town GM and Parts Plants," *UAW Solidarity*, 1992.

3   McClintock, John M. "A Tale of Free Trade and Labor and Money and Power in Mexico." *Baltimore Sun*, March 1, 1992.

4   Ibid.

5   Ibid.

6   Williams, Joel. "Boss Man of the Border: Don Agapito, Mexican Labor Leader." Associated Press, May 6, 1990.

7   Ibid.

8   Ibid.

9   McClintock.

10   Ibid.

11 Reding, Andrew. "Free Trade, Shackled Labor." *The New York Times*, April 18, 1992.

12 Nila Minon, Susana. "Ex-Union Leader of Ford Workers Charged in Attack Against Workers." *El Financiero*, November 1, 1994.

13 "Kansas City UAW Celebrates Solidarity with Mexican Workers," *UAW Solidarity*.

14 "Safety Is a Right for All." *UAW Solidarity*, January–February 2001.

15 "Demand Justice for Customtrim/Autotrim Workers." Coalition for Justice in the Maquiladoras fact sheet.

16 Scott, Robert E. "NAFTA's Legacy: Growing U.S. Trade Deficits Cost 682,900 Jobs." Economic Policy Institute, December 17, 2013.

17 Ibid.

18 Ibid.

19 "NAFTA at 20." Public Citizen's Global Trade Watch report, January 2014.

20 Elsila, Dave. "No More NAFTA's." *UAW Solidarity*, April–May 1997.

21 Ibid.

22 Ibid.

23 Ibid.

24 Vindell, Tony. "Union, Maquiladoras Lock Horns Again." *Brownsville Herald*, February 15, 1989.

25 Ibid.

Chapter 14

1 Ham, Melinda. "Defying the Dictator." *Africa Report*, May–June 1992.

2 Chihana, Chakufwa. "Malawi: Prospects for Peace." Keynote address delivered at a conference of Zambian exiles at Lusaka, Zambia, on March 20, 1992, to assess their prospects for democratic change in their country. Referenced in Kahn and Chihana, note 8 below.

3 Ham, "Defying the Dictator."

4 "Chakufwa Chihana: Malawi's 'Father of Democracy.'" Obituary, The Scotsman, June 29, 2006.

5 Ibid.

6 Ibid.

7 Human Rights Watch report, 1993. See: www.hrw.org/reports/1993/WR93/Afw-04.htm.

8 Kahn, Melvin A. (Wichita State University), and Enoch Chihana. "Foreign Student Lobbying in America: The Impact on Malawi Politics." Paper delivered at Southern Political Science Conference, Jan. 6, 2006, in Atlanta, Georgia, from which I drew for this chapter

9 "Ignoring Calls for Change." Lawyers Committee for Human Rights, New York, November 13, 1992.

10 Kahn and Chihana, "Foreign Student Lobbying."

11 Ibid.

12 Ibid.

13 Human Rights Watch, 1993.

14 "Human Rights in Malawi." A report of a joint delegation of the Scottish Faculty of Advocates, the Law Society of England and Wales, and the General Council of the Bar to Malawi, September 1992.

15 Stearns, Scott. "Malawi Government Pressured to Reform." *Christian Science Monitor*, May 26, 1992.

Chapter 15

1 Piscopo, Vince. "Local 774 Member: Honor Son's Sacrifice by Ending Wars." *UAW Solidarity*, May–June 2011.

2 Ibid.

3 *People's Weekly World*, March 1, 2003.

4 "UAW Local 600's Opposition to War." *Counterpunch*, March 4, 2003.

5 Fletcher, Bill, Jr., and Fernando Gapasin. *Solidarity Divided*. University of California Press, 2008.

6 Elsila, Dave. "The Race That Can't Be Won." *UAW Solidarity*, July 1982.

7 Ibid.

8 Halloran, Richard. ""Pentagon Draws Up First Strategy for Fighting a Long Nuclear War." *The New York Times*, May 30, 1982.

9   Elsila, "The Race That Can't Be Won."

10   UAW President's Report, 1970, p. 125.

11   Lichtenstein, Nelson. *The Most Dangerous Man in Detroit*. Basic Books, 1995.

12   Ibid., p. 423.

13   Ibid., p. 437. I relied on Lichtenstein's book for this section on Reuther.

14   Koscielski, Frank. *Divided Loyalties: American Unions and the Vietnam War*. Taylor & Francis, 1999.

15   "Unionists Examine Effects of the Arms Race." *UAW Solidarity*.

Chapter 16

1   Pan, Philip P. *Out of Mao's Shadow*. New York: Simon and Schuster, 2008. Pan did some of the best reporting on labor and human rights abuses in China for *The Washington Post*. I drew on detailed descriptions of the Yao Fuxin case in his excellent book for this chapter.

2   Ibid.

3   Ibid.

4   Ibid.

5   Ibid.

6   "Paying the Price: Worker Unrest in Northeast China." Human Rights Watch, August 2002.

7   Pan, *Out of Mao's Shadow*.

8   Hilton, Ronald. "Corruption in China: Shenyang," quoting correspondence from John Pomfret, WAIS Forum on China, March 6, 2002.

9   Pan, *Out of Mao's Shadow*.

10   Ibid.

11   "Paying the Price," Human Rights Watch.

12   Pan, *Out of Mao's Shadow*.

13   Ibid.

14   "Paying the Price," Human Rights Watch.

15   Ibid.

16   Pan, *Out of Mao's Shadow*.

17   "The Liaoyang Workers' Struggle: Portrait of a Movement," *China Labour Bulletin*, July 2003. The China Labour Bulletin published by Han Dongfang was a major source of information about labor inside China.

18   "330th Report of the Committee on Freedom of Association." International Labor Office, 286th Session, March 2003.

19   "The Liaoyang Workers' Struggle," *China Labour Bulletin*.

20   Ibid.

21   Ibid.

22   Pan, Philip P. "Crowd at Courthouse Highlights Mounting Problem for Communist Party." *The Washington Post*, January 16, 2003.

23   "The Liaoyang Workers' Struggle," *China Labour Bulletin*.

24   "Imprisoned Labor Activist Threatened with End to Family Visits if Abuse Is Revealed." Human Rights Watch, December 1, 2004.

25   Testimony of UAW President Ron Gettelfinger before the U.S.-China Economic and Security Review Commission, September 23, 2004.

26   Scott, Robert E. "The China Toll." Economic Policy Institute, August 2012.

27   Scott, Robert E., and Hilary Wething. "Jobs in the U.S. Auto Parts Industry Are at Risk Due to Subsidized and Unfairly Traded Chinese Auto Parts." Economic Policy Institute, January 31, 2012.

28   "China Can Wait." *UAW Solidarity*, March 2000.

29   Brown, U.S. Senator Sherrod. "Marking Ten Years Since China Joined the WTO." Press release, December 13, 2011. http://www.brown.senate.gov/newsroom/press/release/marking-ten-years-since-china-joined-the-wto-sen-sherrod-brown-co-chairs-hearing-on-chinas-broken-trade-promises.

About the Author

Don Stillman served as Director of Governmental and International Affairs for the UAW for more than 20 years. President Leonard Woodcock hired Stillman in 1975 to run the union's Public Relations and Publications Department, which he did until President Doug Fraser asked him to move to the Washington, D.C., office in 1982.

Earlier, Stillman worked for Jock Yablonski, who opposed Tony Boyle for the presidency of the United Mine Workers. Following Yablonski's murder, Stillman joined in creating Miners for Democracy. He helped topple the UMWA's corrupt leadership in 1972.

Stillman's work as editor of the *United Mine Workers Journal* won it the National Magazine Award. He later was the recipient of the Research and Writing Award of the MacArthur Foundation, as well as the Samuel Gompers Award from the graduate school of the City University of New York. Stillman holds a B.A. with high honors from University of Redlands in government and an M.S. from Columbia University's Graduate School of Journalism.

Stillman has taught at Oxford University, where he served as visiting fellow at Magdalen College and co-taught the labor seminar held at Oxford's Institute of Economics and Statistics. He also lectured at Harvard's Institute of Politics as part of its study group seminar program.

He was founding editor of *WorkingUSA*, an academic journal dealing with issues of labor, class, and gender. Stillman has been published in *The Wall Street Journal*, *The Washington Post*, *Life* magazine, *Progressive*, *Columbia Journalism Review*, and other publications.

His two books are *Since Sliced Bread: Common Sense Ideas From America's Working Families* and *Stronger Together: The Story of SEIU*.

Stillman is a member of UAW Local 1981. He now serves as president of Labor Rights Now, the human rights group that campaigns on behalf of imprisoned worker activists throughout the world.